She felt like being cruel to her brother, to break through his shell of denial. If she was potentially Destruction, and Kindrie was becoming Preservation, then Tori must be Creation. Without all three of them aware of and accepting their roles, however, the Tyr-ridan would fail and with it the Kencyrath's god-given mandate to defeat Perimal Darkling—a battle so old that many Kencyr seemed to have forgotten all about it. She could shatter Tori with truths he couldn't bear to face. Perhaps she should. Or was that just the destroyer in her speaking?

A rush of sparrows outside the window made Jame flinch back. They were fleeing the shelter of the vines in a shrieking mob, to be snatched up by the wind and carried away. She leaned out and looked down, shielding her eyes with a hand. At first, she thought that wind and hail were thrashing the ivy; then she saw that it was crawling slowly up the wall. Rootlets groped for cracks and dug into them. Ice sliced through puffs of mortar dust, as the mass of greenery dragged itself up inch by inch.

"Destruction begins with love," Torisen said through stiff lips, in a harsh voice not his own. "The power that seduces, that betrays. . . They are creatures of the shadows, poisoning men's dreams, sucking out their souls . . . Cursèd be the lot of them . . ."

"Who, Tori?"

"Shanir. Women. You."

❦ Baen Books ❦
By P.C. Hodgell

The Kencyrath Series
Seeker's Bane (omnibus)
Bound in Blood
Honor's Paradox
The Sea of Time
The Gates of Tagmeth

The Godstalker Chronicles (omnibus)

The Gates of Tagmeth

By

P. C. Hodgell

THE GATES OF TAGMETH

A Baen Books Original

Baen Publishing Enterprises
P.O. Box 1403
Riverdale, NY 10471
www.baen.com

ISBN: 978-1-4814-8354-4

Cover art by Eric Williams
Map by P.C. Hodgell

First Baen printing Trade Paper Back, August 2017
First Baen printing Mass Market, October 2018

Distributed by Simon & Schuster
1230 Avenue of the Americas
New York, NY 10020

Printed in the United States of America

10 9 8 7 6 5 4 3 2

Dedication

to Liz
and Marc
and all of the horses
we have known

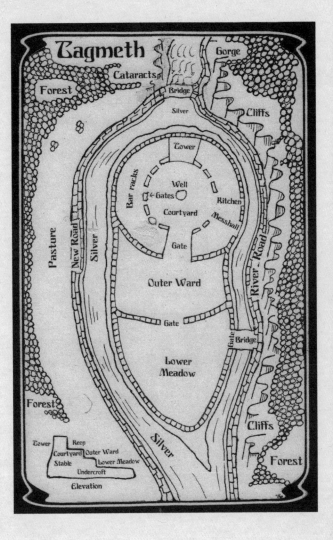

The Gates of Tagmeth

ᚱᛊᚺ CHAPTER I ᛊᚺᚱ
Gothregor
Spring 50—Spring 60

I

JAME PAUSED in the doorway of her brother's tower study, blinking into the gloom. The room seemed empty, yet it breathed fitfully as the wind ebbed and flowed through it. In the open western window, up the chimney, through the doorway to the spiral stair in which she stood, out again, ahhhh . . .

Papers rustled on the desk. Embers flared on the hearth, the last of a fire set on this chill evening in late spring.

Perhaps I won't have to face him just yet, she thought. *Oh, first, for food, sleep, time . . .*

"Tori?"

"Here."

His voice came from the shadows near the window, where he stood so still that her eyes had slipped over him. Back turned, hands clasped behind him, he was staring down into the inner ward, as perhaps he had been ever

3

since she and her tired, hungry ten-command had ridden into Gothregor at dusk. Below, Brier Iron-thorn would be dismantling their little caravan, the cadets sent to dinner, their meager baggage to their new quarters, their mounts to the subterranean stable. The wind gusted again, bringing a grumble of thunder.

"So you've come at last," he said.

"As you see."

Or would, she thought, *if you turned around.*

But he didn't.

"I won't ask if you had a pleasant journey. How is your shoulder?"

Jame flexed it and winced. The broken collarbone would have healed by now if not for the past thirty-odd days in the saddle, despite Bel-tairi's gentle gait. As for riding the rathorn colt Death's-head, forget it.

"Never had a broken bone before, have you?" Harn Grip-hard had said. "Everything will seem worse than it is until you get used to it."

Get used to it? Did one ever?

"We made the best time we could," she said, trying not to sound defensive. "There were delays in Kothifir. Then it's a long way north to the Riverland."

"So I remember, having ridden it many times."

Was he reminding her that, despite the fact that they were twins, he was at least ten years her senior? They had been allies as children, but that was long ago, before their father had ripped them apart. Now he was Lord Knorth and Highlord of the Kencyrath while she was only a second year randon cadet. Despite all that she had accomplished, the gap between them kept widening.

"I thought we had agreed," she said, then bit her lip, vexed. She hadn't meant to lash out so soon, if at all; sometimes, though, he made her so very angry, and she had waited a long time to tell him so.

Torisen's shoulders twitched. "Agreed," he said. "On what?"

"That I was to qualify as a randon officer, if I could, with your approval and support. But I have a year of training yet to go—if the Randon Council doesn't kick me out, and they may. Your summons has cost me my last season at Kothifir."

"From what Harn Grip-hard tells me, you caused quite enough trouble there with the time that you had."

Jame choked back a retort. Dammit, that wasn't fair. She hadn't triggered the failure of the Kencyr temple, or the civic disorder that had followed, or the descent of the Karnid horde upon Kothifir. Things simply happened whenever she was around. Should she tell him that she was potentially one of the three Tyr-ridan expected for millennia by their people? Worse, she was a latent nemesis linked to That-Which-Destroys, the third face of their despised god. Even without trying, how could she help but cause trouble?

. . . *some things need to be broken* . . .

That was hard to explain, however, when standing up to one's knees in the rubble that had been someone else's life.

And Tori hadn't helped matters by summoning her back to Gothregor prematurely.

Renewed unease and anger pricked her. Perhaps he meant to sabotage her chances with the randon, she thought, not for the first time. If they finally accepted her, he would no longer be able to strip her of the rank that she had fought so hard to achieve—not, at least, without insulting the Kencyr warrior class who, so far, supported him and whom he held in high regard. Without that status, though, what prevented him from dumping her back into the Women's World where Highborn girls were nothing but chattel to be contracted out for the greatest political gain?

Maybe, however, the Matriarchs could stop Torisen from foisting her on them again. No doubt they remembered all too well the miserable winter that Jame had spent in their halls when she had first rejoined the Kencyrath. A certain young sewing instructress was still prone to hysterics whenever her name was mentioned, or so Jame had heard.

A faint aroma made her stomach growl. Her brother's dinner, untouched, sat on the table in a nest of papers— cold roast chicken, bread, and cheese. Although it was hard to tell with his back turned, she thought that he looked thinner than when she had last seen him, almost a year ago, and he had always been slender. They shared that trait; people always underestimated them because of it. But this time, perhaps, it was something else.

When Torisen's steward Rowan had delivered his order that Jame attend him immediately upon her arrival, the scar-faced randon had added in a low voice, "Blackie hasn't been quite himself since the end of winter. Walk wary."

At winter's end, Tori would have learned about Brier.

Dark shapes flitted past outside the window as sparrows came home to roost in the vines that climbed the tower. A breeze rustled ivy leaves. On the table, the haphazard pile of correspondence stirred. Jame noted that on many of the scrolls, the wax seal was intact. She wondered if their cousin, Kindrie Soul-walker, was still acting as her brother's scribe. They had decided not to make it common knowledge that the white-haired Shanir was in truth a pure-blooded, legitimate Knorth, one of only three survivors of that ancient house from which the Highlord had always come. People might get ideas.

If Torisen had pushed Kindrie away again, though . . .

Their father, Ganth, had taught him to fear those of the Old Blood. Like Kindrie. Like Jame herself. She knew that, in some moods, she was indeed to be feared, but surely her twin brother with his bound household was Shanir himself. How could he not see that? She had walked in his dreams and in his soulscape, had felt the tension between harsh childhood lessons and adult responsibilities. He was a good man at heart, she told herself, doing his best to manage the flawed society which the Kencyrath had become. He needed her to sweep away the dead wood of the past and Kindrie to preserve that which was still worthwhile, but how could he while the ghost of their father whispered poison through the door in his soul-image which she herself had locked?

A drop of blood trembled on a knife's tip, falling into a cup of wine:

Here, son. Drink to my health.

Had Ganth tried to blood-bind the young Tori as their foul uncle Greshan had his younger brother Ganth? Did that explain the festering paternal splinter in Tori's soul? If so, how did one root out such a thing?

Ah, ha, ha, ha . . .

"You spoke?" said Jame sharply.

"I said, 'Don't touch those.'"

Without thinking, she had reached out to steady the shifting mound of papers. She drew back her hand.

"You claim that we had an agreement," he said, his back still turned, his voice roughening as if it caught in his throat. "If so, it was based on the assumption that you could be trusted. Father said you would steal my people, and he was right. Whom else have you suborned besides the Southron Iron-thorn?"

"If you think that anyone could corrupt Brier," she said, trying to keep her voice light, "you don't know her very well."

"I have known her since she was a child."

And so, of course, he had. Brier was the daughter of Rose Iron-thorn, who had died helping Torisen escape from the dungeons of Urakarn when he had been little more than a boy. He must be remembering that too: His hands had tightened behind his back. A flare of firelight caught their lacework of white scars drawn taut over fine bones.

Jame remembered Brier drunk and raging in the Kothifir barracks, trying to drown the memory of the muffled snap of a baby's neck. Its mother had flung it out the window of a burning tower. Brier had caught it. It had looked merely asleep in her arms, rosy with the heat, its tiny hands just beginning to relax, but it had been dead.

"She said to hold its head just so . . ."

The Highlord is kind, but do I deserve kindness? Do I trust it? Rather give me strength, even if it is cruel.

"She was in despair," Jame said to her brother's back. "She needed support. You were too far away to give it."

And too weak, she nearly added, but was that true? As much as they might fight about other things, she and Torisen shared a deep respect for the Kendar and a reluctance to take advantage of them . . . or was that merely a failure of leadership, as the former Caineron Brier seemed to think?

"I need you," Jame had said to her, oh, in so many ways.

That night, Brier's bond to the Highlord had broken and a new one to his sister had formed.

But am I strong enough to do her justice, Jame wondered now. *If it comes to that, am I sufficiently cruel?*

She felt like being cruel to her brother, to break through his shell of denial. If she was potentially Destruction and Kindrie was becoming Preservation, then Tori must be Creation. Without all three of them aware of and accepting their roles, however, the Tyr-ridan would fail and with it the Kencyrath's god-given mandate to defeat Perimal Darkling—a battle so old that many Kencyr seemed to have forgotten all about it. She could shatter Tori with truths he couldn't bear to face. Perhaps she should. Or was that just the destroyer in her speaking?

The wind came again, alternately bearing the tang of snow high on the surrounding mountain peaks and a promise of rain much needed since the failure of the southern wind earlier that season to bring moisture. The pile of scrolls shifted again. Some rattled to the floor and rolled in among the glowing embers. Parchment scorched, then burst into flames.

Torisen glanced over his shoulder at the flash of light, his eyes a clouded silver gleam in his shadowed face.

"I didn't touch them," said Jame.

"You didn't have to. Filthy Shanir . . ."

"What?"

But he had turned back to the window. The wind built, lifting the wings of his hair, weaving black and silver threads, and careened around the room as if trapped there. Thunder rolled closer. Rain spattered the window ledge. More scrolls tumbled into the fire, and smoldering logs near the back burst into flames. By their uncertain light, Jame thought she saw movement on the plate bearing Torisen's dinner—mold crawling over the bread, maggots over the cheese and meat.

Am I doing that?

It was suddenly much colder, making her exhaled breath smoke. The rain turned to sleet, then hail that drove into the room and bounced off the floor, while overhead, the slate roof rattled. It must be pelting Torisen in the face, but he didn't turn away from it. Jame thought she heard him mutter something, but his words were lost in the general uproar. She crossed the room to stand beside him.

The hail was now whipping sideways, all but obscuring the view. A rush of sparrows outside the window made Jame flinch back. They were fleeing the shelter of the vines in a shrieking mob, to be snatched up by the wind and carried away. She leaned out and looked down, shielding her eyes with a hand. At first, she thought that wind and hail were thrashing the ivy; then she saw that it was crawling slowly up the wall. Rootlets groped for cracks and dug into them. Ice sliced through puffs of mortar dust as the mass of greenery dragged itself up inch by inch.

"Destruction begins with love," Torisen said through stiff lips, in a harsh voice not his own. "The power that seduces, that betrays. . . . They are creatures of the shadows, poisoning men's dreams, sucking out their souls . . . Cursèd be the lot of them . . ."

"Who, Tori?"

"Shanir. Women. You."

And he looked up at her through Ganth's sullen, raging eyes.

For a moment, Jame was rendered speechless. Then, without thinking, she slapped him as hard as she could.

He jerked back and blinked. His rigid expression seemed to melt with the rain that ran down his hollow cheeks and streamed off his beard.

"Jame? When did you get here? What was I saying?"

Scrabbling vines reached the window ledge and hesitated, tendrils waving uncertainly. Beneath them, loosened stones ground together like teeth, spitting out mortar dust, and the tower shivered.

"Stop it," said Torisen to Jame. "Get out. Now."

She opened her mouth to protest, then closed it, gulped, and fled.

II

THE STORM PASSED that night, leaving havoc in its wake.

Until then, it had been a mild spring and the crops

were well advanced despite the lack of rain. Tomatoes, peas, and strawberries were now smashed down in their furrows, along with all new grain less than four inches high with undeveloped roots.

Animals, too, had suffered. Horses and cattle in the fields had stampeded in panic. Lambs, foals, and calves that hadn't been brought into shelter had been trampled or pummeled with hail the size of a child's clenched fist. One clutch of chicks was found pounded into the mud, rendered virtually boneless but still feebly cheeping.

Jame and her ten-command helped wherever they could—in the water meadow, until someone unlatched the flood gate and the inrushing Silver nearly carried them away; in the subterranean stable, until the horses spooked and, led by Torisen's black stallion Storm, battered down the partition walls; around the old keep, until a workman replacing mortar above nearly dropped a loosened stone on Jame's head. No one seemed to be deliberately trying to hurt her, but things kept happening. Finally, on the tenth day after their arrival, Rowan sent them to the relative safety of the apple orchard north of Gothregor, to save as much of it as they could.

The trees had been in bloom when the storm struck and had suffered as much from the sharp, accompanying frost as from the wind and pelting hail. Some were completely blighted, with leaves and blossoms turning black. Many had broken limbs. Others lay on their sides, gnarled roots clutching at the sky. All needed either pruning or removal.

"Heads up!"

A branch crashed down through brittle leaves, almost

hitting Damson. The stocky cadet glowered up at Dar, who yelped and lost his grip on a high limb.

"Damson . . ." said Jame, in a warning tone.

The Shanir cadet made a face and turned away. Jame already knew that Damson could cause considerable damage by tweaking others' minds, especially their sense of balance. Worse, she seemed to enjoy doing so and had, as far as Jame could determine, no conscience whatsoever except where her command-mates were concerned. Instead of now hanging upside down by his knees like some improbable fruit, Dar could have fallen like a stone on his head.

Rue prodded the branch with a toe. "Look. The wood is rotten and . . . ugh." She drew back as black beetles swarmed out of it. The bark collapsed with a papery rustle on its hollow core.

Jame remembered Tori's dinner teeming with mold and maggots. Perhaps the firelight had fooled her eyes, but reports had been coming in for days about disease and insects covering damaged crops.

"Trinity," Rowan had muttered when Jame had told her, in part, what had happened in the tower that first night. "That's worse than I've seen. I only meant to warn you that Blackie has been unusually short-tempered and preoccupied of late. You had better stay out of his way until he sorts himself out. Trust me: he always does."

This had struck Jame as very good advice. She had since seen her brother at a distance, but in general the latter days of spring had passed without the twins crossing paths even though they dwelt, more or less, under the same roof.

In the meantime, Jame thought a good deal about what had happened in the tower, without understanding it at all. She might be a potential nemesis, and she had been very angry that night, but she was usually aware when destruction flared in her. There was a cold, ruthless joy to it, a surrender to forces that seemed beyond her control. At such a moment, one could do anything, no matter how terrible, before conscience pulled her back. If nothing else, her retractile claws emerged. In that context, slapping Tori hardly seemed to count.

How, though, could he be responsible? He had manifested some Shanir traits in the past, true, whether he admitted them or not, but how could That-Which-Creates cause such destruction?

Jame shivered. The closer the three surviving Knorth came to fulfilling their destiny—if they ever did—the more terrifying the prospect became. Would she, Tori, and Kindrie still be themselves, or only puppets of their hated god, possessed by his power? Honor guided them now. Would it protect them then?

"So, how do you reckon the ratings will go?" asked Killy as he tossed an armload of shattered branches into a waiting wagon.

The horse in the shafts shifted from one shot hip to the other, sighed, and went back to sleep. In the wagon bed, the hunting ounce Jorin protested at being woken from his nap. The other cadets groaned.

Of course, they were deeply concerned about how they ranked after their year in Kothifir and how that would effect their third and final year of training. However, they had already picked this topic to pieces and most felt that it was bad luck to bring it up again so close to learning their fates—tomorrow, in fact, on Summer's Day. Killy could be maladroit at times, though. Now he was so again.

"If we pass," he said, cheerfully plowing on, "we'll all become ten-commanders, in charge of regular Kendar or of other cadets. Just think of that!"

"Or five-commanders," said Quill, "which, either way, is barely a step up from where we are now. You mark my words: everything we've done to mess up over the past two years will come back to haunt us. You shouldn't have put a spear through that instructor's leg at Tentir, Killy."

"Ah, who's going to remember that?"

"The instructor, I should think."

"Anyway," said stolid Erim, "the Randon Council will decide according to what skills they think we still need to prove. What good does it do to second-guess them?"

Nonetheless, they were off again despite themselves, wondering out loud where they would be bound on the morrow.

"Tentir for Dar and me as third-year mentors, we hope," said Mint.

The others hooted. During the ride north, she and Dar had at first tried to conceal that they had become lovers, then responded to teasing by flaunting it. The randon college frowned on such attachments, although they were far from uncommon there.

"Special duty for me," said Quill. "I'd like to accompany a diplomatic mission to the Central Lands now that the Seven Kings are riling up against each other again."

"Back to Kothifir," said Erim, "on Harn Grip-hard's staff."

When pressed, quiet Niall spoke wistfully about a ranger assignment. Given his experiences in the slaughter at the Cataracts, no one wondered that he would yearn for the quiet of the wilderness.

Rue had already made it clear that she intended to continue as Jame's servant, no matter what anybody said.

Damson remained silent, although Jame felt the dart of her small eyes. Well aware of her oddity, this disconcerting cadet had announced that she would henceforth look to her Highborn ten-commander as a model—a prospect that filled Jame with profound misgivings.

No one asked the Southron Brier Iron-thorn. She, like Rue, would presumably go wherever Jame did, whatever she felt about it.

Jame hoped that her ten wouldn't suffer for her faults. After all, they had proved themselves over and over in one unlikely situation after another, ending with the defeat of the Karnid horde before Kothifir that had resulted in her own broken collarbone.

She herself had hardly been idle, but not in ways that might count among the randon, assuming they ever learned of them. Harn Grip-hard had his suspicions. So did Sheth Sharp-tongue. Still, they were only two members of the Randon Council, made up as it was of one war-leader from each of the nine major houses.

Jame wondered if Tori already knew what the Council had decided. Surely so, since the randon would have consulted with him as they did with all lords, each of whom had his own special needs for this new crop of cadets. Her brother must already be thinking about possibilities. She hated being at his mercy, especially when their father might at any moment glare at her out of his eyes.

Oh, Tori, what has happened to you, and what does it mean for all of us?

Dar had righted himself on a tree limb. "You should see this, Ten," he called down to her.

Jame considered the apple tree's trunk. Boughs flung wide their arms from it, offering a ready ladder—that is, assuming more of it wasn't afflicted with rot. Her shoulder twinged.

"Here."

Brier stepped between her and the tree, offering cupped hands. For a moment, Jame looked into the Southron's eyes, as green and unreadable as malachite. Even bound as they were, would they ever understand each other?

She put her foot into the offered stirrup of laced fingers without giving herself time to think and was flung upward. Leaves and twigs whipped her in the face. A flailing hand struck a major limb and clung by its claw-tips. Then her feet found purchase. Dar reached down and pulled her up to his perch.

"Look," he said.

Blinking away black spots—crumbled leaves, surely—Jame stared out over the orchard. From ground level, the damage had seemed random. From here, it appeared that the wind and hail had raked through the trees like fingers, leaving parallel tracks of destruction. Those trees on the southwestern edge were blighted and broken. Others leaned together behind them in rows as if seeking shelter, no doubt aided by a vernal touch of arboreal drift. Those that had fallen must have leaned too far. Jame's eyes followed the sweep of destruction, which curled around the foot of Gothregor. She couldn't see over the fortress's high walls, but memory showed her the bands of hail that had fallen across the inner ward, melting in the next day's morning sun. No doubt about it: the Highlord's tower had been the epicenter of the storm.

Movement caught her eye down on the River Road— a troop of travelers approaching the Knorth fortress from the north. From their bright clothes, she judged that they weren't Kencyr.

"Those must be the emissaries from Karkinaroth," said Dar. "I hear that they passed through here around the Feast of Fools, headed for Restormir."

"Why?"

"Folk say that their new prince wants a contract with a Caineron Highborn."

Jame snorted, then reconsidered.

As rare as such an occurrence was, it had happened once before, when Caldane had sent his young daughter Lyra Lack-wit south to the ill-fated Prince Odalian. Then, what the Karkinorans had really wanted was a military alliance with the Kencyrath, and they had gotten something of the sort when the Waster Horde had marched on the Cataracts. Never mind that poor Odalian had been replaced with the darkling changer Tirandys, Jame's former teacher or Senethari, for whom she still mourned.

The visitors disappeared around the foot of the mountain spur upon which Gothregor was built. Horns echoed off the opposite mountain slope, announcing their arrival.

By now it was late afternoon. The sun had set behind the western Snowthorns, and shadows were beginning to pool in the river valley. The cadets threw their last armloads of branches into the wagon, scrambled in after them (again displacing Jorin), and woke the drowsy horse. As soon as the latter realized it was stable-bound, it roused and took them through the northern gate at a bone-jarring trot.

As they passed under the shadow of the gatehouse, a bucket full of hammers fell from above, clipping the horse's flank and smashing on the pavement at its heels. It bolted through into the wasteland that had been the inner ward's garden, sending several cadets tumbling off the back of the wagon into the churned-up mud.

"Sorry!" a voice called after them from above.

"This is getting ridiculous," Rue muttered to Dar as they scrambled to catch up.

The mess hall was already full and boisterous by the time they reached it. Surrounded by towering Kendar, Jame didn't see that someone was already sitting at their table until she was almost upon him, and then he was hard to miss, being large even for one of his kind. She noted, amused, that the table bobbed slightly as it balanced on his raised knees. Marc had aged some over the past year, his red hair thin and receding at the temples, but he was still hale and fit with the muscles of a warrior turned artisan in his late middle age. How old was he now? In his mid-to-late nineties, probably. Jame dropped a kiss on the top of his balding head and sat down on the bench beside him. Since they had first met in Tai-tastigon nearly four years ago, he had been her dearest companion and the moral compass of her turbulent life, sorely missed during her sojourns at Tentir and Kothifir.

Brier sat down on the big Kendar's other side with a nod to him, which he returned with a warm smile. Jame felt an unfamiliar twinge of jealousy. Brier might be his great-granddaughter, but that didn't count for much since they were only related by the paternal line and had barely seen each other since Brier's childhood.

"How was your day?" Jame asked to regain his attention. "Still shutting down the kilns?"

He popped a chunk of bread dripping with gravy into his mouth, chewed, and swallowed. "Yes. Mind you, I'm nowhere near done, but I've run out of raw materials for the moment."

On her last night in the Women's Halls two years ago, pursued by shadow assassins, Jame had accidentally shattered the huge stained-glass map that made up the eastern wall of the High Council Chamber. Ever since, Marc had been trying to repair it, and doing a remarkable job, considering his only knowledge of glassmaking was hearsay gained from the secretive artists of Tai-tastigon. He had discovered that sand, ash, and lime taken from various parts of Rathillien, not to mention traces of such native elements as cobalt, copper, and gold to add color, created glass unique to that area.

Contiguous pieces in turn fused together spontaneously, allowing him to fit them into the upright window frame. The result was spectacular, but it didn't look at all like a map unless one knew how to read the mineral traces. Bits of it glowed where Torisen had mixed drops of his blood into the molten glass, to what purpose, no one was yet sure. Also, there were holes in it: despite over three thousand years on Rathillien, the Kencyr had not yet explored all parts of their new world.

"That reminds me," said Jame. "It's odd that this never occurred to me before, but the original map only showed the Central and Eastern Lands."

Marc frowned, wiping his beard. "I didn't think of that either. There's no room for the Western Lands on the new map either, and that's not just because I have no raw materials for them. It's as if they no longer existed."

Jame shivered. One could go a long while, even a lifetime, without thinking about Rathillien's endangered status as the threshold world closest to Perimal Darkling, ancient of enemies. The Kencyrath had retreated down the Chain of Creation for some thirty millennia, ever since The Three-Faced God had created it to fight the shadows that crawled. How many worlds they had lost, not even the scrollsmen of Mount Alban knew for sure, nor how close they were to losing this last refuge. Most agreed that Rathillien was round, and that the other side of it had already been swallowed. The Barrier lay within sight of the Haunted Lands keep where Jame and Tori had been born, also just north of the Merikits' land and south of the Southern Wastes. There were also "thin" spots such as the White Hills where it dwelt just under Rathillien's surface. How close had it crept to the west? The Tishooo, otherwise known as the Falling Man, one of Rathillien's four elementals, had gone to see. Jame wondered if he would ever return to tell her.

No one had yet served the cadets their dinner.

"D'you suppose they've forgotten us again?" Quill asked, craning to look around.

It had happened at almost every meal. The odd thing was that the neglect didn't seem to be deliberate. People simply forgot that they were there.

Under the table, Jorin impatiently butted her knee with his nut-hard head. He was hungry too.

Belatedly, a cook rushed out of the kitchen carrying a streaming cauldron of soup, its bottom still ruddy from the fire. Clutching its handles through his bunched-up apron, he dodged around the diners, trying not to splash anyone. As he neared Jame's table, however, he tripped. His grip on the pot held, but its contents went flying. Marc knocked her backward off the bench, out of the way. Soup flew over her head in a scalding brown sheet that seemed to boil in midair. It hit the back and exposed neck of a Knorth Kendar seated at the next table, who jumped up with a startled yelp of pain. The cook dropped the kettle and bustled over to administer to his enraged victim. The pot, meanwhile, rolled under another bench and over assorted feet. As chaos spread, Jame regained her seat.

"Has this sort of thing happened often, since you returned?" Marc asked.

"Huh. More so than it should."

The big man regarded the remains of his meal, then pushed them aside.

"Kendar are often vulnerable to their lords' health and moods," he said. "It comes with the bond between them."

"I know that."

Hadn't she seen Lord Caineron inflict his vicious hangover on his helpless bondsmen at Restormir? Worse, wasn't her father Ganth said to have imposed his madness on his followers in the White Hills when he had sought to avenge the slaughter of the Knorth ladies on the Seven Kings, never mind that they were the wrong target?

The very thought made her feel sick. The so-called Highborn shouldn't have such power over the perforce servile Kendar. Damn their god anyway, for having made the Kencyrath so.

Some things need to be broken.

"That which can be destroyed by the truth should be," Kirien had said, never mind that it had been in the grip of what amounted to an academic berserker fit.

But what was the truth?

If the link between the Three People suddenly disappeared, what would become of them? The catlike Arrin-ken would probably go their own way, as they had for the past two millennia. The competent Kendar could no doubt manage by themselves. Only the proud Highborn would be left helpless. Fair enough. However, if the Kencyrath did break, who would be left to oppose Perimal Darkling? She thought again of shadows hungry for life crawling out of the Master's House, out of the Haunted Lands, out of the Southern Wastes, and she shivered.

The mess-hall fracas had grown around them, spilling from table to table. Some Kendar leaped up with curses, upsetting benches, as their neighbors barged into them. Others shouted for order, and raised fists to enforce it.

When someone bumped into him, Killy half rose, but Brier's hand on his shoulder pressed him back down. The ten-command sat wide-eyed in the midst of chaos, once again forgotten.

All in all, it was one of the strangest fights that Jame had ever seen.

Kendar sometimes reflected their lords' moods.

Tori was doing his best to ignore her, but behind that Jame sensed that he was angry, confused and, yes, perhaps even frightened, Ancestors only knew why. He didn't want to hurt her. Neither did his people. However, accidents kept happening. Of course, except for Brier, her ten-command were also bound to the Highlord, but they knew her better than they did him, and as twins she and Tori had much in common. So far she seemed to be providing them with an adequate substitute.

"We should leave," Jame said to Brier, under the uproar, both of them ducking a flung bowl. "Without us here, they may calm down."

She had been resting her forearms on the tabletop, sleeves rolled up to her elbows after the day's heat. When she rose, she saw that the wood which she had touched was bumpy with knotted whorls as surely it hadn't been before. What, now she was giving the very furniture hives? Time to go, indeed.

ᚱᚱᚱᚱ CHAPTER II ᚱᚱᚱᚱ
Departure
Spring 60—Summer 15

I

AS THEY TRUDGED ACROSS the muddy former garden, Jame glanced up at the keep, oldest of Gothregor's structures, which stood between the inner ward and the forecourt of the Women's Halls. Light streamed through the surviving stained-glass windows of the third-floor Council Chamber. Tori must be entertaining the Karkinoran emissaries. A dark silhouette stood framed by the central panel that depicted the Knorth's rathorn crest. Jame knew instinctively that it was her brother. Was he watching them pass below, hungry and tired, driven out of his hall? She almost called out to him, but choked back the words. He seemed to wait a moment, then turned and retreated into the chamber's interior.

Feeling miserable, she plodded on. Ever since she had returned to Rathillien, fleeing the Master's House and Perimal Darkling, her one goal had been to rejoin her twin brother. They belonged together. Even as squabbling children, she had known that, and thought that he did too. Since her return, however, he had pushed her away again and again, and Kindrie too: She had learned that the Shanir healer was still at Mount Alban, apparently in no hurry to return.

Someone's stomach growled. The others chuckled, but Jame knew they must all feel just as hungry. What kind of a leader was she, who couldn't keep her own troops fed?

Their quarters were located in the thickness of the outer wall, a long, narrow chamber with cots lining one wall and windows the other, overlooking the inner ward. As they entered, Jorin's ears pricked. Jame's quarters were at the far end of the hall, set off by a wooden partition. The ounce disappeared through its doorway. When Jame caught up with him, he was under her bed, all but for the tip of his twitching tail. From beneath the frame came a muffled shriek.

Brier moved quickly past her, with Damson a pace behind her. Picking up the bed by its head and foot, they swung it away from the wall. All the cadets stood in the doorway, staring at the figure curled up on the floor, trying to fend off the ounce's inquisitive nose and dabbing paw.

"Jorin, back."

Jame helped the girl to her feet. She was dressed, or rather almost undressed, in a welter of white ribbons, the fashionable sleeping attire of a young Highborn lady. A lacy mask shadowed rather than concealed her face.

"Why, Lyra, I didn't know that you were at Gothregor."

Caldane's young daughter surged forward, tripped

over a stray ribbon, and fell into Jame's arms, jolting her
sore shoulder and almost knocking her over. As she
steadied them both, she nodded to Brier over the girl's
shoulder. The Southron cadet withdrew from the tiny
room and discreetly shut the door after her. Jame sank
down on the displaced bed, still holding Lyra.

The young Highborn was almost in tears.

"Oh, I'm so glad to see you!" she cried. "Everything
has been so dull here, until now. I've been in the Women's
Halls all spring. Kallystine says I must learn how to be a
proper lady, but I want to be like you and have
adventures!"

Kallystine had once been Torisen's limited-term
consort, before one of her potions had backfired and
withered her face. Jame hadn't heard anything more
about her over the past two years.

"Great-grandma Cattila is ill," explained Lyra, looking
suddenly doleful. "Sister Kallystine has taken over her
duties until she's better."

The Caineron Matriarch was possibly the oldest
woman Jame had ever met, short of the Earth Wife
herself, who sometimes acted as Cattila's spy, or Ear. At
her age, she might well be dying. Kallystine must be back
in her father's favor to have claimed the matriarch's role,
even temporarily.

"That still doesn't explain why you were hiding under
my bed," she said.

Lyra's expression changed again, stricken by sudden
recollection. She gripped Jame's arms, making her wince.
"They're coming! They're coming! Oh, please don't let
them take me away! I was so miserable there, until you

rescued me, with only Gricki for company. The Prince was kind, but I hardly ever saw him. And then he changed."

Jame sorted this out. "Gricki" had been Lyra's half-breed servant in the palace at Karkinaroth, before she, Jame, had accidentally bound him and given him a new name. Graykin was still in Kothifir, acting as her spymaster. The hapless prince had been Odalian, whose place the changer Tirandys had taken before the battle at the Cataracts.

"You're afraid that the new prince's agents mean to take you back to Karkinaroth."

"Why else are they here? When they came through before, going north, they brought me all sorts of pretty trinkets, but they talked over my head to the Matriarchs as if I were a child or an idiot. How Karidia smirked and simpered. Everything must be just as dear Kallystine desires. Oh, she made me so mad!"

The Coman lord was part Caineron. Karidia, the Coman Matriarch, clearly believed that any additional alliance or favor done to that powerful house reflected some of its glory onto tiny Kraggen Keep, her own home. She was about as annoying a person as Jame had ever met, like a small dog that wouldn't stop yapping.

"Have you heard from your father that he's made a new contract for you?"

Lyra sniffled. "Why would he tell me? You know how Highborn ladies get passed around, like sweets after dinner. It shouldn't be that way, should it?"

"Of course not. Still, there's something odd about all of this."

Someone tapped on the door. "Ten, Five says that there's a bunch of people headed this way," said Erim, outside, keeping his voice low. "She thinks one of them is the Coman Matriarch."

Lyra gave a little shriek. "Oh, she knows I'm here! I thought I was so clever, sneaking out, but I must have been seen. Don't let her have me! Oh, please!"

Jame held her, thinking. She couldn't deny that Lyra was here—that would be a lie, the death of honor. There wasn't a back way to smuggle her out, either. Refuse to hand her over? The Coman had no right to a Caineron, whatever Karidia thought, but then neither did a Knorth. At the least, it would cause a fracas, and then Tori would have to get involved. She didn't want to meet her brother again under such conditions.

Someone knocked on the dormitory's outer door. Then came a pause, then a barrage of petulant rapping, then Brier's steady, courteous voice.

"Matriarch. To what do we owe this honor?"

"I know that chit is here. Produce her at once!"

"What chit?"

"Lyra Lack-wit, as if you didn't know!"

"Why should a Caineron be in the Knorth barracks?"

"Because she idolizes that hoyden your lord has been fool enough to make his lordan. A disgrace to all Highborn ladies, that wretched girl. Everyone knows that all Knorth are mad, and you were fool enough to desert the Caineron for them. For shame, you turn-collar! Now let me pass!"

Yap, yap, yap.

Jame could almost see the Coman Matriarch stomping

an impatient foot on the threshold—something not so easily done given her tight underskirt. With luck, she would fall over.

Lyra was clinging to her. "Don't let her take me. Oh please, don't! Something bad is going to happen tonight. I just know it!"

Jame made up her mind.

"Lyra, be quiet," she said, giving the girl a shake. "Listen. This is what we're going to do."

II

BRIER HELD HER POSITION, patiently blocking the door while the plump little matriarch shouted up into her face. Over Karidia's head, she regarded the Coman guards who had accompanied her from the Women's Halls. They were all female, of course, and singularly blank of expression. What would they do if their mistress ordered them to invade the Knorth barracks? Brier knew what she would do if they tried and silently told them so, eye to eye.

A rustle of cloth made her look over her shoulder just as a slim figure muffled in a hooded cloak slipped forward between the watching cadets. Gloved hands held the garment shut. White ribbons fluttered around its hem.

Brier raised an eyebrow, but stepped politely out of the way.

Karidia pounced upon her prey and led her away with a tight grip on her arm, scolding incessantly.

III

". . . AND STAY THERE!"

The bedroom door closed, the lock clicked. Karidia
yapped some more through the keyhole, then went away.

Jame let the cloak drop to the floor. She was fairly sure
that Lyra's bed clothes shouldn't be wrapped so
haphazardly around her or tied with such hasty, clumsy
knots, but there hadn't been much time for finesse.
Doubtless Lyra had maids to help her in such matters of
dress, but Karidia had sent them all away, leaving only a
few candles lit against the coming night. Jame tugged at a
loop, which came apart in her hand. She felt like a badly
wrapped package, and more naked than if she had been
stripped to the skin.

Lyra's quarters were full of expensive trinkets and
luxurious appointments, as one would expect for the
daughter of a rich house. Jame wandered about it,
examining a handful of gems casually scattered across the
top of a dressing table, a golden bird that ruffled metallic
feathers as she passed, and a bent silver flute. Lyra would
appear to be an impatient student of music. Likewise, a
pack of gen cards with simpering images had been thrown
into one corner and dismembered clothes into another—
attempts, it seemed, to transform court dresses into
divided skirts such as the Brandan Matriarch wore, to the
chagrin of her colleagues.

Jame wondered what she was doing here. Short of
turning Lyra over to Karidia, it was the only solution that

had come immediately to mind. True, in the morning the ruse would be exposed unless she escaped during the night, but that would only postpone the hunt.

More than that, though, she felt that there was something odd about Lyra's sudden contract, if indeed there was one. Surely Karidia would have mentioned it. A prospective bride hiding under a bed should have provoked some comment, assuming that the matriarch was sharp enough to see the irony.

However, if Lyra was right . . .

The curse of the girl's position in the Women's Halls was that there was no Caineron Matriarch to protect her, even less so if Cattila was sick at home and the reins had fallen to Kallystine. The Matriarchs collaborated on some things, but each was primarily out to profit her own house. When Jame had been an inmate of the halls over that terrible winter three years ago, of course there had been no Knorth Matriarch nor even any other Knorth ladies to support her. She had been put entirely in Kallystine's power with the aim, she guessed, that she be baited into showing the worst of her nature. The sudden appearance of a mysterious Highborn Knorth must have alarmed the Matriarchs, given what the Kencyrath had suffered from that house during her father's reign as highlord.

In the end, though, it was Kallystine who had betrayed herself.

Jame touched her cheek. Through Lyra's dainty mask she would feel the scar left by Kallystine's razor-ring. There had been fears, at the time, that such a vicious, unprovoked attack would lead to a blood feud between the Knorth and the Caineron, but subsequent events had over-shadowed the injury. Jame herself seldom thought about it. She had never been nor expected to be a beauty, so why fret?

But Lyra was so young, so innocent, so vulnerable, and no favorite of her older half-sister.

Well, she would sort things out in the morning. Perhaps the Jaran Matriarch Trishien would tell her what was going on, or even the Brandan Brenwyr, if she was in residence.

Jame tried Lyra's bed, but it was so soft that she felt swallowed by it. Instead, she chose a white bear skin on the hearth and curled up on it under her cloak.

Uneasy sleep led to dreams. Someone lay under the cloak with her, back to back. Tori, she thought. They had always fitted together, whatever posture they took. Her long, black hair flowed over her shoulders and down his chest, now as it had then when as a child Tori had sometimes wrapped himself in it. Shifting tension on her scalp told her that he was fingering its ends. It felt as if they had been arguing for hours, in circles.

". . . what do you know of leadership?" he was saying. "You may be a randon cadet, but whenever you can, you've handed over your duties to someone else—Brier Iron-thorn at Tentir, Marigold Onyx-eyed at Kothifir. You've missed many lessons, once twenty days of them at a time. You're always running off, Perimal only knows where, leaving your ten-command, your entire house, to fend for themselves. No wonder the randon question your competence, or at least your commitment."

They did? With a sinking heart, she remembered that

tomorrow was Summer's Day, when her fate for the next year would be decided. When Tori would decide it.

"You had Tentir. I would have given anything for that. And you threw it away."

Tug.

"I did not! Anyway, there are other things besides lessons and barracks duties." She tried not to sound defensive, wanting to turn the conversation. "And I seem to be the only one doing anything about them. 'Fear the One, await the Three, seek the Four,' or so the Arrin-ken say."

"What's that supposed to mean?"

Tug.

Had she explained this to him before? He had so much power over her, but knowledge was power too, and she hadn't shared everything she knew or guessed. Perhaps, if she did, she could break through this new, strange barrier between them.

"You know the Four," she said, "or at least you saw the Burnt Man once, at Kithorn, and you met the Earth Wife in her lodge. She was the one hanging by her feet from the rafters while I tried to jar her molten fat back into place. The other two are the Falling Man and the Eaten One. The Arrin-ken went looking for them. The Dark Judge has some sort of an alliance with the Burnt Man, Mother Ragga is friends with the Caineron Matriarch, and Timmon's half-brother Drie got swallowed by his lover, the Eaten One. I've encountered all four, but don't really have an understanding with any of them. To them, the Kencyrath is as much an invader as Perimal Darkling. They speak for Rathillien, but in a confused way. Each was an individual who found him- or herself cast into one of these roles according to the nature of their imminent deaths when our temples activated on this world."

"Are you saying that we created them?"

He sounded dubious, and a bit scornful. Jame began to regret telling him anything.

Tug.

"Ow. Tori, stop it. In a sense we did, the way that the uncontrolled power of our temples made the New Pantheon gods possible, except that the Four rose out of the Old Pantheon, the gods worshiped on Rathillien before we came."

"This is getting complicated. I imagine that the Three are the Tyr-ridan, who speak for our own wretched god, or will when they deign to show up."

Jame gulped. "Tori, there are three of us Knorth now. I—I think I'm a potential nemesis, about to become Destruction incarnate."

"That doesn't surprise me at all. Then who, pray tell, is the One?"

She noted that he skipped over the other two potential Tyr-ridan, Creation and Preservation. However, a nervous tremor ran through him. That was unusual, as she knew from their childhood when they had often shared a bed. This was a dream. They had often shared those as well. Something more was going on this time, though, and that made her increasingly uneasy.

"The One is the Voice of Perimal Darkling, which Gerridon is under pressure to become," she said, all the time testing the link between them. They were currently in the dreamscape. Dared she probe beneath that to the soulscape? The thought made her shudder. Just keep talking. "You see, the Master is running out of Kencyr souls to maintain the immortality he gained by betraying us all during the Fall. Perimal Darkling will sustain his eternal life if he agrees to speak for it, but that also means being consumed by the shadows."

Torisen twitched again. In her mind, his voice began to take on a peculiar undertone, as if someone sought to speak with or through him. "The randon say he led the Karnids against Kothifir. Why is he still fighting for Perimal Darkling if he doesn't want to serve it?"

"It isn't quite like that. He will do anything to avoid paying for the Fall. You talked to him when you were a boy serving in Kothifir, didn't you? You know he has no honor or conscience. He wants Rathillien and the Kencyrath for himself, to make a stand against the shadows. He will sacrifice anything and anyone to obtain that goal."

"Then there are three forces: the Three-faced God, Perimal Darkling, and Rathillien. Each is seeking its own voice, its own manifestations."

"Yes. It will come down to individuals acting for greater powers. Oh, Tori, don't you see? It all seemed so far away, so long in coming, but come it will, soon, and we aren't ready!"

He laughed, with a sob caught on his voice.

The undernote swelled into a throaty, avid whisper.

"Foolish, foolish child. As if it were given to you of all people to know the truth. Oh!"

And Tori's voice returned, half strangled.

"Shut up, shut up, shut up! What good is that, or

anything else, if the Kencyrath falls apart first? It needs a strong leader. Now. Father says . . . Father says . . . you will destroy me if you can. Destruction begins with love. I love . . . I love . . . no! I refuse to be driven mad or to harm my sister. I refuse to listen."

"What? Tori, stop it! You're hurting me!" He had wrenched at her hair, jerking her head back. She clutched it to ease the strain.

"The door is shut, the door is shut!" he cried, pulling harder.

They twisted face to face. His hands were knotted in her hair; she barely restrained hers from clawing through his beard, into his eyes. Wake up, wake up, wake up . . .

And so abruptly she did, alone, tangled in the cloak, cold with sweat.

IV

THE ROOM WAS DARK, the candles burned out. It took Jame a moment to remember where she was. Parts of the dream were already beginning to fade, as tightly as she tried to hold on to them. Something important had happened—hadn't it?—but what? Oh, schist.

"A dream," she muttered. "It was only a dream."

But something had woken her. A sound. The soft click of a key in a lock.

The air currents in the room changed. Feet shuffled. Several muffled figures had entered the apartment and now loomed over her.

"Come, little lady," one of them murmured in a voice

thick with a Southron accent. "We will take you to your prince."

And hands reached down.

So Lyra had been right, thought Jame as she allowed her kidnappers to hustle her down the steps, bundled up in her cloak, and out of the Caineron compound. Something bad was happening tonight. Still, the situation baffled her. Did the Karkinorans think that they could escape the Riverland with their captive, fifty miles past three keeps? For that matter, how did they even mean to get out of the Women's Halls?

They hurried her down the northern arm of the gallery that lined the forecourt, under the shadow of the old keep. Ahead was the gate that gave access to the inner ward, but where were its guards?

The bulk of the Women's Halls lay to the south, housing the Edirr, Danior, Ardeth, Randir, Jaran and Coman. Some commotion was going on there, shrill voices raised in alarm or protest. No doubt the gate-wards had gone to investigate.

The gate swung open. A dozen figures waited with saddled horses at the head of the ramp leading down to the subterranean stable. Close by was the northern gate, which gave access through the thickness of the wall to the ravaged apple orchard.

Jame had gone as far as she intended to go with her would-be abductors. She drew a deep breath and unleashed the rathorn battle-cry of her house, a shattering scream that sank to a bone-rattling roar. The men holding her flinched. She slipped out of their grasp, reversing a wrist lock on one of them. When she twisted it, he flipped over its fulcrum of pain. The other scrabbled to regain his hold. She stomped on his toes—a less effective move than if she had been shod—then drove her elbow into his stomach and met his chin with her fist as it jerked down.

Warning shouts sounded as dark figures ran down the gallery and across the forecourt, the guards returning to their posts. Outside the gate, horses shrilled and reared. On both sides of the wall, Kencyr scythed through the intruders, leaving them on the ground still or groaning.

Jame had retreated down the arcade. She had wrenched her barely healed shoulder, and it hurt. For once, let someone else have all the fun.

A parcel of matriarchs arrived in a flurry of skirts, following their house-guards. Jame imagined that the windows above must be full of curious eyes, not that the girls there could see through the gallery's tin roof. Some of the brawl had spilled out into the forecourt, though, no doubt to their delight.

Karidia arrived, scolding. Jame noted that she was fully dressed, unlike her colleagues in their flowing nightgowns. Ribbons, apparently, were reserved for the very young, and tight underskirts for daytime wear.

The crowd of ladies on the arcade parted and the Ardeth Matriarch Adiraina passed through it, supported by the Danior Matriarch Dianthe. Adiraina walked carefully, running her free hand along the gallery rail. Her sleeping mask was embroidered with shut eyelids. Pearls like tears hung in a fringe from long, silken lashes. She turned her blind face toward the battleground, where only Kencyr now stood.

"What is the meaning of this disgrace?"

Karidia stepped forward, blustering. "It's only that Prince Uthecon's emissaries have come to fetch his bride. This unpleasantness would not have been necessary if Lord Caineron had been more reasonable."

"Caldane did not approve of his daughter's proposed contract, did he?"

"Humph. We of the Women's World should have the say in such matters."

"But we do not, not since the Fall. Was this Kallystine's idea?"

Karidia huffed. "I'm sure that dear Kallystine acted in the best interests of her house."

"No doubt," said Dianthe dryly, "in exchange for a magnificent bribe."

"So they gave her gifts, as is only proper."

Jame became aware of a growing, silent crowd just outside the gate. There was Brier's tall frame and Marc's, which overtopped both her and everyone else. Torisen stood between them, looking as slight as a boy by comparison.

"This is all very well," he said, with a touch of amusement, "but what does it have to do with kidnapping my sister?"

Incredulous eyes turned to Jame, who removed Lyra's mask and stepped forward.

Karidia raised pudgy fists as if to flourish them in her face. "You . . . you . . . wretched creature! What right have you to meddle with the affairs of true ladies? Leave our halls at once! In fact, kindly leave this fortress!"

"Point of law," said the Jaran Matriarch Trishien. She had come up quietly and stood at the edge of the throng, stray flickers of light reflecting in the lens sewn into her mask. Jame wondered if she wore them night as well as day, the better to read in bed when the urge took her.

"We are the Highlord's guests," Trishien said. "He can order us to leave but not we him or, I think, his sister and lordan. I have reminded you of this before," she added, sounding somewhat apologetic.

Meanwhile the Karkinorans were slowly recovering themselves, except for several who had to be lifted from the ground and supported.

"This is a most unseemly treatment of guests," said the leader, glaring at Torisen.

"Honorable guests do not attempt to steal from their host."

"Nonetheless, our prince will hear of this."

"I daresay he shall. Soon. By sunset of the day now dawning, I request that you quit the Riverland."

"What, travel fifty miles in a day?"

"Ride fast."

They left the forecourt, some stumbling, others carried. Their horses had been caught and quieted. Mounted, the leader scowled down at Torisen.

"You may yet regret this, my lord. The time will come, soon, when you seek employment for your mercenaries in our court."

"Be that as it may, goodbye."

They rode out.

The ladies departed with sidelong looks at Karidia, whose face in the growing light was dark red and pop-eyed with ill-swallowed chagrin.

"See me before you go," Trishien murmured as she passed Jame.

Go where?

The crowd outside the gate also dispersed, except for Torisen.

"Such a long night," he said to Jame. "Still, we need to talk."

V

UP IN THE TOWER STUDY, Burr had kindled a fire against the morning chill. Jame curled up in a chair beside it and began absentmindedly to pluck off her ribbons.

Torisen stood by the window looking out as he had on that first night, but with only a hint of that fearful flare of power around him. On the whole, he seemed to be more self-possessed than she had yet seen him, but also bone tired.

"One thing," he said wryly over his shoulder, "life is always interesting when you are around. Where, pray tell, is that prize nitwit, Lyra?"

"In my quarters, I assume." One by one, she flattened each ribbon and rolled it into a compact ball. "She really doesn't want to go back to Karkinaroth."

"Now she won't have to, unless Caldane changes his mind. I rather think, though, that he has other plans for her. She's something of a prize, you know, and a useful bargaining chip. Kallystine overreached herself. Do you know why?"

Jame shrugged. The cloak had slipped off her shoulders and she was glad of the fire's warmth.

"Kallystine is ambitious and vengeful, but not very

bright," she said. "However, with Cattila ill, there will be an imbalance of power at Restormir. I think Lord Caineron both respects and fears his great-grandmother. Without her to check his behavior, however slightly, he might do anything."

"I hope not," said Torisen, with a shudder, "given his past behavior. Hard times are coming. That Karkinoran was right. With King Krothen cutting back on the Southern Host, less money will funnel back to the Riverland."

Jame looked up, startled. "I thought Kroaky meant to keep his Kencyr forces intact, whatever happened."

"So he said. Repeatedly. However, Kothifir's glory days are over and we will all suffer for it."

Jame thought about her journey across the Southern Wastes, back in time, to the lost city of Languidine and of its destruction in one terrible night, due to the awakening of the Kencyr temple around which part of its royal palace was built. It had all been part of Kencyr history unfolding, in an unguessed-at way. Perhaps it was appropriate that the Kencyrath of the present should also reap that bitter fruit. However, life in the Riverland had never been easy. The fields, pastures, and orchards of the river valley simply didn't provide enough food or raw materials for the nine major houses located there. Mercenaries' pay allowed their lords to buy needed supplies in the Central Lands.

Quill had mentioned that the Seven Kings had started to squabble again. In the past, before Ganth's fall in the White Hills, Kencyr mercenaries had done much of their fighting for them. Not since. Now Prince Uthecon of

Karkinor wanted a renewed contract with the Caineron that might extend to military support. She saw where Tori's fear lay. Would he or any lord be forced to hire out fighters to support their Riverland keeps? And if they did, might these Kencyr be forced to meet each other on the battlefield, as had happened in the White Hills?

"I'm sorry," she said, hardly knowing for what.

Torisen squared his shoulders. "We have suffered worse, and survived. Now, for today's business. I have the Randon Council's recommendations."

Jame sat up with a jerk. After a moment, she remembered to breathe. "What of them?"

He turned back to the table and tapped a long finger on a stack of unrolled scrolls held down at their corners by smooth river rocks.

"You will be glad to hear, no doubt, that all of your ten-command has passed. Dar, Mint, Niall, and Damson have been promoted to ten-commanders. Erim, Quill, Rue, and what's-his-name, oh yes, Killy, are now five-commanders. I will make up the rest out of Kendar either stationed here or on their way back from Kothifir, with an assortment thrown in of second-year cadets who otherwise would be going south."

"And Brier?"

"From what I hear, Iron-thorn filled the role of master-ten, second-in-command to you, both at Tentir and Kothifir. That will now be made official. Rue will remain your servant. You may wish to promote her to chamberlain." His lips quirked. "You may find that one hard to shake off."

"And . . . what about me?"

"A one-hundred commander. There's a hitch, though. The randon question your competence." He paused and gulped. "We've had this conversation before, haven't we?"

How much of the dream did he remember? Enough, apparently, to be embarrassed, as well he should be.

"We both know that you can't stay here, not as things are."

What things? she wanted to ask, but the words caught in her throat. The floodgates unexpectedly opening, the horses stampeding, the mess-hall table breaking out in hives at her touch . . . Was he right to blame her for everything that had gone wrong? No, dammit. Not this time.

"You think I'm a danger to our Kendar," she said, leaning forward. "You want me as far from them as possible. But I'm your lordan, your heir. You can't send me off into the wilderness, say, as a ranger, or cast me off altogether without admitting to the other lords that you made a mistake."

Torisen rubbed his temples. He was apparently getting a headache, and Jame wasn't entirely sorry.

"You are the Highlord's heir," he said, "therefore more is asked of you than of other lordan. This is what I have decided. You will take your new one-hundred command and reclaim one of the Riverland's abandoned keeps. There are six of them, three more or less intact. Chantrie is closest, just across the river. Don't look to me for help. Survive on your own for your third year as a cadet and no one will ever question your skills as a leader again."

Jame sat back, momentarily speechless. Life would be hard enough in the major keeps over the coming winter.

How could she hope to provide for her people? It would be like her failure tonight to feed her ten-command, only a hundred times worse, quite literally a matter of life or death. Was he setting her up for failure yet again?

"As you will, my lord," she said as she rose. Putting the ball of ribbons on his table, leaving her cloak behind, she stalked out of the tower study.

VI

THE NEXT nine days passed in a blur of preparation.

To staff the base of her new hundred-command, Jame had ten ten-commands, four under the charge of her former team mates Dar, Mint, Niall, and Damson. The fifth was that harsh-voiced Kendar Corvine, once an oath-breaker, now newly returned to the Knorth. The sixth through the ninth were new to her: cheerful Jerr, dour Talbet, as well as a pair of older identical twins except that one was fair and the other dark: Berry and Huckle.

The tenth commander came as a surprise.

Stepping out of the west wing barracks into a bright, cloudless morning, Jame glanced across the inner ward at the square tower of the old keep. She had talked to her brother several times over the past few days about setting up her soon-to-be-launched expedition. He had remained courteous and tightly controlled, his face pinched with the headache that now seemed to be his constant companion. She had heard him burst into rants against Rowan and other Kendar, only to pull himself up short and tersely apologize. Their dreams, when they crossed, left her tense and unhappy, although she couldn't remember on waking what they had been about.

How could she help him when he shut her out so completely? If only Harn and Grimly were here, they might have broken through to him. Perhaps he talked to his servant Burr, but she doubted it, and cousin Kindrie was still at Mount Alban, not that he and Tori were completely comfortable with each other yet, as how could they be while Tori's deeply entrenched hatred (or was it fear?) of the Shanir remained?

Someone was tramping across the newly replanted vegetable garden of the ward toward her.

"Char?" she said in surprise. "When did you get here?"

He glowered at her. "Last night. I'm reporting to you as ordered . . . ran."

"I'm not a randon officer yet, but you should be. What happened?"

Char had been a third-year Knorth cadet at Kothifir, one of several who had tried to force Jame out of the Southern Host with challenges. He had also been at the Cataracts and, along with the rest of his surviving classmates, had been promoted on the battlefield from second to third-year status. That had probably been a mistake. Having missed most of Tentir, the jumped-ahead cadets were noted both for their arrogance and for a touch of immaturity. Nonetheless, Jame had thought, after the thwarted Karnid invasion, that she had won Char's grudging acceptance. Now here he was, looking at her askance with loathing in his eyes.

"The Randon Council decided that I don't yet know how to follow orders," he said, "so they ordered me to repeat my third year. You wouldn't know anything about that, would you?"

"Of course I don't."

"Of course." With a lopsided sneer, he turned to go.

"Char." Her voice, though quiet, stopped him as if he had run into an invisible wall. "Your new command is gathering in the north barracks. You will have one of my old command, Killy, as your number five—and no, he isn't my spy."

Char shook his head as if to clear it. "Did you hear the results of the vote?" he asked, somewhat hoarsely.

"What vote . . . oh."

She had completely forgotten. Throughout her year at Tentir, all cadets had been tested over and over again, mostly by the randon. At Kothifir, it had been the cadets' turn to pass judgment on their peers: Who would they most willingly follow into battle?

"We chose Brier Iron-thorn," said Char, and walked away, stumbling a bit.

Jame considered this somewhat blankly. It made sense, of course: Brier was a born leader. And it was good that the Knorth cadets had finally accepted the former Caineron rather than seeing her as a turn-collar.

But it also felt like a slap in Jame's face.

I still have to win their approval, she thought, dismayed, *as well as Tori's and the Randon Council's.* Would these tests never end?

Her mood lifted, however, at the sight of Marc approaching along the northern edge of the ward. He, at least, knew better than to trample newly planted crops.

"Have you changed your mind?" she asked as the big

Kendar loomed over her, his thinning hair a back-lit halo in the morning sun.

"No. As I said before, there's nothing more I can do here for the moment. I've filled in the map's blank space with cullet—not satisfactory, of course, but I hope that it will hold the whole in a lead frame until I have more to work with. So I'll go with you . . . if you still wish it."

Jame smiled up at him. "Of course I do. I'll need a steward, won't I?"

He looked startled. "I'm not a randon, you know. I've never been anything but a common soldier."

"There's never been anything common about you."

His brow creased with thought as he thumbed his bearded chin. "If I'm going to run your household, I'd better start thinking about provisions. Where are we going, by the way?"

So far, Jame hadn't told anyone. Most assumed, as did Tori, that she was removing to Chantrie just across the river, within easy reach of help if needed, never mind that to ask for it would be to admit failure.

"Tagmeth," she said.

Marc blinked. "That will put us north of Restormir, with the Caineron as a neighbor, in a ruin that they tried to reclaim before Caldane's great-grandfather consolidated the family in the home keep. Why not keep going, up to Kithorn?"

"That's Merikit territory now. I'm sorry. Of course you would like to go back to your old home."

Marc considered this. "Well, maybe not. There are too many memories."

Jame knew that he was thinking about his family

slaughtered by the Merikit and wondered how he would feel, being so close to his old enemies again, never mind that the massacre had been the result of a misunderstanding.

"Tagmeth it is, then," said Marc, pulling his mind back to the present and future.

Jame watched him walk off, deep in thought. After losing Kithorn, he had served as a Caineron yondri or threshold-dweller for many years before walking all the way to East Hold in search of a new lord. Turned out there, too, he had reached Tai-tastigon in despair, ready to die, only to stumble across her, an apprentice thief who was also Kencyr, also questing. In himself, he embodied the tragic fate of many Kendar under the rule of fickle lords. This whole project would be worth it if only to give her old friend the first home he had known since his boyhood.

Home.

She had told Brier that they were going there when they had left Kothifir. That had turned out not to be true, as she should have known it would. All her life, she had been searching for a place to belong. Tai-tastigon and Tentir had come closest, Gothregor and Kothifir never, much less the Haunted Lands keep where she and Tori had been born or the Master's House in Perimal Darkling where she had grown up—a place still mercifully vague in her memory.

Home had also meant rejoining the Kencyrath, only to find that she must forge her own place there, in a society that otherwise had none bearable for her.

Most of all, home had meant Tori, a return to her

other half. Well, she was working on that, despite her brother's current strange and shifting mood.

That reminded her: the Jaran Matriarch had asked her to visit before her departure. Now was as good a time as any, while she had a moment to spare.

She found Trishien in her summer quarters on the top floor of the Jaran compound within the women's quarters.

"The guards didn't want to let me in," she said.

Trishien almost slammed her book shut but restrained herself, closing it gently and resting her thin hands upon it.

"That wretched Karidia. Her order that you be banished from the Women's Halls was supported by Adiraina, who should have known better. They can't shut you out any more than they can your brother. I told them that."

Jame sat down in a chair facing the matriarch. "Is it my imagination, or have there been changes in the Women's World? Kallystine usurping Cattila's role—that can't be normal."

"Nor is it. We don't know what is going on within the Caineron, or the Randir, for that matter. I suppose the balance tipped when Rawneth more or less took over her house. Her son Kenan may officially be Lord Randir, but none of his people seem to be bound to him."

"That was my impression, too. Kindrie says that besides Rawneth personally binding Kendar, some are bound to lesser Randir Highborn, even within the Priests' College."

"Ah. I had wondered."

Trishien's ink-stained fingers restlessly tapped the book's cover. She put it aside with an impatient moue and picked up a loose skein of multicolored yarn from a basket at her feet. This she draped over Jame's hands and began to wind it up.

"For that matter," said Jame, obligingly tilting the skein back and forth, "everything has been in flux since Jamethiel Dream-weaver helped to cause the Fall. The balance swings one way, then the other. She had power. Then women were stripped of it. Now there's Rawneth, Brenwyr, Cattila, and you."

Trishien smiled. "You flatter me."

"Not at all. Kirien values you, and she will be the next head of the Jaran, a lady instead of a lord, the first since the Fall, with her house's consent."

"And you . . ."

"Yes. The Highlord's lordan. I don't think, though, that anyone actually expects me to succeed him."

"On the contrary, it is what some fear."

Jame was surprised. Despite having been her brother's declared heir for two years now, she hadn't thought of herself as a potential political power.

"I suppose, if I survive the next year on my own . . . By the way, you're wrapping that yarn around your fist."

Trishien shook free her now club-like hand and ruefully regarded the resulting rainbow tangle in her lap. "You should see my attempts at knitting."

"The Earth Wife, that is, Cattila's sometime Ear, tried to teach me, using a half unraveled foxkin. The lesson did not go well."

The Jaran Matriarch dumped the mangled skein back

into the basket as if gladly washing her hands of it. "Your brother is struggling with his attitude toward you, as you no doubt have noticed. He gives chances, but then seems to withdraw his support."

Jame snorted. "'Seems'?"

"Think. He could have slapped you down, hard, any number of times. What he withholds, he does in part because the Kencyrath can only be pushed so far, so fast. I will own, though, that his current mood perplexes me."

"About that . . . lady, I'm worried. Has he confided in you?"

"No. He used to, sometimes, but not since his return from Mount Alban after the Feast of Fools."

"That was when he found out that I had bound Brier Iron-thorn."

"That, no doubt, is part of it but not, I think, all. I feel . . . I feel . . ." She shook her head, helpless, baffled. "Something is wrong. Whatever it is, though, he must deal with it himself. The pressure has been building for some time between what he knows and what he cannot bring himself to admit. Whatever is going on now, it plays into that."

"I can't tell you how many times I've wanted to slap him silly . . . or sane."

Jame rose to leave, but paused in the doorway.

"How did you know that I wouldn't be staying at Gothregor?"

Trishien smiled sadly. "Can destruction dwell with creation without preservation?"

"Oh," said Jame blankly. "Is it that obvious?"

"Only to those who know how to think. Fortunately—or perhaps unfortunately—at present, that excludes most of the Kencyrath. Fare you well, child."

VII

MORE KENDAR returned from Kothifir to fill out the new command's ranks, also some second-year cadets newly graduated from Tentir.

In addition to her core ten-commands, Torisen had picked out nine officers each with expertise in a particular field who would have supervision over the tens in rotation, but would hold none of their own. Brier, Rue, and Marc came first, of course. After them, there was leather-faced Corva as horse-mistress, a Southron master cook named Rackny, hunt-master Tiens, Fen the Farmer, Swar the Smith, and Torisen's favorite herbalist, Kells. Their absence would ease some of the pressure on Gothregor as its people returned, but still these were among the fortress's best. Perhaps Tori wanted her to succeed after all.

Nonetheless, she wondered about their loyalty since all, except Brier, were bound to her brother. Maybe the fact that she and Tori were twins would again work in her favor. As she met her new command one by one, though, she was struck by their stony response. It had been a strain for those stationed at Kothifir to be so far from their lord. Arguably, Brier's bond to the Highlord would not have broken if she had been part of Gothregor's garrison. Tagmeth was closer than Kothifir, but still uncomfortably far afield. Would they give her the support she needed? Could she engage their enthusiasm in establishing a keep that none of them, at least at first, would see as their home? Only time would tell.

On the fifteenth of Summer, the new one-hundred command assembled at the foot of Gothregor's steps.

"Ready, lass?" asked Marc. Too big to ride a horse, he was prepared to walk the entire way.

Jame looked in his twinkling eyes, level with her own, mounted as she was on the delicate Whinno-hir Bel-tairi, and drew strength from them. Then she twisted in the saddle to gaze back at her people. How odd to think of them as such, except for the faces of her erstwhile ten dotted among their ranks.

"I'm not a leader," she wanted to protest. "Who would be such a fool as to follow me?"

But that answer would not satisfy the randon. She was trapped in the expectations of her people, if not of her god-damn god.

"Forward, then," she said.

Brier Iron-thorn raised a hand. As it fell, horses stepped out, oxen-wains rolled, and boots scuffed the stones of the River Road. The small herd of black, bad-tempered cows that were going with them raised hoarse bellows of protest, answered by the shrill chiding of caged chickens and the howl of dogs from the hunting pack. Geese honked. Sheep bleated. Swine squealed. Horses snorted.

Back in the ranks, someone began to sing:

"Oh, I have come from the far White Hills,

My home to seek, my kin to greet.
Oh, where is my lord on the gray, gray heath?
Gone, gone away, forever . . ."

CHAPTER III
Northward Bound
Summer 15—25

I

SOME FORTY LEAGUES lay between Gothregor and Tagmeth. A rider using post-horses could have covered that distance in twelve hours. Kendar running would have taken two days. However, Jame hadn't considered her newly acquired livestock.

"These cows will move about ten miles a day, if you're lucky, and the oxen less," Char pointed out with ill-concealed glee. "That is, if the former don't stampede. Then you either have to round them up or leave them behind. And they will need a midday break to graze."

Jame considered the herd of tossing black heads and red-rimmed, truculent nostrils that jammed the road at the end of the column. How many were there anyway? Thirty? Forty? They seemed to form one bad-tempered beast with many horns and hooves. Her command had barely left Gothregor before the problem had become obvious, as indeed it should have before they had even set out. All those conferences and consultations, all those hours spent lying awake, trying to think of everything that could go wrong . . .

She had hoped to keep their mission a secret, or at least their destination, so as to reach Tagmeth before potentially hostile keeps along the way learned what was afoot. Small chance of that now.

"Do we go back?" asked Char, lifting his reins as if about to turn.

"No," said Jame. "Since you know so much about cattle, I put you in charge of them. See that they keep up."

Char glowered. "I didn't train at Tentir to become a cowherd."

"You barely trained at Tentir at all," Dar pointed out with a grin.

Jame rode back to the head of the column, past so many watchful eyes.

"Already we're off on the wrong foot," she muttered to Brier. The keeps lay some twenty-five miles apart. "Send word ahead to Falkirr that we will be there on the sixteenth, to Shadow Rock on the eighteenth, to Tentir on the twentieth, and to Mount Alban on the twenty-second. After that, we'll hope to sneak past Restormir on the twenty-fourth."

"D'you think we can?"

Jame shrugged. "We have to try."

II

CHAR WAS RIGHT: they only made it half way to

Falkirr on that first day, and the cattle barely that. More docile animals would have moved faster, but these were the ill-tempered, barely domesticated kine native to the Riverland, distant cousins to the wild yackcarn of the north. They had been lagging since their midday browse, adopting a mule-like trudge punctuated by random dashes into the bush that lined the road. When Char's sweating, cursing ten-command drove them into camp after dusk, they charged among the tents, trampling some and overturning cooking pots, before finally being corralled into a sullen mob.

"Really, Char?" said Jame, regarding them.

Char glowered. "Really, Ran."

"I told you, I'm not . . . oh, forget it. Just keep up."

She supposed, riding away, that the herd could be left to follow at its own pace, but somehow she didn't think that it could make it past Wilden alone, much less past Restormir. Did she really need such a fractious charge? Well, yes, for milk as well as for meat if the winter should prove as harsh as she feared it would.

III

THE NEXT EVENING they arrived at Falkirr.

Brant, Lord Brandan, greeted Jame and her officers in his hall. A weathered man in a patched coat, he was used to working shoulder to shoulder with his Kendar in all seasons. Now they were preparing for the mid-summer Minor Harvest to bring in the hay as fodder for the winter to come. Jame supposed that it was too late to plant anything at Tagmeth that could be harvested this year. They would have to carefully ration the grain now bulging the supply wagons.

Brant's sister Brenwyr swept into the hall as they were sitting down to a plain but hardy dinner.

"So you are striking out on your own," she said to Jame as she spread her full skirt around the chair that her brother had risen to offer her. Jame noted that the Iron Matriarch's skirt was divided for riding—no tight undergown for her, to the other Matriarchs' distress, although she did wear the traditional mask.

"Yes. It remains to be seen, though, if we can last the winter on our own."

Brenwyr's brown eyes snapped at her through her mask's slits. "I should think you can do anything you set your mind to, child. Is Torisen being unreasonable?"

Jame accepted a bowl of stew in which chunks of vegetables and venison bobbed.

"I don't know," she said thoughtfully, breaking off a hunk of bread and dipping it in the broth. "I'm only just learning what work is involved. The Kendar will advise me. I hope. How is Aerulan?"

"Besides being dead?" Brenwyr gave a harsh laugh, but her face softened. She ran gloved finger tips down the front of her stiff, rust-brown jacket, flicking open buttons. When she spread the garment to reveal its lining, Jame saw her late cousin's face smiling at her over the Brendan's shoulder.

"You reworked her death banner?"

"Only enough to make it fit."

She gave herself, or rather Aerulan, a brief hug, and

shivered. Perhaps her long-dead lover had returned the embrace.

Pages brought in the second course—fish stuffed with almonds and baked in pastry. Jame slipped her half-eaten bowl of stew under the table to an eagerly waiting Jorin.

Aerulan had been slain by Shadow Assassins, her throat slit, her blood soaking the dress she wore, which had subsequently been unraveled and woven into her death banner. No one at the time had realized that the blood had trapped her soul in the weave. Jame wondered if such use as this would eventually rub off the dried flakes, but decided not to mention the possibility to Brenwyr. It was good—and exceedingly rare—to see the Iron Matriarch happy.

IV

THE NEXT DAY they crossed the Silver to its western bank and continued north on the New Road.

It was beautiful, early summer weather. Clouds drifted southward overhead against an azure sky. Wind plaited meadow grass. Late spring flowers spangled the slopes that ran down to the river. Deer bounced off the road into trees as the cavalcade came into sight, causing the gazehounds to whine and pull at their leashes, upsetting the lymers who hadn't yet caught the scent. Glittering jewel-jaws danced over the grass to feast on unseen carrion. Jorin trotted off to investigate, but Jame called him back. No need to borrow trouble. Occasionally she caught a flash of white between trees upslope. By the bond between them, she knew that the rathorn colt Death's-head was keeping pace with her, and that it irritated him she was going so slowly.

At a break for lunch beside a waterfall, Jame sought out Marc.

"We've come at least thirty miles so far," she said, "with ninety more to go. How are you holding up?"

The big Kendar grinned at her from his seat on a mossy rock. His boots were off, his feet turning wrinkly white in the cold water. He wriggled gnarled toes with evident pleasure. "This is a pleasant summer's stroll, lass. For a long time I've been looking for a chance to stretch my legs."

Then it was up again and back on the New Road, just as Char's charges caught up with them again.

V

THEY NEARED Shadow Rock soon after sunset.

First, one saw the lush bottomland meadow, already sunk into shadows, the disputed ownership of which had nearly brought the Danior and the Randir to war with each other two years ago. The Silver still ran in its new bed, putting the land firmly on the Danior side. Good. As one of the smallest houses in the Riverland, one-eighth the size of its rival, the Danior would never have survived a full-out conflict with the Randir. Arguably, only their close connection with the Knorth had kept them intact so far.

Jame's eyes were drawn across the river, up the slot

valley that housed the Randir fortress. Wilden always reminded her of a wedge-shaped jaw full of sharp teeth with streams that trickled down from the lower moat like drool. Tall, bleak buildings clustered in compounds divided by steep, jagged roads, all under the shadow of the Witch's Tower on the upper terrace. So, too, was the shed-like entrance to the subterranean Priests' College, although it was not visible from this distance. That made Jame think of Kindrie, who had spent his benighted childhood there.

Benighted, too, seemed to be the entire fortress on this early summer evening. The streets and courtyards were empty. If lights had been kindled within, shutters had also been closed. The only movement was a trickle of smoke or mist emanating from the tower, rising to hang still in the now windless air. The sight made Jame feel tense, breathless. Wilden might have been some great beast frozen in a crouch.

Shadow Rock, on the other hand, bustled happily. Workers were coming in from the fields, hunters from the hills. Bright flags hung motionless from its towers, or perhaps that was laundry. Silver flashed on the wall, followed by the faint, tinny sound of a horn. The visitors had been sighted.

"We heard you were on your way," said Cousin Holly, Lord Danior, greeting Jame and her officers in his small inner ward. "There isn't much left by way of wine, but the cider is especially good this year. Come in and partake."

They drank the welcome cup while Holly's young son pelted around the hall shrieking "Kitty! Kitty!" and Jorin slunk from one hiding place to another. Jame caught the boy as he hurtled past, pleased to note in doing so that her shoulder now took the strain without complaint.

"Cousin Jame, Cousin Jame!" he shouted in her ear, then wiggled free.

Jorin fled.

Holly had been Torisen's heir apparent before Jame's arrival, and his son after him, but he didn't seem to resent her accession as the Knorth Lordan.

"That would be foolish," he had once told her. "As if I could impose my will on the entire Kencyrath, or would even want to."

Dinner was a sparser affair than at Falkirr. By early summer, last year's harvest had almost run out and this year's was yet to be gleaned. Still, the hall was bright and cheerful, except that Holly seemed preoccupied.

Jame slept in Shadow Rock's guest quarters, but uneasily, waking in the dark with a start. Jorin grumbled in protest and snuggled deeper into the blankets against the night's chill. She lay there waiting for her heart to stop pounding, trying to remember the dream that had so disturbed her. Then she eased out of the bed to more sleepy protests from the ounce, wrapped herself in a cloak, and climbed barefoot to the top of the keep tower.

Someone was there before her. She recognized Holly's profile as he half-turned at the sound of her approach. They stood side by side in silence at the parapet, looking out across the dark water meadow, the river gleaming swift in its bed, the steep slope beyond, running up to black bulk of Wilden.

As earlier, no lights showed there, nor any sign of life.

"What's going on?" Jame asked in a hushed voice. The breathless tension had returned, pressing down on her.

Her dream: cold, dark, claustrophobic . . . *let me out, let me out, let me out . . .*

Let whom out, from where?

She sensed rather than saw Holly's shrug.

"I don't know. Things have been strange ever since shortly after the Feast of Fools. As soon as the sun sets, everyone goes into hiding. Maybe Lady Rawneth has been conjuring again."

The Witch of Wilden, who had been responsible for the massacre of the Knorth ladies, including Aerulan and the matriarch Kinzi, and who had yet to pay their blood prices.

Someday, thought Jame, making a silent promise to those long-dead kinswomen. Soon.

The trickle of mist that still rose from the tower had gathered into a hazy cloud lit by a gibbous moon. The shape was vaguely disturbing.

"It looks like a face," said Holly, staring.

So it did, with thinner, darker patches for eyes and a gaping mouth that seemed silently to scream in rage or fear, impossible to tell which. As the cloud rose above the encompassing walls of the valley, a breath of air elongated it. The forehead and eyes sheered off. The mouth stretched and tore. Soon it was gone, but still nothing moved below.

"There was fog the night that Tori stayed here on his way back from Mount Alban," said Holly. "It flowed down the streets of Wilden and pooled in the valley. Fingers of it reached as far as Shadow Rock. I thought I saw . . . but no: that was only a dream. It's fading now."

Like her dream, thought Jame. Never mind. If it was important, she would remember later.

VI

THE NEXT DAY they set off again, and on the second night thereafter arrived at Tentir.

It seemed strange to be back at the randon college, where Jame had spent such an eventful year. On the one hand, she felt as if she could walk back into her quarters in the Knorth barracks, back into her old life, but on the other hand all the cadets were now strangers who looked like children and eyed her askance. The instructors were largely the same, except that Corvine now followed her as a ten-commander rather than acting as a randon sargent. The commandant this year was the Coman war-leader, who regarded her haughtily as if to say, "If I had been in charge when you were here, you would never have tricked me into letting you graduate."

That was probably true. She had been remarkably lucky to have had the Caineron Sheth Sharp-tongue as her superior officer, as much as that had at first looked like a disaster.

After a tense dinner, she retired to the guest quarters in Old Tentir rather than to the Knorth compound, although Rue told her that the lordan's apartment there had been unoccupied since her departure the previous summer.

VII

IN THE MORNING, the one-hundred command again crossed the river, back to its eastern bank and the River Road.

Toward noon, another, faster cavalcade passed them, traveling north on the opposite New Road. By the device on their standard, a golden serpent devouring its young, they were Caineron. By the litter swinging perilously between a team of four high-stepping horses, they were escorting a Highborn lady. Which one became clear when Lyra leaned out between the curtains and waved furiously at them until someone pulled her back inside. Her father Caldane must have summoned her home. Jame wondered why.

So far, Char had managed to keep up with the herd.

"You're lucky," he told Jame grudgingly when she sought him out in camp that night. "The cows are antsy, which keeps them moving. A lot of them lost newborn calves to the hailstorm and have since come back into season. When one does that, they all tend to."

"You really do know a lot about cattle, don't you?" said Jame, regarding him curiously.

He answered without looking at her. "I should. I grew up with them. If you must know, my father was your father's head herdsman." He paused to scrape off a boot on a rock. "When I qualified for Tentir, I swore I would never step in shit again. Huh."

Jame grinned. "Cow pies and horse apples. Manure happens."

VIII

AT DUSK on the twenty-second they reached Mount Alban. Lights greeted them, spangling the upper reaches of the Scrollsmen's College, which was built into a hollowed-out cliff face. The one-hundred command settled in at the cliff's foot. Jame noted that they avoided the circle of stones that marked the foundations of the old hill fort. That was where Tori had met the Deep Weald wolver known as the Gnasher, Yce's homicidal sire, and slain him. The Wolver Grimly could have told her what had happened, but he and Yce had both gone south to the Deep Weald to establish Yce as her father's heir, and Harn remained with the rapidly diminishing Southern Host.

Poor Tori, Jame thought, to be missing his best friends at such a time as this.

As what?

There it was again, that twinge of anxiety.

"Most dreams mean nothing," said Kindrie, when she told him later, "and most slip away by morning. Still, 'let me out, let me out'? Are you sure it wasn't your father speaking?"

Kindrie knew that some fragment of Ganth was trapped in Torisen's soul-image. When Tori had offered to bind his cousin, the Shanir healer had found himself being offered the bolt to the door that imprisoned that raging madness. Wisely, he had refused to take it.

"I don't think so," said Jame.

They had met in Mount Alban's library, surrounded

by niches full of priceless scrolls reaching from floor to ceiling. Night pressed against the windows, held at bay by a chandelier full of guttering candles. Molten wax dripped on Kindrie's wild mop of white hair. He ignored it. The muted noise of the college rose from below.

"I see you!"

"No, you don't!"

A rush of ascending footsteps followed, and an elderly man burst into the library—a singer, judging by the intricate gold embroidery on the cuffs and collar of his belted robe.

"Shhh . . ." he said, raising a gnarled finger to his chapped lips, and scrambled for cover behind the room's largest desk.

A pudgy, panting scrollsman burst into the room on his heels.

"Which way did he go? Which way did he go?"

When neither Jame nor Kindrie answered, the little scrollsman said "Tsk!" in disgust and rushed away, his robe flapping.

The singer emerged from cover and slunk after him, pausing to give Jame and Kindrie a mischievous, gap-toothed grin.

Jame remembered climbing the twisting ironwood stair that led through the college's irregular levels. Scrollsmen had been tiptoeing across landings, peering into rooms and around corners. In their wake, there had been a scurry of singers seeking new hiding places.

"What's going on?" she asked.

The answer came from the doorway as the Jaran Lordan Kirien entered the library.

"The singers have hidden various scrolls throughout the college," she said. "If a scrollsman catches a singer, he or she has to tell them where a specific manuscript is. It's their somewhat harebrained response to Caldane trying to destroy certain valuable scrolls this past spring. Index is beside himself."

So the old scrollsman would be, thought Jame; his reputation was based on his knowledge of where every scrap of parchment was.

Candlelight caught the delicate bones of Kirien's face as she emerged from the shadows, her profile as fine as any engraved on an antique coin. Although both a Highborn lady and a scrollswoman, she wore neither dress nor mask nor robe, but rather pants and a plain, belted jacket of good material. At first glance, one might have taken her for a handsome boy. She ignored Kindrie despite his involuntary step toward her.

"We heard that you were coming," she said to Jame, echoing Holly.

"The entire Riverland seems to know," said Jame ruefully.

"Of course. Whatever you and your brother do is of interest to the rest of us."

She still hadn't even glanced at Kindrie, who subsided, looking perplexed and unhappy.

"I suppose Matriarch Trishien has kept you up to date."

Kirien touched a pocket distorted by the slate on which she and her great-aunt communicated by far-writing.

"Aunt Trishien is worried," she said. "The Highlord's

behavior lately has been . . . mystifying. My impression is that he is trying to act properly, but under great stress and no, I haven't any idea what is wrong."

A scrawny old man bustled into the library and thrust a rolled parchment into Kirien's hands.

"Hello, Index," said Jame.

The ancient scrollsman glared at her.

"Here again, are you?" he spat. "So, what falls apart or down this time, eh? Or maybe a nice fire . . . no." His gaze wandered up the shelves of frighteningly flammable parchment. "Don't you dare."

Not waiting for an answer, he scurried out again.

Kirien returned the parchment to its niche.

"No," she said to the singer who arrived on Index's heels. "This was fairly returned and so is out of the game. Really," she added to Jame as the singer departed, disappointed, "it's like dealing with a houseful of children. Still, I will miss them when I become Lady Jedrak."

"Wasn't that the name of the former lord, your great-great-grandfather?"

"So we have called every leader of our house since the Fall, as a sort of joke. It's High Kens for 'servant,' or, more loosely, 'one who has no time to read.' I suppose that we've always tried to distance ourselves from the burden of leadership. 'The Jedrak,' we say, sometimes. My great-uncle can't wait to become simple Kedan again."

"Will you have to leave Mount Alban?"

"Not altogether. After all, Valantir is just across the river. But the head of a house has other responsibilities than scholarship, which is why no one else wants the job."

Jame thought ruefully about her own duties as the Knorth Lordan, which in the past she had barely met.

Perhaps thinking along similar lines, Kindrie twisted a handful of his blue robe nervously. "I should have gone with Cousin Torisen back to Gothregor," he said. "I've stayed here too long."

Kirien regarded him for the first time, with exasperation. "D'you really think you can help him? Aunt Trishien had the right of it: First, he has to help himself."

"Nonetheless . . ."

"Then go! What good d'you think you're doing here?"

With that, she turned and stormed out.

Kindrie looked helplessly at Jame.

Jame shrugged. "Don't ask me."

IX

FOR ONCE, Jame didn't partake of a keep's hospitality, despite invitations both from the Director of Mount Alban and from Jedrak, Lord of Valantir until Kirien came of age.

Instead, she ate with her one-hundred command and then, after dinner, walked into the ring of ancient hill fort stones. It was eerily quiet there, muffling the sounds of the nearby camp. A mist had risen from the river, but it didn't intrude within the circle. Rather, set aglow by the light of campfires, it traced the outside of the old keep as it had once been, walls, windows, doors, as if looking at the inside of an invisible mould. All had fallen long before the Kencyrath had arrived on this world, giving way to the border forts of Hathir which had cannibalized the older ruins.

Then Hathir and its rival west bank empire, Bashti, had ceded the Riverland to the Kencyrath.

Movement caught Jame's eye, a bright something scurrying along the floor of the phantom, glowing hall where it met the wall. Long tail, quivering whiskers, big ears—a mouse, or rather the ghost of one. It sat up and seemed to peer at her. Dead these four thousand years. Perhaps to it she was the specter of a future which neither it nor its many times great-grandchildren would live to see.

Turning up her collar against the night chill, Jame stepped out between the standing stones. No light shone behind her as the ruins sank back into shadow, leaving only the smudged fires of the camp ahead. Something tapped her upturned face and trickled down her cheeks like tears. It had begun to rain.

X

THE NEXT DAY an overcast sky drizzled and drifting clouds cut off the upper slopes of the surrounding Snowthorns while the Silver smoked in its bed.

The one-hundred command plodded on. To the Kendar this was a minor inconvenience, given the well-made River Road on which they trod, but the horses, dogs, and cattle walked with heads listlessly bowed. If they could have grumbled out loud, they would have.

The day after was worse.

A damp mist settled in the valley, as dense, almost, as wet white feathers. Soon one could see no more than a dozen feet in any direction, and the column closed ranks to keep in touch with each other.

Toward late afternoon on the twenty-fourth of Summer, they paused just short of Restormir on the opposite bank. There was no question about seeking hospitality in the Caineron fortress. Once enclosed by it, Jame doubted she would ever willingly be released, such was Lord Caldane's hatred of her. She smiled, remembering their first clash at the Cataracts. He had thought she was a typical Highborn girl, another Lyra Lack-wit. She had slipped him a potion found in the Builders' city in the Anarchies. It had given him the hiccups, and with each "hic" he had risen farther into the sky. Kendar were often afflicted with height-sickness. So too was Lord Caineron. The sight of her ever since had threatened to launch him again.

"Go ahead," she told a scout. "Tell me what you see."

The rider was soon back, emerging suddenly out of the fog.

"There's what might be a Caineron one-thousand command blocking the road," she reported. "I eased through the edge of their ranks, but the bulk of us won't get past them without a fight."

Jame glanced back at what she could see of her one hundred. Fighting was not an option, even if they weren't so heavily outnumbered, not without risking an internecine war.

"Stay here," she told Brier, and rode forward.

The mist hovered around her, muffling the sound of

Bel's hooves, making it seem as if they were moved in place. Then the hoofbeats doubled. Jame first saw four white socks approaching, then the bulk of a stocky chestnut gelding. Gorbel sat on it like a sack of potatoes. They drew up head to tail.

"Don't tell me," said Jame. "You heard that I was coming. I didn't know you were back in the Riverland."

Gorbel harrumphed. With his bulging brow, small eyes, and long, down-turned slash of a mouth, he looked more than ever like a dyspeptic bullfrog.

"My father doesn't know what to do with me," he said. "He only made me his lordan and sent me to Tentir because you were there and I was the only son of the right age. We Caineron weren't to be left behind, oh no."

"Well, you showed him, didn't you?"

Gorbel gave a sound that was half croak, half mirthless chuckle. "Too right I proved myself, at least to the Randon. Now Father can't demote me without insulting them. Sounds rather like your own situation, doesn't it?"

It did.

"So," said Jame. "Here we are. Now what?"

"Father claims Tagmeth. His great-granduncle did a lot to restore it, oh, a hundred years ago or so, before my grandfather started gathering all Caineron back into Restormir. No more cadet branches striking off by themselves. Kithorn was the last, and look what happened to it. I won't say the recall was a good idea. We're wickedly crowded. But that's what he did and my father holds by it."

"Tagmeth isn't on your side of the Silver," Jame pointed out. "For that matter, neither are you."

"Strictly speaking, the old keep is on an island in the middle of the river. And we Caineron go where we please, here about. D'you want to make something of that?"

Any other Caineron would have been belligerent; Gorbel simply wanted to know her intentions. They had had a strange relationship ever since their days at Tentir, with grudging mutual respect but also the awareness that any change of politics could turn them into mortal enemies.

Jame considered her situation, wishing she had asked more questions at Mount Alban. Surely some scholar there would know the rules governing such matters, as there had been during the dispute between Wilden and Shadow Rock.

"I suppose it depends on who holds Tagmeth," she said.

Gorbel gave a volcanic sneeze that made his horse jump.

"Damp," he said morosely, wiping his nose on his sleeve, leaving a slimy smear. "And cold. Kothifir suited me better."

"I never liked the heat. Besides, I'm dressed for this climate."

Gorbel was not. His ornate court coat, crimson stitched with swirls of gold, might have served in the over-heated banquet hall which he had just departed, judging from the fresh stains down the front.

"Sorry to tear you away from dinner," Jame said.

"More like from a twenty-course breakfast that never ends. Most days are like that at Restormir, what with all of my brothers crowding in to vie for notice, huh, even that fool Tiggeri who thinks he's so funny. They all believe that my days as lordan are numbered. Everything is a dead bore, and there sits Father in the midst of it, goading everyone on, as sleek and fat as King Krothen."

Jame thought of that incredibly obese monarch, and wondered if his svelte alter-ego Kroaky had also begun to swell now that, presumably, he could no longer play the scamp in low dives. "Truly?"

"Well, not quite. He can still stand up, with help. Anyway, regarding possession of Tagmeth, Father has sent a one-hundred command north to occupy it. They left this afternoon, when we heard of your approach. You'll never catch up with them, though, given that cow-tail you're dragging behind you."

So he had also sent out scouts.

There being nothing more to say, Jame gave him a rueful salute, turned, and rode back to her own command, all the time thinking hard, making up her mind.

Jeers followed her from the unseen Caineron as word of her retreat spread. Her own troops heard. Disgruntled grumbling rippled through their ranks as she rejoined them.

She told Brier what she had learned.

"That's it, then," said the Southron.

"Not necessarily. We're going to leave the road and bypass Gorbel on the upper slopes."

Corvine had ridden up. "Not a good idea," she said in her hoarse croak of a voice, around long-since axe damaged vocal cords. "You know how tricky the Riverland is away from the keeps. People get lost in the wilderness all the time, if they're fool enough to go there. Many never find their way out."

That was true. Any unoccupied part of Rathillien had a tendency to live its own secretive life. Jame wasn't sure if it actually changed, apart from occasional arboreal drift, or just seemed to. However, only natives such as the Merikit and animals knew how to navigate it. Another example, she thought, of how unwelcome this world had made itself to her kind.

"Agreed," she told Corvine, "but up-slope there are also folds in the land. Those are our only chance to beat the Caineron to Tagmeth."

Other ten-commanders had joined them and were listening with profound unease.

"I've heard of those folds," said Jerr, "but I always thought they were myths. I mean, shortcuts though the landscape from one place to another—how likely is that?"

"It's a matter of correspondences. If one spot resembles another in some way, geological or psychic, they tend to overlap. Likely or not, the folds exist. I've used them."

Yes, mostly with a wise horse like that equine mountain-range Chumley to find the way. But now she had the Whinno-hir Bel-tairi, and the rathorn colt Death's-head, and no other choice.

The caravan retreated about a mile, far enough, Jame hoped, for Gorbel's scouts to give up on it, then cut eastward off the River Road. Here there were water meadows swimming in a soup of fog, and finally the stony toes of the Snowthorns, discovered when the lead horses tripped over them.

By now, the sun had set and night was falling. As they climbed out of the fog and drizzle, at first the western sky over the Snowthorns glowed cobalt and then, as color faded, the stars came out. It was the dark of the moon, the heavens a vault spangled with tiny diamonds. Looking up at them, Jame wondered what it would be like if they ever went out. Legend said that when Perimal Darkling swallowed a threshold world like Rathillien, first the moon disappeared and then, one by one as the shadows spread, the stars. How far away were they? What were they? How much, truly, had been lost with each defeat of her people? The very thought made her dizzy.

Then darkness began to spread across the sky, coming from the north.

It was only the wings of high, tattered clouds, Jame told herself, after the first jolt of fear.

However, their shadows cast a black, velvet cloak over the land beneath. Kencyr have good night-vision, but they must have some light. Now hands groped unseen and feet stumbled over invisible obstacles. Brier ordered that the horses be roped together and that the foot troops hang on to the nearest stirrup. To be separated now was to risk being utterly lost. Jame clung to Bel's mane as the mare's movement beneath her anchored her to the earth. Somewhere in the void, Jorin wailed. Blind since birth, the ounce used her eyes to see, and found the current situation deeply upsetting.

"Jorin, here."

A moment later, his weight landed scrabbling on Bel's rump. She started, nearly throwing both of them, before settling again into her cautious pace.

Weirding mists also came from the north, Jame remembered uneasily, and the south wind, the Tishooo, had been absent all season to sweep them away.

Pale illumination swept down on them—a momentary parting of the clouds. Before, they had looked down on the mist-flooded valley of the Silver. Now they were surrounded by hills and cliffs. A ripple of unease passed down the column. Lost. . .

Not yet, thought Jame. So far, Bel had not hesitated. Moreover, she was leading them through this trackless wilderness by a way that allowed the jouncing supply wagons to follow, if with difficulty.

Darkness silently returned, and went, and came again. The night went on and on, as if it would never end. Already tired from a day on the road, horses and Kendar alike began to stumble over undergrowth until they found themselves among tall trees whose leaf canopy cut off most light to the bare forest floor.

An eternity later, they stopped to water the horses at a rushing mountain stream.

Word came from the back of the column that Char's ten and the herd had vanished.

"Damn," said Jame. "Of all times to fall behind . . ."

The night had been eerily still. Now a strange, muffled cry sounded in the distance, like a bass squeal sinking to a series of barking grunts: *"Squeeee . . . huh, huh, huh."*

Horses froze, heads up, ears pricked.

Brier wheeled, trying to face the sound, but it might have come from any direction.

"Squee . . . huh!"

"Have you ever heard anything like that before?" Brier asked Corvine, who had spent more time in the Riverland than she had.

"No."

"Yes," said Jame. "Once."

She had been hunting with the Merikit north of their village.

"You saw the yackcarn stampede," their leader, Chingetai, had said to her. "By the Four, you and that white brute of yours were in the middle of it. But those were only the cows. Yes, only the females migrate. The bulls stay up in the hills. You can hear them trumpeting in season for the mates who climb to seek them out. Oh, they must be magnificent!"

"You've never seen one?"

"No one has." Chingetai had puffed out his tattooed chest with pride. "Such is the mystery and grandeur of the male."

At the time, Jame had reflected wryly that, despite his title and pride, the Merikit chieftain was actually subordinate to Gran Cyd whose housebond he was, as long as she should care to keep him.

Could a yackcarn bull actually be stalking Char's herd, so far south of his usual territory and so far below the snowline? True, what a lure an entire herd of cows in season would be, even if they weren't yackcarn, but still . . .

She remembered the stampede thundering down on her as she wrapped her legs around Death-head's barrel and Prid clung to her waist from behind the saddle. The rathorn reared, but still his head only came to the shoulders of the oncoming behemoths. Four-foot horn spans, ropes of lather swinging from mouths agape, small mad eyes all but buried in bulging, warty foreheads, the stench of them, rolling on before . . .

Jame dismounted.

"What are you doing?" Brier asked sharply.

"I have to find Char."

"No," said Corvine. "You led us here. Into the wilderness. Into the folds of the land. You can't abandon us."

Jame hesitated. She read the same judgment in Brier's hard, malachite eyes. She was their commander. Her place was here, with the nine-tenths of her force whom she had brought into such danger.

Delegate, the randon would say . . . but to whom?

Corvine had caught Bel by the bridle, but the Whinno-hir shook free and drifted away. On the edge of visibility, she paused, no longer an equine but a woman with white, flowing hair that masked the half of her face seared by Greshan's fiery brand. Jame had never been quite sure if she actually shape-changed or only seemed to.

"Follow her," she told Brier and Corvine.

They looked, and their expressions changed.

The Whinno-hir's disfigurement and presumed death had haunted Tentir for decades. It was a terrible thing to defile one of her kind, an innocent, who had been with the Kencyrath almost since the beginning, never mind that she had also been bound to Kinzi, the last Knorth Matriarch, whom the Shadow Assassins had subsequently slain. Her presence reminded them all of the depths of their past, which many now did their best to forget.

See, she might have said. *We are more than the present moment, our duties beyond mortal reckoning.*

"All right," said Brier in a choked voice. "Go."

Jame cut away from the column, moving perpendicular

to it. She didn't want to see those incredulous eyes following her apparent desertion.

Dark fell again. The sounds of the column faded as if they too had been muffled by the night. Nearer, hooves crunched on the previous year's dead leaves. Even though Jame was prepared, she jumped when Death's-head snorted down the back of her neck.

"Don't *do* that!" she exclaimed, spinning around to face him.

His ivory mask hung in the gloom like the visage of a demon, greater horn curving back from his forehead, the shorter nasal tusk all but pricking her under the chin. She might have impaled herself on it. Blood-bound to her as he was, he couldn't deliberately harm her, but he never tired of offering her chances to hurt herself.

The rathorn had stopped next to a big rock. Jame used it as a mounting block to swing onto him, bareback. She hoped that he, like Bel, like Chumley, would know how to navigate the folds of the land, especially since he was a true native of Rathillien.

"Squeee . . . huh."

Whatever it was, they were close to it, and to the voices of Char's ten-command calling out to one another among the trees.

Death's-head nearly ran into a cow. The beast brandished her horns at them and shied away, back into the night. All around them cattle were lowing. They sounded urgent. Cloud shadows chased each other over the ground, alternating dense midnight with patches of faint starlight. What Jame saw then, she saw only briefly, but the image lingered:

A cow on her knees, rump in the air. Something clung to her haunches, moving. A warty, furrowed brow; horns, one snapped off short; wrinkled skin with gray tufts of bristles, crisscrossed by scars; a short tail sticking straight up and quivering like a pennant . . .

"*. . . huh, huh, huh . . .*"

"What in Perimal's name . . . ?"

Char had come up behind Jame, with someone behind him. Who . . . oh, Killy, Char's five-commander, once a member of her own ten. Odd, how he always seemed to slip everyone's mind. Together, they stared at the spectacle before them.

The cow gave a startled snort and lurched to her feet, the other still clinging to her from behind. Her rear legs folded and she sat down.

"*Huh!*"

Stumpy limbs shot straight out and small, piggy eyes bulged. A knobby member that would have done justice to a stallion emerged with a plop and jutted skyward.

Then darkness fell again. In it, the cow lumbered off while another of her sisters lowed plaintively nearby for attention. When star-light returned, the clearing was empty.

Killy had turned away. Even in the gloom, one could tell that his face was suffused with embarrassment. Char made an impatient sound. Jame leaned over Death's-head's neck, helpless with laughter.

"I shouldn't, I know," she gasped, "but oh, it was so funny!"

Char glared at her as if she had affronted his dignity. Again. "All right. I know what happened—more or less—but what was that thing?"

"Something never before seen: a yackcarn bull."

"Don't be ridiculous. Everyone knows that they must be huge."

"'Such is the mystery and grandeur of the male.'"

"Stop laughing, damn you!"

"All right." She straightened, wiped her eyes, and stifled a hiccup. "Mind you, I had no idea that one of them might mate with a domestic cow—to the extent that this lot are domesticated. This fellow looked pretty old and scruffy, though. Maybe he's been driven out of the hills."

"Damn him, too. We've got to collect the herd and catch up with the rest of the column."

No argument there.

The rest of the night was spent routing cows out of the undergrowth where they had settled to sleep. At least, their need remedied, they were easier than before to handle. Jorin proved unexpectedly adept at herding them, probably because he saw it as a wonderful game, and they were too sluggish to gore him. Death's-head rousted the more stubborn with his horns and scent, both capable of causing panic. The clouds had blown southward, leaving a sable sky sparkling with points of light. Toward dawn, the sky began to glow over the peaks of the eastern Snowthorns, then dazzling light tipped the western range.

From somewhere ahead came the sound of rushing water. Death's-head slashed through undergrowth and stopped on top of a cliff that overlooked the Silver. To the north, the river tumbled down a series of falls in the raucous throat of a gorge. The River Road continued, carved out of its eastern bank, joined by the New Road at the foot of the cataracts over the back of a bridge.

Below was an island in the middle of the river, roughly shaped like a teardrop. Its high, broad prow breasted the swift current, and crowning the rocks were the ruins of a shell fortress. Its trapezoidal tower keep faced the waterfall. Most of its roofs were gone, exposing a honeycomb of intramural rooms circling a center court. However, it was in better shape than Jame had expected, thanks, no doubt, to the efforts of Gorbel's great-granduncle.

"Tagmeth," she breathed.

An unexpected chill ran down her spine. All of her life, she had been looking for a place to call home. Was this it?

Char pushed through the bushes on foot.

"You're blocking the way," he said, then saw where they were.

Below the castle was a walled outer ward set with a double gate; below that, a lush meadow tapering to the island's nether point. Some horses grazed there while others, including Bel, warily regarded the Kendar who blocked the island's only bridge, which spanned the Silver to the River Road. Jame saw Brier's dark-red helm of hair and Corvine's cropped gray. She couldn't see whom they faced.

Char stretched out on the cliff top and peered down.

"A flag," he said. "Gold on crimson. So, the Caineron have arrived."

"Can you hear that they are saying?"

"No."

His hand dislodged a rock as he shifted his weight. A shout of protest came from below.

In the meadow, Bel looked up and gave a silvery cry of welcome.

The rathorn snorted in answer and pawed at the rim. More stones fell. Before Jame could stop him, he reared, screamed, and came down again, hard, driving his fore-hoofs into the loosened soil. Char scrambled back as the cliff top gave way. Death's-head also tried to retreat, but then he was sliding down on his hocks and rump in an avalanche of debris with Jame clinging to his neck. Caineron troops scattered below. Rathorn and rider thumped down on the River Road in a cloud of dirt. Death's-head shook himself vigorously. Jame fell off.

"Well," she said, climbing unsteadily to her feet and slapping dust off her clothes with shaking hands. "Here I am."

Everyone was staring at her.

"So we see," remarked the Caineron commander dryly.

A tall, elegant man riding a tall, gray stallion that Jame had once . . . er . . . borrowed to race across the bloody tatters of a battlefield. . . . From above Cloud's pricked ears, the dark, sardonic face of Sheth Sharp-tongue gazed down at her.

"Commandant," she said, drawing herself up with a jerk into a salute.

"Not at present. My Coman counterpart currently has charge of Tentir, as I believe you discovered on your way north."

This was, of course, true. However, Jame could scarcely say in front of such an audience that in her opinion Sheth Sharp-tongue and Harn Grip-hard were the only commandants of either the randon college or the Southern Host who mattered.

"How can I help you, Ran?" she asked instead.

"I was just about to request that your people turn this keep over to us. As you no doubt know, the Caineron claimed it many years ago and spent considerable effort restoring it."

"Then they abandoned it. I'm sorry, Ran, but the Knorth hold Tagmeth now."

Movement caught the corner of her eye. With exquisite timing, someone had raised the rathorn banner over the tower keep. Sheth Sharp-tongue regarded it with the flicker of a smile.

"Indeed," he said. "Well, we hardly came equipped for a siege and we certainly have lost the element of surprise."

He reined, about to go.

"Lord Caineron won't be pleased," said Jame with concern. The commandant was already in trouble for letting her graduate Tentir and for releasing his brother Bear into the wilds.

Sheth glanced back and smiled again, crookedly this time. "Let me worry about that, child. Fair warning, though: m'lord won't give up Tagmeth easily."

As the Caineron column reversed and retreated, Brier joined Jame on the River Road.

"A mess," she said, regarding the tumbled debris of the landslide. "As usual."

Death's-head bared his fangs at her and hissed through them. Jame swatted him on the nose, bruising her hand in the process.

"Still," said Brier, "it could have been worse. What d'you suppose Lord Caineron will try next?"

Jame sighed. "I have no idea. We need to set up sentries as soon as possible, though. Now, how are we going to get the herd down off that cliff?"

⊱⊰ CHAPTER IV ⊱⊰
Visitors
Summer 45—55

I

JAME WOKE, stretched, and considered the sky through the tower's broken roof. It was early on the forty-fifth of Summer, twenty days after their arrival at Tagmeth. The sun had not yet risen over the eastern Snowthorns and a few stars still flickered overhead, but she could already hear activity below in the courtyard.

My keep, she thought. *My . . . home?*

It seemed as if every adventure had the latter as its goal. How often she had said to Marc, or Brier, or herself, "We are going home," but so far she had never arrived. Always the outsider, always the misfit. Was this how the Kendar felt? But then, they felt at rest wherever their lord was. Her link to Tori, both as Highlord and Lord Knorth, didn't seem to work that way. It had drawn her back to the Kencyrath, but not to an actual roof or to a place to set down roots. Perhaps Tagmeth would become that. In the meantime, it was at least her responsibility, and she the ultimate authority over it.

The thought gave her a twinge of apprehension.

Yesterday she had been up on the guardhouse roof with the thatchers, doing what she could to help, mostly getting in the way. She remembered the moment when a bundle of reeds had disintegrated under her weight and she had shot down the steep slope, scrabbling for a handhold. Claws weren't much good on loose straw, which also tended to jam sharp ends under them. However, they did catch on the top of the wall as she went over its edge. The jolt had wrenched her newly healed shoulder, which still ached. If someone hadn't grabbed her wrist, she might have fallen two stories to the outer ward.

The accident wasn't much in itself, but it stirred a deep-seated unease: was it possible for someone aligned with That-Which-Destroys to create something new, if one looked at the restoration of Tagmeth that way? True, she had participated in acts of creation and preservation before—take, for example, the resurrection of Gorgo the Lugubrious in Tai-tastigon and helping to save the Res aB'tyrr, the inn that had become her adopted home. Someone (who?) had suggested that potential Tyr-ridan would attract all three aspects of the Three-faced God until they settled into their personal avatar. No doubt about it, though: over the past three years she had manifested more destructive tendencies than anything else.

"The Riverland reduced to rubble," she muttered, "and me sitting in the midst of it, looking apologetic."

Enough of that.

Rising, she dressed in the workaday clothes that Rue

had left out for her—a coarse shirt, a sturdy jacket, pants, and boots. The gloves made her pause. Everyone knew by now about the retractile claws which she had kept hidden for so long as a guilty secret. Their acceptance of this Shanir trait still amazed her. True, the Kendar minded less than the Highborn, perhaps because none of the former were similarly cursed. Except for Bear. But that was because, like his brother Sheth, he also had a touch of Highborn blood. She wondered where her former teacher was now and if that hideous cleft in his skull had continued to close. No one had reported seeing him since he had fled Tentir for the wilderness, with his brother's blessing and against Lord Caineron's orders. Sheth was no doubt in trouble for that too.

"Huh," she said, and put the gloves aside.

Feeling oddly naked, she descended to the courtyard, taking care to avoid various rotten steps. The yard was paved, its cracks recently cleared of weeds. Like most Riverland keeps, Tagmeth was built around ancient hill fort ruins. In this case, they were actually embedded in the inner wall of the shell keep, a circle of white arches bricked up with various colors of stone. All had traces of runes carved above them, but so weathered as to be unreadable. Jame reckoned that her people were the fourth to occupy this site—first, the Merikits' ancestors; then the Bashti (or was it the Hathir? Tagmeth, after all, was set in the middle of a river); then Gorbel's great granduncle; and now the Knorth.

Brier approached as she was washing her face in cold water drawn up from the well set in the middle of the yard.

"I took a closer look at the thatching that came loose yesterday," the Southron said without preamble. "The birch twigs weren't knotted properly."

Jame wiped her dripping face on her sleeve. On one hand, she was glad that it hadn't, after all, been her fault. On the other, she remembered the various "accidents" that had plagued her ten-command back at Gothregor. She had never been entirely sure if they were deliberate or not.

"I hope we haven't brought a practical joker with us," she said, "or, worse, a saboteur. Still, not everyone on that roof was an expert."

"Some of the twigs were also notched."

"Oh dear. Well, we shan't say any more about it for now. Perhaps nothing else will happen."

Brier gave her a hard look. "D'you really believe that?"

Jame sighed. "No. How could I, given my history? What else can we do, though, except walk wary? Now, what are our tasks for today?"

Brier told her. It was a long list.

Besides roofing, the masons were out in search of stones to mend the walls, which had been damaged sometime recently by earthquakes. They had hoped to scavenge the remains of whatever keep had opposed Tagmeth, those in the Riverland always coming in pairs, but there were none. Probably the Caineron had used them up in their own restorations.

Explorers had discovered Tagmeth's cellars by falling into them.

"A fire-timber hall?" Jame asked hopefully.

"No. There are two levels. The upper can be adapted

into a subterranean stable for winter. The lower is at the same depth as the riverbed and partly flooded."

Loggers working under Farmer Fen were in the upslope forest cutting timber to replace rotten woodwork and to build a smokehouse adjacent to the kitchen, in hopes that their hunters would merit it.

As her new steward, Marc was organizing the larder, helped by Rue. Jame suspected that Jorin was with them, no doubt begging for his breakfast.

Meanwhile, Kells was out walking the hills to supplement his collection of herbs. Yesterday he had reported back that he had found some unfamiliar to him, leaving the garrison devoutly to hope that he wouldn't experiment on them.

Tiens and Cheva had led the hounds and horses out before dawn.

"These hills are rich with game," said Brier, "but it has the knack of slipping away when the dogs try to close with it. This place has been wild too long."

Jame had been afraid of that. It would take time to master the intricacies of this strange new land, perhaps more than her garrison had. Of course, all the unoccupied regions between the Riverland keeps were peculiar, but Tagmeth felt more so in its isolation, almost like a border fort. Things might come at it out of the wilds that even the nearest keep, Restormir, would never see. Already there had been reports of huge pug marks beside a nearby stream, like those of some gigantic cat, which had baked and shattered the clay upon which they trod. That suggested the presence of the blind Arrin-ken known as the Dark Judge. It would be just her luck if she had landed in the heart of his territory, given that he was set on judging all Shanir bound to That-Which-Destroys and that he was also quite insane.

About the lay of the land, though, she might ask the Merikit for help, if they would give it about something so important, even sacred, to them. Or maybe she was just looking for an excuse to visit their village to see her friends and unlikely family there. But she didn't dare leave her people again so soon after abandoning them, as many saw it, in the wilderness on the night of the yackcarn.

"And Char wants to talk to you," Brier was saying, as if in echo of her thoughts.

"I suppose, then, that I'd better start with him. No one else particularly wants to see me . . . do they?"

Brier didn't answer. She simply stared down with hard green eyes at this eccentric Highborn to whom she had so unexpectedly become bound.

Jame threw up her hands, startled for a moment to find them naked. "All right, all right. I'm going."

Now that the Kendar were settled, doing work that they understood, those regulars who didn't know Jame tended either to patronize or dismiss her, and some didn't trust her at all. No doubt they had all enjoyed many a good gossip about their peculiar lordan. After all, they weren't randon, who should know better—those, at least, whom Jame hadn't left completely bemused. Then too, since childhood she had been used to looking up into their blunt, good-natured faces. To them, however, she must seem as small as one of their own children, and nowhere near as sturdy. Tori had had a similar problem. He still did, as far as Jame knew.

Oh well. Either she would earn their respect or not. In the meantime, she would observe, and learn, and try not to trip anyone.

Tagmeth in effect had three gatehouses: one set in the shell wall between the courtyard and the outer ward where the chickens now lived, one between the ward and the lower meadow, and one at the head of the bridge connecting the island to the east shore.

Not being directly linked to the west bank was a nuisance, but valuable, Jame supposed, in case of an attack. So it had certainly proved when Sheth had had to bring his troops into the east bottleneck at the foot of the bridge. For all she knew, he had had to ford the river as far south as Restormir.

Bel called inquiringly to her as she passed, but she waved the Whinno-hir back to grazing among the other horses, which she had adopted as her herd.

The debris from the avalanche had been cleared away. Stripped of soil, the cliff face now rose sheer and rocky above the River Road.

To the north, the Silver frothed down the steps of the cataract within the throat of its gorge.

Jame paused on the bridge that spanned the river at the base of the falls. Spray had turned its stones slick with dappled moss. The air shook with thunder. Underneath, water swirled in a devil's cauldron before dashing downstream to where the end of the island cleaved it like a ship's prow.

On the other side of the bridge was the New Road wending southward. Above it, a steep meadow stretched up to the dark margins of a forest. Black cattle dotted this lush expanse, horned heads bowed to graze. The cows looked up as Jame approached. She slowed, wondering if they would charge her, but here came Char, stepping confidently among them, slapping this sable haunch or that heavily muscled shoulder.

"They seem to like you," she said.

"I know them, and they know me. You should avoid them on your own, though."

From upslope, back in the forest, came the sound of rending wood and then a mighty crash.

"My ten are up there," said Char, "helping Farmer Fen. Yesterday, my Five—what's-his-name, Killy—notched a tree on the wrong side, then barely dodged its fall."

Char's command was unique at Tagmeth. The other nine independent officers had no ten-teams permanently assigned to them, but Jame hadn't removed Char's when she put him in charge of all livestock. His Five, Killy, somewhat haplessly carried on as his surrogate as his ten rotated under various de facto master tens, who had learned to dread its advent.

"I keep forgetting that Killy was yours, once," said Char.

"He still is. So are you. Brier says that you wanted to talk to me. What about?"

One of the cows ambled up and butted him. Avoiding her three-foot span of horns, he scratched the hairy thatch between her eyes.

"A good third of them are pregnant," he said.

"Really? Well done, bull!"

"Er . . . yes. I think you were right, though, that this one is too old to compete with the younger males.

Normally, they mate and leave. Our boy may be lost and lonely. I've heard him huffing through the woods at night, maybe waiting for a chance to service the rest of the herd, which is no longer in season. If he tries prematurely, they will kick him to death. He also keeps trying to chase that rathorn of yours away."

Death's-head had never preyed on the local livestock, chickens excepted, and even then he preferred them roasted. Moreover, Jame couldn't imagine him letting himself be driven away from anywhere he preferred to be, and said so.

"I think it's more of a game for them both. He came prancing through a clearing yesterday evening, all glimmering ivory and flowing tail, with that scruffy yackcarn panting after him. Then back they came going the opposite way, this time with the stallion chasing the bull."

Jame wondered if Death's-head was also lonely, now that Bel was spending most of her time with the remount herd and she, Jame, was so busy in the keep. If so, she was glad that he had found a friend, however unlikely.

Horns sounded to the south—the sentries, announcing unexpected visitors.

Below on the island, Kendar ran out of the keep and down to the meadow where they caught horses and swung up onto them, most without bothering about tack. As they galloped over the bridge and up toward the falls, some nine or ten men and women appeared around the curve of the New Road to the south, running. One of them carried a bundle that might have been a child. A ten-command of Caineron charged after them.

"Damn," said Jame. "That's Fash."

She was off down the slope before Char could stop her.

The lead horseman leveled a boar-spear on a lagging runner and thrust it into his back up to its wings. The man cried out, threw up his hands, and fell. With a whoop, the rider wrenched free his weapon as he passed and spurred after the other refugees.

Jame plunged down onto the road between the pursued and the pursuers.

"Not on my land, you don't," she said through her teeth.

Fash leveled his spear at her. She slipped past its point with a wind-blowing move, caught the shaft, and swung up in a high fire-leaping kick that knocked the Caineron cadet out of his saddle. She was on him before he could recover, her hands around his throat.

"Well, Fash," she panted. "Have you run out of Merikit to hunt?"

The other riders swirled around them. Lances came down, clashing, in a steel-tipped ring.

"Easy . . ." said Char behind her.

Only then did Jame realize that her claws were out, needle points resting on the throb of the cadet's carotid arteries, thumbnails poised over the jugular. Beads of blood gathered where she had pierced his skin. He was holding very still, trying not to gulp.

"Move," she said to him. "I dare you."

With a rush, other horses surrounded the intruders. There was Brier on her tall chestnut gelding without saddle or bridle, and Corvine, and Marc huffing up on foot at the head of another unmounted contingent. Horns tossed behind them. The herd had come down to see what all the excitement was about.

Jame stood up, dizzy, feeling her heart hammer in her chest. She hadn't been so close to a berserker flare in a long time. When Fash tried to rise, she kicked his legs out from under him almost absentmindedly.

"These are escaped Caineron *yondri*," he said, glaring up at her. "You're interfering with a legitimate hunt."

"First, this land belongs to Tagmeth, not to Restormir. Second, *yondri* are threshold-dwellers with no legal status. If you don't acknowledge them, how can you claim them?"

"No one leaves Restormir without the permission of its lord."

"Brier did." Jame glanced up at her master-ten. As usual, the Southron was expressionless, but she tapped a knotty bough that she had snatched up as a club against her boot.

Fash jeered. "Oh yes. Brier Iron-thorn. And how did your brother like it when you snatched her away from him? I can tell you, the other lords didn't like it at all. You over-reached yourself there, girl, and now your precious Highlord will pay for it."

He tried to rise again. This time, Char knocked him down. "Watch what you call our lady, boy."

Jame touched Char's shoulder to restrain him. "Let him be. You"—this, to Fash—"leave, and don't come back."

Fash stood up warily, mounted, and wheeled back to the south, followed by his sullen ten-command. At the bend in the road he turned and shouted, "You'll see, you scrawny bint. You'll see!"

Brier led riders after them to make sure they kept going. Marc went to collect the fallen Kendar. The cows dispersed. Jame turned to Char.

"'Our lady,' eh?"

He kicked a pebble, not looking at her. "Should we accept Caineron insults?"

"Apparently not. All right, then. Let's go see what Caldane has dumped on our plate this time."

The fugitive Kendar waited for them farther up the road. Most sat on the ground, wan with exhaustion, but all rose as Jame approached. Muffled to the eyes, the slight figure they had carried now drew back as if to hide behind them. Shy? Afraid? Guilty? Jame thought that she had never before seen such a mix of hope and fear as appeared in these Kendars' expressions. One stepped forward, a young woman with a thin face and large, desperate eyes.

"Lady," she said in a husky voice, then coughed and remembered to offer a shaky salute. "We have come to join your household."

II

"THEY CAN'T, OF COURSE," said Brier, taking the mug of cider that Rue offered her. "What were they thinking of, to try?"

"Escape. And a chance to belong. You of all people know how bad life under Lord Caldane can be, especially for those with no rights. Also, since I bound you, a former Caineron, why not them?"

"You know the answer to that."

Jame sighed. "Of course I do. Tori would be furious. Well, more furious. He would also probably recall all of us and dismiss me as his lordan. Then the rest of the High Council would laugh at him and say, 'We told you so.' He's got trouble enough as it is without that."

Bits of that first night at Gothregor came back to her, but she pushed them away. She was still angry at Tori for saddling her with so much responsibility and so little support. These days, she didn't even seek him in dreams.

It was dusk. Brier and Marc had joined Jame in her tower apartment for the evening meal—the ubiquitous bread, cheese, and bowl of stew, served by Rue. The garrison were also at dinner, no doubt discussing the same topic that they were. Their guests had camped in the island's outer ward, among the chickens, between two gatehouses, both of which were closed. Marc had supplied them with tents and food. After all, he had said, they couldn't be left to starve—or, others had muttered, to deplete the poultry. No one trusted them within the shell keep itself. Caldane was devious. He might have sent them with secret orders, although Jame doubted it.

"Besides," said Brier, following her own thoughts, "the garrison is edgy enough as it is about their own bonds to your brother."

"Why should this threaten that?"

Brier considered. "It shouldn't. But you are a strong counterweight to him. A potential rival."

"I don't mean to be."

"You can't help it. We all felt it in Kothifir, with the Highlord so far away and you so close. I broke my bond to him. They might too, under stress, unintentionally. Then too, your brother can only bind so many Kendar before he starts to forget their names. There is no place in his household for these fugitives."

Marc sat by the fireplace, absently prodding the blazing logs. Nights this far north were cold, even in midsummer, especially with a hole in the roof. Jorin stretched out on the hearth on his back, his fore-paws curled up against his snowy chest, his hind in the air. A branch snapped. The ounce jerked, opened his moon-opal eyes, and sniffed. Then he rolled onto his feet and trotted out of the room.

"As Torisen's lordan," said Marc, watching him go, "you should be allowed to bind people in your own right. Look at the Caineron. There are so many of them because Caldane has seven established sons, each with his own household within Restormir."

Jame laughed. "I don't think he's yet extended that privilege to Gorbel, who is his heir."

"Until Caldane changes his mind," said Brier. "I don't think Gorbel's brothers see him as a serious threat."

"The more fool they. Then too, he isn't of age yet. Neither am I. Nor is Timmon. I'm not sure that any of us can actually inherit until we turn twenty-seven. Kirien can't. That's why her uncle is acting as her regent. It all gets pretty complicated, when you think about it. Someone once told me that the strongest Highborn in a house always, eventually, becomes its lord, and the strongest is the one who can bind the most Kendar."

"How does that account for Lord Randir? No one seems to be bound to him at all."

"I did say 'eventually.' Kenan couldn't stand up to the true heir, Randiroc, in a casual encounter. I doubt if he will do better in a serious one."

"So you could say," said Marc, reverting to the previous comment, "that the followers make the leader."

"I suppose you could. But how does that help me with our current guests?"

"It doesn't," said Brier. "Ignore them. Sooner or later, they will go away."

"Go where? Not back to Caldane."

"Maybe the Danior or the Jaran will take them in, if they can get past Restormir. They aren't our problem."

Soon after that, Brier and Marc left. Rue fussed around the room for awhile, setting it straight, but Jame stopped her when she began to remove what was left of the meal.

"That's right," said Rue, eyeing her. "Finish it up later. You don't eat enough, and that's the truth."

"Are you calling me skinny?"

"That," said Rue, "would be a compliment." And she left.

Jame leaned against the mantelpiece, staring down into the fire. With one thumb hooked in her belt, she ran fingertips over her side. Yes, she could feel the ribs through both shirt and jacket, but still . . .

Famine's foal, someone had once called her. Oh well.

But those fugitives, not her problem? She wasn't sure about that. They had risked their lives to get here. One of them had died. She remembered the desperation in that young woman's eyes. Damn their god anyway for making the Kendar so dependent on the Highborn. Surely that made them every Highborn's responsibility, whatever Brier said.

The followers make the leader.

Wise Marc.

Still, what could she do without risking her own people?

Jorin slipped back into the room and went to the table, nose raised and wrinkling at the delicious odor of the cooling stew.

"You may as well come in too," Jame said to the muffled figure hesitating on the threshold.

It advanced, shoving back its hood from a mass of tangled black hair and a smudged face.

"I'm so hungry," said Lyra Lack-wit.

"Then eat."

The Caineron girl went quickly to the table, sat, and began to wolf down all that the dinner party had left. Jorin raised a paw to tap her knee imploringly.

"How did you know I was here?" she asked, through a full mouth.

"I saw you on the road this morning. And Jorin has been with you for the past half hour. How did you get from the outer ward into the keep proper?"

"Oh, that was easy. A wagon came out loaded with stuff. When it went back in, I snuck in under it."

"I see that I will have to speak to my guards. Lyra, why are you here?"

The girl held out a chunk of beef. The ounce balanced on his hind legs and delicately took it from her fingertips.

"Well," she said at last, not looking at Jame, "after all

that excitement at Gothregor, the Matriarchs sent me home, and I was glad to go. We passed you on the road. Did you see me wave? Back at Restormir, Father put me up on top of the Crown to look after Great-gran."

"How is Cattila?"

Lyra's expressive face drooped. "She says, as long as someone has to keep an eye on Father, she isn't going anywhere, but I don't think it works like that . . . does it?"

Jame remembered the Caineron Matriarch with her toothless grin and her face like an apple dumpling gone bad. Those tiny, wicked eyes, that iron will . . .

"Who knows," she said. "Maybe with her it does. Why did you leave her?"

"Oh, it was too awful! Father has made a contract for me with Dari of Omiroth."

Timmon's cousin and rival, who was pressuring Tori to make him Ardeth lordan regent over his failing father Adric. He with the terrible breath, who was allergic to his own teeth. He whom no woman contradicted twice.

If Caldane was offering him his daughter, he must intend to support Dari's claim.

"So you ran away," she said. A terrible thought struck her. "Lyra, don't tell me: you promised those *yondri* that, if they brought you here, I would give them a place."

"Oh no! Of course not!"

But she still wouldn't meet Jame's eyes.

"What, then?"

"I . . . I may have told them that . . . that you would be grateful . . . oh, Jame!"

She sprang up, ignoring Jorin's squall as she stepped on his foot, and threw herself into Jame's arms.

"Where else could I go? Who else could protect me? Oh, don't throw me out! I'm sorry if I'm being a nuisance. I'm sorry . . ."

And, with a hiccup, she began to cry.

Jame held her, considering. This was worse than when Lyra had thrown herself on Knorth mercy at Gothregor. Caldane would be furious enough when he found out to rip Tagmeth apart stone by stone, and her allies were too far away to help. If he found out. Fash hadn't known whom he was chasing or surely he would have said something. No men were allowed on top of Restormir's Crown where Cattila held court. Quite possibly Lord Caineron didn't know yet that his daughter was missing, and then would he guess where she had gone?

Then again, if Kallystine had undertaken Cattila's duties, would she be aware that her half-sister had fled? Maybe not if Cattila didn't tell her, and somehow Jame didn't think the Caineron Matriarch would even obliquely help her despised great grandson.

"All right," she said to the sobbing girl, whose tears were beginning to soak through her shirt. "We'll think of something."

III

THEREAFTER, the summer turned hot. Occasional thunderstorms rumbled down the valley, rendering the stones of the New and River Roads slick, and washing the cliffs above until they gleamed. Flies gathered in the sloping pasture where the cattle grazed among a sprinkling of flowers. The meadow at the lower end of the island turned a lush green. Work continued on the keep, whose walls and roofs were now mostly repaired. But was it enough? Not unless the garrison could also provide for the coming winter. Jame woke each morning with a panicky sense of precious hours slipping away.

The sun beat down as she made her way north toward the bridge that spanned the river.

"Wait for me! Wait for me!"

Jame sighed as Lyra skipped up to her, swishing a patchwork skirt. The girl had arrived in clothes stained and tattered from her flight from Restormir with the *yondri*. No one at Tagmeth had had anything to offer in her favorite color, flame red, so she had settled, pouting, for a shirt and a pair of dark britches whose seams had been ripped open and re-sewn to fit her slender figure—more or less.

"These are hot!" she complained, fanning her open collar against fair, flushed skin. "Let's take a picnic lunch and go wading."

"The Silver is too dangerous."

"Oh, but there's that darling pond down-stream. You know, the one that gathers among the rocks before it spills into the river. You promised!"

"I said, if there was time. There isn't. Not today."

"Then when?"

Jame sighed. Lyra was proving a tiresome houseguest, always demanding to be entertained. If no one paid attention to her, she whined, as if to be left on her own was a sign that no one wanted her. Jame supposed that she understood. The girl was still terrified of being sent back to Restormir, and apparently unaware that this was no way to endear herself to her new hosts.

They crossed the bridge. Lyra lingered, leaning on the rail to drink in the cool mist that breathed down the gorge. Jame would have done the same if she had been alone, but now she went on, back into the heat of the valley.

From the tower keep, she had seen a stocky figure trudging up the New Road and had been too impatient to wait for his arrival. Now he approached, a middle-aged Kendar built like the stump of some mighty tree, short of leg and barrel-chested.

"I don't understand it," said Fen, taking off his wide-brimmed straw hat and wiping his forehead with a sleeve. The upper quarter of his face was pale, the rest the permanent leathery brown of a farmer. That, indeed, was the role that Torisen had sent him to fulfill in the new keep, to his growing frustration.

"I've been up and down the Silver for some ten miles each way, and there are precious few arable fields. Everything is thin soil over rocks, barely fit to graze."

"What about that?" Jame asked, glancing across at the island with its green lower margin.

"That's another strange thing. The soil there is about a foot deep, but it must have been carted in. Where did it come from? We could turn out the horses and plant it, I suppose, but it isn't very big. You need one or two fertile acres to support each individual for a year. True as my hat, I don't see how Tagmeth has ever been able to sustain itself."

"I know how they did it," said a husky voice behind Jame.

She turned to find the *yondri* who had first spoken to her. The young woman looked ready to bolt, but febrile determination anchored her.

Fen snorted. He obviously had no more use for the runagate Caineron than the rest of the Knorth Kendar did, nor for Lyra. Bored with eavesdropping, the Highborn girl had begun to gather pebbles by the roadside.

"One moment," Jame said to the *yondri*, and turned to finish her conversation with Fen. When he had trudged away, grumbling, she turned back.

"Must," said the *yondri*, with a gulp.

"Must what?"

"That's my name. Must. Short for Mustard."

"I see. Well . . . er . . . Must, what have you to say?"

"What I said. I know."

Jame sighed. This was getting nowhere. "Explain."

"My grandfather was one of the Caineron who helped to restore this keep back a hundred years or so ago. He told me the secret."

"Which is?"

Must gulped again. Jame could almost see her digging in her toes.

"First, you have to promise."

"Promise what?"

"To take us in."

Jame took a deep breath, controlling herself. "This really won't do," she said. "You can't blackmail me. What kind of an arrangement would that be?"

"D'you think I care?"

"Obviously not, but I do. Go back to Lord Caldane."

She had turned away when Must's voice, half-choking, stopped her.

"All right. All right. It was a bluff anyway. Grandfather and the rest survived on supplies sent from Restormir."

Lyra laughed, and threw a stone. It hit one of the grazing cows, whose head jerked up with a snort. Small, bloodshot eyes glared downhill at the group on the road. More heads raised. Sunlight gleamed on an array of menacing horns.

Jame gripped both women by their shoulders and turned them around. "Walk," she said through her teeth. "Don't run."

They regained the bridge after what felt like an eternity.

"Whoop!" said Lyra, with a breathless giggle.

"Listen to me, both of you," Jame said to them. "Leave. Me. Alone."

And she stalked off.

IV

JAME DIDN'T SEE LYRA or Must again for the rest of the morning. At first this pleased her, but then she began to wonder where they were. Must, she learned, had gone off with the rest of the Caineron *yondri* to gather firewood in the west bank forest. No one had given them this chore. They had apparently taken it on in an attempt to make themselves useful.

"Or, more like, to ingratiate themselves," said the Kendar who told Jame, with a snort.

Not until almost noon did she have news of Lyra.

Apprentices scurried about the keep's kitchen, preparing the midday meal. Off to one side, Marc was learning how to prepare lamprey soup.

"Now, I've taught you how to dress this slippery fellow," the little master cook was saying, obviously pleased to have no less a person than the keep's steward leaning attentively over him. "Repeat."

"First, you bleed it through the mouth and cut out its tongue," said Marc, with the air of someone counting steps on his fingers. "That last is to stop it from screaming. Save the blood, for it is the fat. Then scald it as you would an eel."

"Yes! And here it is."

The cook thrust a long-handled fork into a seething pot and drew out a dark, lank form, not unlike a boiled snake.

"Oh, what a beauty!" he exclaimed, turning it so that it flopped this way and that, its tongue-bereft circular mouth grimacing with rings of bared teeth. "Caught it myself, I did. I've never seen its like."

Probably he hadn't, thought Jame. Such fish weren't known in Kothifir, from which, judging from his walnut tan, the cook had recently come.

"Then thread it crosswise on a very thin spit in one or two loops, like this, and roast it. Meanwhile, what spices do you prepare?"

"Ginger, cassia, cloves, nutmeg, grains of paradise . . . what's that, by the way?"

"Never mind. We don't have any. If we had some parsley, we could turn the broth bright green, but it's supposed to be thick and black. 'Mud,' we call it."

Jame regarded the sinuous loop crackling in the flames and seeming, stealthily, to writhe.

"That's not a lamprey," she said. "It's a blackhead."

The little cook blinked at her. "A what?"

"They come from the lake that's the source of the Silver, under the shadow of Perimal Darkling. When they bite their prey, they lay eggs in its flesh. These hatch and compel their host to migrate downstream, even while they devour its flesh from the inside out. Finally it explodes, releasing them to a new stretch of the river. I've seen them infest a man who ate an infected host. It wasn't pretty."

As the cook stared at her, aghast, Marc reached over his shoulder and slid the creature off the spit, into the devouring flames.

"There, there," he said, patting the little man kindly on the back. "Why don't you teach me how to make a nice parsnip pottage instead?"

The cook tottered off.

"I suppose nobody told him that one doesn't fish in the Silver," Marc said, turning to Jame. "For that matter, this is the first I've heard of blackheads myself."

"I thought they'd been stopped at the Steps, but it seems that they weren't."

She remembered Chingetai's friend vomiting a tide of black, writhing forms into the river as his flesh melted away and he shrank to nothing but bones in a loose sack of skin. The parasites had next attached themselves to the Eaten One, one of Rathillien's elemental Four, but then had melted into ribbons of shadow. This world apparently had ways of protecting itself, if not completely. She wondered whether the Merikit might be having similar problems upstream.

"You think they come from Perimal Darkling?" Marc asked.

"You can see the Barrier from the top of the steps, across the lake, and sometimes up to the threshold of the Master's House."

Marc ran a calloused hand through his thinning hair. "I keep forgetting that the shadows are so close."

"I've felt them looming over me all of my life," said Jame wryly, "when I wasn't actually under them."

She gulped as the truth suddenly swelled up inside her. Her past held so many secrets. No wonder the Kendar didn't trust her. Who could she tell, though, if not this, her oldest friend?

"In fact," she heard herself say, "did I ever tell you that I grew up in Perimal Darkling, in the Master's House?"

He regarded her steadily, and her heart caught in her throat.

"No, you didn't," he said at last, "but I sometimes wondered. Never mind. You're here now."

He patted her on the shoulder, then turned to manage the kitchen until its master chef stopped shaking.

Jame leaned against the mantelpiece, waiting for her breath to slow.

There, she thought. *That wasn't so bad, was it*?

Yes, dammit, it was, like ripping open an old sore.

To follow that simile, though, the wound that was her childhood had never properly healed, and wouldn't as long as she could remember so little of it.

Another thought struck her. If she was here, now, so

was Marc. When he had talked about her supposed right to bind Kendar, had he meant himself? She knew that Torisen had offered him a place in his service at Gothregor, but he had refused it. He was waiting, he had said. Of course. For her. Anyone else in his position might have been jealous of Brier, but not Marc, and neither of them knew about Graykin. How had she come to place them both before her old friend, who deserved a place so much more than either? Chance. Need. Somehow, she would bring Marc into the fold too where, in her heart, he had been all along.

Attendants were carrying platters of bread, cheese, and onions into the mess hall where Kendar were already gathering. They would eat as they arrived, or take food back to wherever their work awaited. Dinner was the more social meal of the day.

Jame scanned the room. Lyra wasn't there, which was odd because she never missed a meal. Jame stopped a server to ask.

The man sniffed. "Oh, the little lady came in earlier and asked for bread and cheese in a sack. No onions, thank you very much. Then she left."

Her picnic lunch.

Jame left the hall, the keep, the island, moving fast. That little fool. But Lyra was her responsibility, unlike the Caineron Mustard, and her earned name wasn't Lack-wit without reason.

The pool of which Lyra had spoken was about half a mile south of Tagmeth above the eastern bank. Jame first saw its lip, which thrust out over the River Road and projected a waterfall directly into the Silver. Stone steps led up. She climbed two at a time, slipping and sliding, then paused, breathless, at the top. Here a swift mountain stream had hollowed out a wide basin where water swirled before plunging out over the falls. Lyra sat on a rock beside the pool, looking disconsolate. She jumped up when she saw Jame.

"Oh! You finally came! Can we eat now?"

Jame ignored the untouched sack of provisions lying at the girl's feet.

"Lyra, didn't I tell you this was dangerous?"

Lyra pouted. "You said that about the Silver. Lots of people must come here, or they wouldn't have built those steps."

True enough, as far as it went. Jame eyed the swirling water. It would take a strong swimmer to fight that current hence, no doubt, the challenge.

"Come away from the edge," she said.

Lyra flushed with indignation and started to scramble to her feet. "You think I'm just a silly child."

Her foot caught in her skirt. She exclaimed again, this time with alarm, and tumbled into the water.

Jame lunged after her. The basin's margin was shallow, but even so close to the shore the current was fierce. Trapped air puffed up Lyra's skirt. Before Jame could reach her, she had been swept away, crying.

"Help, help! I can't swim!"

The current swirled her around the pool, just out of reach. Swearing, Jame tore off her jacket and kicked off her boots. During that short delay, Lyra was borne toward the waterfall. She disappeared over it with a shriek.

Jame ran around the edge of the basin, jumping from

rock to rock. At the head of the falls, she anxiously scanned the river below. Lyra bobbed up, already some fifty feet downstream, then sank again.

Jame dived in, wondering belatedly, in mid-air, if she was about to break her neck. From above, one could see the river's rocky bed. Once in, however, the bottom seemed to fall away, just as it had at the foot of the Steps when she had gone in, through blocks of shifting ice, to rescue the Merikit girl Prid.

The water was ice melt, shockingly cold, the current swift. Jame surfaced, sputtering, and struck out downstream. How could she hope to catch up? This was a stupid thing to do, but what else could she have done?

She had the impression that someone was on the New Road, keeping pace with her. Yes. A golden horse, its rider shouting and waving, but she couldn't make out who it was or what he was saying. She tried to point him downstream. A surge of water closed over her head. When she broke the surface again, horse and rider were gone. The river swept her around one curve, then another, then another, and there was the horse, now riderless.

Two heads, one dark, one fair, bobbed as the water surged around them. As Jame swept down on them, they disappeared. Her flailing hand caught a taut rope. It led back to the horse, attached to his saddle. It rasped through her fingers as the horse was dragged, feet braced, toward the river bank. Something was pulling the two swimmers down. Jame took a deep breath and dived, keeping her grip on the rope.

Hand over hand, she pulled herself down. As her eyes adjusted to the murky depths, she saw a clotted shadow near the bottom that resolved itself into Lyra and her would-be rescuer, tangled in the rope and in each other's arms.

Beneath them, the river bed appeared to be paved with shield-sized scales. Trinity. It must be the River Snake, whose head lay under Kithorn, its heart at Hurlen, and its tail in the Eastern Sea, one of the Chaos Serpents that underlay much of Rathillien, whose writhing convulsed the earth.

She was nearly out of air. Soon she must either strike for the surface or breathe water. While the latter should kill her, this apparently was sacred space. Letting out the last of her breath, she sniffed in a nose full of water, then choked as the icy fluid flooded her lungs.

There was a moment of panic: *Was I wrong? Am I drowning?*

But the next breath was easier, if no less painful. The two below had no doubt already, perforce, discovered this.

Now Jame could make out a puckered orifice between the scales, fringed with twisting serpentine forms. Several of them were wrapped around one leg of the fair-haired swimmer. With a jerk, they drew him and Lyra farther down. The orifice dilated. Within were ring upon ring of teeth.

Jame groped for her boot knife, then remembered that she had left it (and her boots) beside the pool. She swarmed down the others' bodies, unsheathing her claws.

Something flickered past her in the water. Blackheads. She slashed at them and missed. A vast body brushed past her, whiskers tickling. The parasites fastened on it, then dissolved. A huge fishy eye regarded her solemnly askance.

BLOOP, said the Eaten One, and swam away.

The River Snake's tentacles withdrew.

Freed, the rope jerked them up to the surface and onto the shore, where the horse had backed himself into a thicket and was snorting among its thorns.

All three lay on the ground, retching up water.

The blonde boy clutched his side where the rope had drawn taut. "I think . . . my ribs . . . are broken," he gasped. "I thought . . . I was going to be . . . torn in two. Who's . . . the drowned rabbit?"

Lyra glared at him through bedraggled strands of wet hair. "I am not!"

"Which?"

"Either!"

Jame gingerly drew a breath and spoke hoarsely. "Lyra, meet Timmon, the Ardeth Lordan. Timmon, meet Lyra Lack-wit of the Caineron."

⟨⟨⟨ **CHAPTER V** ⟩⟩⟩
Dreams and Deeper
Summer 55—64

I

TIMMON gingerly shifted in the chair, mindful of his sore sides.

"I've heard a lot recently about that girl's knack for getting into foolish scrapes," he said, "often with you getting her out of them. The Karkinorans really tried to kidnap you in her stead? I pity them. Did Lyra tell you that she's about to be contracted to my dear cousin, Dari?"

"Yes."

They were in the ground story of the tower keep, which the Kendar had hastily prepared for their new Highborn, guest. Lyra's apartment was on the second floor, Jame's on the third and highest. Jame leaned against Timmon's mantelpiece, regarding him. Even in pain and disarray, he was an uncommonly handsome young man about her own age with tousled blond hair—an unusual color for a Kencyr—and charming features. Indeed, "charm" was his outstanding characteristic. When Jame had first met him at Tentir, he had used this Shanir trait unstintingly to make people like him and to get his own way. No one had gotten away with more than Timmon. It had baffled him that, as hard as he tried, he couldn't charm his way into Jame's bed. That, instead, she had found him funny was, to him, incomprehensible.

Then again, sometimes Timmon's antics were anything but humorous.

She remembered the cadet Narsa whom he had seduced in part to make her jealous. Desperate, pregnant, the girl had hanged herself over Timmon's bed, to his profound shock. That, perhaps, was the first time he had ever been brought face to face with the consequences of his actions. It was certainly the first sign Jame had seen that he might someday grow up.

However, he didn't lack for physical courage, as he had shown when the Karnids had marched on Kothifir. That in itself had gotten him past his second year as a randon cadet.

Timmon might not have broken his ribs in the tug-of-war between the River Snake and his horse, but Kells suspected that he had cracked several of them. Certainly, the resulting band of bruises was impressive. It also hurt him to draw a deep breath, so the herbalist had bound them to prevent him from doing himself further injury. There seemed to be no other treatment but time and rest, short of calling in a healer like Kindrie.

"What I don't understand," said Jame, "is why you are here at all. This is a long way from Omiroth."

Timmon grimaced and tried not to squirm. Patience was not one of his virtues, such as they were.

"Ever since I got back from Kothifir," he said, "Mother has been keeping me close. Grandfather Adric is fine some days, completely soft on others. The thing is, if—when—he truly goes over the edge, there's going to be a battle for the succession."

"But you're his declared heir."

Timmon snorted. "Dari doesn't put much stock in that. Truth be told, he runs Omiroth these days and only wants me to keep out of his way. Of course, Mother fights that. She's always scheming, always pushing me to the front. I hate it."

"If you don't succeed your grandfather, though, what will you do?"

"I don't know. Fall back on my randon status, perhaps."

"What assignment have they given you for your third year as a cadet?"

He made a face. "I'm supposed to command the household guard. They gave me a pretty uniform, which Mother adores, but mostly I'm ignored."

"Oh, Timmon."

He had always been inclined to dodge responsibility. As a child, he had even been given a whipping boy in the person of his half-brother Drie, who now swam with his lover, the Eaten One, if she hadn't already digested him. Jame thought Timmon had more ability than he usually showed. If, however, nobody gave him a job worth doing, he would slide back into his old, lackadaisical ways as, it seemed, he had.

"Gorbel hasn't been sent out to conquer the world either," said Timmon, with a pout that made him look about twelve years old.

"I suppose not, but he will probably find something useful to do."

"You always did like him best."

Gorbel's bulging forehead and down-turned, batrachian mouth filled Jame's mind. She burst out laughing. "Whatever else you say about him, at least he's competent. Usually. How many times has he tried to kill me?"

"Note, without success."

"Points for effort, though. And he was under orders from his father."

It occurred to her that perhaps of the three lordan she was the most fortunate to have been given a chance to prove herself. Timmon and Gorbel were tangled up in house politics. Tori had removed her from that immediate arena, not that she wouldn't eventually have to answer for her performance on her own, to him, to the High Council, and to the Randon.

That last thought gave her pause. What would happen if Timmon and Gorbel didn't find a way to show their mettle? Would the randon still accept them, or perhaps make them repeat their third year as they had Char? She was fond of both, sometimes against her better judgment. More important, she thought she could work with them if they ever did come into power, and with Kirien of the Jaran too. That made three potential new allies for the beleaguered Knorth, one of them both powerful and unexpected.

And don't forget Shade, she thought, not that she exactly saw what Lord Randir's Shanir, illegitimate, half-Kendar daughter could do to help anyone.

Then there was the lost heir Randiroc. Although he chose to live in the wilds, seldom seen, seldom speaking, he was a randon and innately very powerful, as well as a friend, of sorts.

"You still haven't told me why you're here," she said to Timmon, reverting to her first question.

He fidgeted.

"Oh, well, when Dari sent a convoy to claim his new consort, I snuck out of Omiroth and joined them on the road. I know, I know: it was a stupid thing to do, but I was so tired of politics, of . . . of feeling helpless, and being manipulated. Not that the convoy exactly welcomed me. I suppose they sent a message back posthaste to tell Dari that I was with them. Mother will be furious."

"Did you stop at Gothregor?"

He blinked. "Oh. You're thinking about your precious brother, aren't you?"

When she didn't immediately answer, he gave her a sidelong, sly glance.

"Still fighting, are you?"

"Not . . . as such."

"Well, why not? Ever since you returned to the Kencyrath, he's been jerking you around. What, really, do you owe him?"

"I'm his lordan."

"As I am my grandfather's, but only because he thinks that I'm my father, and we both know what a bastard Pereden was. Petulant, weak . . . a third of the Southern Host died because of him."

"You aren't your father."

"What am I, then? What are you? Don't you ever feel

as if the past is rising up to crush you? There's so much of it."

True enough. Neither she nor Tori would be who they were without the looming shadows cast by their ancestors, by their own childhood. How did one distinguish oneself against such darkness?

"No," she said to Timmon. "We are something new. Their choices created our background, but our actions define us against it. You can't surrender responsibility for who you are or you will become your father, reborn."

"Pereden was Grandfather's darling. He would welcome his return. So would Mother. Sometimes . . . sometimes I wake in the night and find her in my bed."

"Timmon!"

He shivered. "She's lonely. She needs, she needs . . . not me. I try and try, but I'm not enough. I never will be. She tells me that, over and over."

"Trinity. No wonder you wanted to get away. Now listen to me: Adric is dying. If you show yourself to be nothing but your father's son, Dari will eat you alive."

"And you?"

"I am myself."

"Then Ancestors help us all."

"Huh. As you say. But about Tori . . ."

Timmon had slid down until he almost cowered in his chair. Now he drew himself up again, wincing at the effort.

"Er, about that . . . no one quite knows what the problem is. Torisen is at least as strong as you are or he would never have become Highlord. His weaknesses are hidden, personal. I get the feeling sometimes that he doesn't shoulder the past as well as you do, or ask himself the same questions about it. Whatever haunts him, he hasn't gotten past it. And it seems to lean more heavily on him since the recent Feast of Fools."

"Why? What's happened?"

"Mostly, I hear things, second- or third-hand. He's shorter-tempered now, although he usually apologizes for any outbursts afterward. He talks to himself, or maybe to someone else who isn't there. And he has bad headaches. There are other things—for example, that hailstorm that destroyed Gothregor's orchard and early crops. Then, after the damp, there was a plague of locusts. Only at Gothregor, mind you. Torisen had to borrow Geri to lead them into the Silver, where they drowned and clotted the river as far south as Omiroth. Dari was furious."

"All of this sounds like a run of very bad luck."

"I haven't even mentioned a murrain on the Knorth cattle."

Jame gave herself a shake. Tori would have to manage on his own for now, as he had left her to do, although a thought lingered: Was it possible that he still had to prove himself as Highlord, just as she did as his lordan? There it was again, the weight of the past—Gerridon's treachery, the Dream-weaver's fall, Ganth's madness—all of which called the present into question.

What if we are among the things that need to be broken?

"So you went on to Restormir to fetch Lyra," she said, pulling herself together. "What happened there?"

"Lord Caldane hemmed and hawed. It seems that his great-grandmother Cattila didn't approve of the match and was sheltering his daughter in the keep's Crown, where no man is allowed to go. Kallystine said she would bring Lyra down."

He paused, and shivered.

"That woman frightens me. She has a wonderful body—I can see why Torisen was entranced by it—but there's something wrong with her face. Anyway, she went up to the Crown but came down alone, shaking. The Caineron Matriarch may be ill, but she can hold her own. And there was someone else up there with her. Her Ear, Gorbel said. We heard shouting. Then the tower began to sway. Caldane turned as white as a slab of lard and started to hiccup. Everyone piled on top of him, but he lifted them all off the floor. If someone hadn't thrown a noose around his foot to anchor him, I don't know what would have happened. Why are you laughing?"

Jame wiped her eyes. "Sometimes I have to remind myself that that man deserves everything he gets. So he still thinks Lyra is with Cattila in the Crown."

"As far as I know. Instead, she's here. Hello, rabbit."

Lyra hesitated in the doorway, looking wary and a bit frightened. She had found a dry dress, which fit her like a sack, and had made an effort to untangle her wet hair, without much success.

"Don't call me that," she said.

"Runagate? Hoyden?" He glanced at Jame with a grin. "That sounds a lot like you."

"I've been called worse."

"I begin to see how you two have ended up together. Are you going to ride the rathorn too, Flopsy?"

"Don't call me that!" Lyra shouted, and fled.

"I'm beginning to like that girl," said Timmon.

"Timmon, this is serious. Can I trust you not to tell anyone that Lyra is here?"

"Who would I tell? Maybe Gorbel. I mean, what are you going to do with her? Somehow, sooner or later, the Caineron will find out and come for her. If Gorbel knew, maybe he could smuggle her back into Restormir."

"And then her father will contract her to your cousin, thereby implying his support of said cousin's claim to the Ardeth when your grandfather dies."

"Well, there is that."

"Leave her alone, Timmon, and give me a little time. I'll think of something."

"You always do." Timmon settled gingerly back in his chair. A faint, inward smile twitched his lips. "Just the same, it would be fun to rob dear Dari of his prize."

II

AFTER THAT, Jame kept a close eye on both of her guests, whenever she could.

Timmon fretted at the pain that kept him from his usual activities and was clearly bored. In the past, that had made him unintentionally dangerous. However, as far as Jame could see, he didn't apply any more charm to Lyra than was typical for him. Mostly, he teased, she blushed and fled, but always came back.

"I don't understand it," Jame said one day to Marc in the kitchen, where he was experimenting with blueberry custard. "If she doesn't like him, why doesn't she just stay away?"

Marc carefully cracked an egg. The white brimmed over his fingers; the yolk settled to the bottom of the shell like a wary yellow eye. He tipped the latter into a pan with milk, corn starch, sugar, and a handful of berries.

"Here," he said, putting the pan over a low fire and handing Jame a wooden spoon. "Stir."

She took the implement with trepidation. "I'm not sure about this. Remember when I tried to make bread?"

That had been in Tai-tastigon, at the urging of Cleppetty. The dough had risen due not to the action of yeast but to the growth of rudimentary internal organs.

"That was before my time at the Res aB'tyrr," said Marc. "I did hear, though, that the resulting loaf had an interesting texture."

While Jame tended gingerly to the mixture, he turned to prepare the ingredients for frumenty. Without molten glass to play with, he had turned to the alchemy of the kitchen. The creative urge could take many directions, Jame noted.

"Concerning Lyra," he said, his back turned, "not that I know much about young ladies, but your friend Timmon is very good looking and she is of an age to notice such things."

Jame snorted.

"There is this, too. I have the impression that Highborn girls are deliberately kept in the dark about some things."

That gave Jame pause. Well, yes. No one had explained the facts of life to many of the girls she had met in the Woman's Halls, to Lyra least of all.

And to her?

So much of her childhood in the Master's House was a mystery. However, she was fairly sure that Gerridon had reserved her for himself, ending in that disastrous encounter beside the red ribbons of the bridal bed.

And Keral?

The changer's lopsided face leered at her out of the past. *Such fun we could have, but you are meat for my master.*

Innocent but not ignorant, the Arrin-ken Immalai had called her on another occasion.

Maybe so. One watched. One learned. There were different kinds of experience.

Yes, Timmon was handsome, but he had never stirred her. Jame thought uneasily of those who had. Bane, her sadistic half-brother; Randiroc, the lost Randir Heir; Tori . . .

Another memory rose, unbidden, unwelcome:

She was a child again, dancing all by herself in the hall of the Haunted Lands keep, but someone watched her from the shadows.

"You've come back to me."

It was Ganth's voice, husky, quivering.

"Oh, I knew you would. I knew . . ."

Then as he stepped forward, he saw her more clearly, and the desperate tenderness ran out of his expression like molten wax. Before she could move, he struck her across the face and slammed her back against the wall. His hot breath roared in her face. His shaking body pinned her to the cold stones.

"You changeling! You imposter! How dare you be so like her? And yet, and yet, you are, so like . . ."

His kiss had bruised her lips. She could still taste it, as sour as vomit.

"Father, no . . ."

Destruction begins with love, he had said and, for him, so it had.

Jame wiped her mouth on her sleeve.

No wonder her thoughts on the subject were so confused. Anyone who involved himself with her was courting serious trouble.

"Lass?" Marc had come up behind her, concerned. "What is it?"

Jame looked down at the pan and gave a shaky laugh. "The spoon appears to be on fire, and the berries are trying to escape."

Sure enough, little puffs of steam and spurts of flame emerged from the thickening custard around the spoon. The berries, driven before the latter, erupted into blue stars and smears as the heat burst them.

"That's rather sad," said Jame.

"Remind me never to make cranberry sauce in your presence."

III

SOON AFTER THIS, Lyra started to disappear for half a day or more at a time, which made Jame even less sure she knew what was going on. One morning, she could have sworn that the girl was on the stair just below her. When she reached the courtyard, however, Lyra had disappeared.

"Oh, here and there," Lyra said when asked where

she had been, vaguely waving a half-eaten piece of fruit in the air.

"And where did you get that peach? I didn't think that they grew in the Riverland."

Lyra stuffed what was left of it into her mouth, swallowed, and choked on the pit. By the time Jame had dislodged it by pounding her on the back, the question had been forgotten.

IV

DUSK.

Light spilled out of the mess-room windows to lie in flickering bars across Tagmeth's courtyard. Supper was done. Now came the time to relax before sleep. The cheerful chatter died as someone began to sing an old riddle song in a plaintive, minor key:

"Oh, where you go is who you are,
  Or so our fathers say.
  But who you are is where you stay,
  Our mothers say, our mothers say . . ."

The inner wall of the courtyard incorporated the arches of the ancient hill fort that had preceded the current structure. The arches' spans had been filled with stone blocks. Fingers crept out of a fissure between them which seemed to expand at their touch, wider, deeper, until a slim figure was able to wriggle out between the crack's parted lips.

Lyra rose and shook out her crumpled skirt. Good. No one had seen her emerge. This, after all, was her secret, gained while lurking around the keep, trying to keep out of the way. Jame didn't want her company? Very well. In turn, she didn't want Timmon's teasing, which made her feel very young and very stupid. Well, she wasn't—stupid, that is—since she had discovered this marvelous secret of Tagmeth's. Nor would she share it, oh no, not until she was given credit for being the clever girl that she was.

> "So who am I, come from afar,
>   Who find myself now here today?
>   Oh mother, say; oh father, say.
>   Where my lord goes, I follow him
>   Though it be far away."

Lyra sniffed her sleeve and made a face. The fabric stank. The place she had just come from had frightened her. She should have returned to the peach orchard or to the oasis, not gone exploring, even if that was what Jame would have done, and she did so want to be like the Knorth Lordan, who was always having adventures. Then again, Jame always survived them. Lyra hadn't been sure she would, this time. What an awful place with its whining, gray grass and hills rolling on and on under a leaden sky and the bloated, dead eye of the moon. Even now, she imagined that she felt the ground drumming under her with hoofbeats, but she hadn't stayed to see what might be coming. Now she was home again, oh so tired, so hungry.

The song ended, to applause. A babble of talk followed.

Lyra's stomach grumbled. She could steal in to raid the kitchen, but didn't want to risk being seen. Instead, she sidled around the edge of the courtyard to the tower keep's door and slipped inside.

She meant to climb to her second-story apartment, but stopped short, goggling, at the sight of Timmon's ground-floor quarters.

The room was illuminated by a blazing fire on the hearth and by a massive chandelier studded with too many candles to count. Flickering light shone on rich tapestries, making the figures depicted there seem to move as they hunted and feasted. What really drew Lyra's attention, though, was the table beneath the chandelier. On it was a golden platter swimming with eels in cream, bowls of exotic fruit, damson tarts, blue custard, spiced brie, capons stuffed with figs, and a roast peacock dressed in its own feathers, among a dozen other dishes, each one more luscious than the last.

Something was wrong here. Before Lyra could think what it was, however, Timmon stepped out of the shadows.

"Welcome. Join me."

In his own way, he was as luscious as anything on the table. Rose-gold hair, a dress coat alive with swirls of scarlet and gold thread, rubies on every finger, and oh, his smile . . .

Lyra shrank back, all too aware of her own dowdy clothes. When she looked down, however, she saw that she was clad in her favorite flame red skirt and a tight crimson bodice embroidered with pearls. Somewhat emboldened, drawn toward the savory smell of so much rich food, she ventured away from the mural stair, into the room.

Timmon's smile grew even more beguiling. "You are hungry, aren't you? Sit down. Partake."

Lyra eased into a chair, watching him warily. His teasing had made her feel like a helpless child, but she wasn't, not with one contract behind her and another ahead, even if the latter made her shudder. After all, she had met fish-eyed Dari and smelled his rotten breath.

"He will break you to his liking," Kallystine had said. Through her thick mask it had looked as if she had no lips at all, just perfect white teeth bared in the cold slit of a smile.

He will break me. What does that mean?

Timmon poured her a glass of spiced wine. Lyra took a sip. Warmth ran down her throat into her stomach, which growled in appreciation. She pulled a leg off a capon, first nibbled, then tore at it. Nothing had ever tasted so good.

"I'm sorry if I upset you before," said Timmon. "We could be such good friends, or more."

The figures in the tapestries drifted away from the feast toward a door, which opened into a luxurious bedchamber. Lyra dismissed both it and them as inconsequential. "More than what?"

"Well, haven't you ever had a . . . special friend?"

"Not until I met Jame."

Impatience flickered across his handsome face. "That's not what I meant. How about Prince Odalian, your first contract?"

Lyra picked up a garlic snail and popped it into her

mouth. "He was nice," she said, chewing, swallowing, "but I hardly ever saw him."

Timmon sat down opposite her, looking thunderstruck. "Jame tried to warn me, but . . . You really don't know what I'm talking about, do you?"

"Humph. You say all sorts of silly things, like calling me a drowned rabbit or Flopsy." Her nether lip quivered. "Everyone thinks I'm such an idiot."

"Don't cry! Look, have one of these candied slugs. They're your favorite, aren't they?"

Lyra hesitated, wary. "Truce?"

"What? Yes. All right."

With a tremulous smile, she reached for the slug, but it crawled away from her, leaving a trail of caramelized slime. The whole table started to move, as if touched by some creeping blight. Eels uncoiled and wriggled off their platter. Fruit rotted. The peacock struggled to its feet, shedding feathers, then sprawled as overcooked legs gave way under it and bones tore through its crispy skin.

Timmon leaped up, shocked, and darted around the table to grab Lyra, who in turn clung to him. Their fine clothes had turned into filthy rags hanging off their limbs. Candles sputtered out. Tapestries rotted off the walls. That stench . . . Lyra had smelled it before, under a leaden sky, but how much worse it was now, in this dank, close space.

Many tables surrounded them, at which sat hunched figures. A voice spoke, as high and thin as a knife scraping bone but distant, too.

"You have betrayed me, you and you and you, who

would have made my son Highlord in my place. But I was too strong for him, for you all, and so he fled. I curse him. I curse every one of you."

"Yes, yes," breathed someone in the shadows, reaching out long fingers to touch the speaker's shoulder. "Make them prove themselves. Their knives are in their hands. Make them use them on you, or on themselves. What price blood on the floor? What price a traitor's guilt?"

"Oh." Lyra drew back into Timmon's arms. He was shaking almost as much as she was.

"This isn't my dream," he said. "It isn't."

A breath of air moved through the hall. The figures crumbled to dust, all but one who still regarded the interlopers from a dim corner with malicious, gleaming eyes. A hand snaked out to grip Lyra's wrist. How cold it was, how tight its hold.

"Children," whispered that chill voice in her ear and, horribly, it seemed to smile. "Little, lost children. Come play with me."

Lyra screwed shut her eyes. She wouldn't listen. She wouldn't. But the floor shivered under her feet, a drumbeat of hooves coming closer and closer. Not over rolling hills, though. Rather, it was descending the stair.

"Whose dream is this?" said a sharp voice. "Lyra? Timmon? Tori, wake up!"

Lyra blinked. She lay huddled in her bed, gripped by strong arms that were not Timmon's. Looking up through frightened tears, she saw the line of Jame's chin, drawn taut with anger. Likewise, in the dim light the Knorth's silver-gray eyes seemed to rage with cold fire. There was the thin white line of a scar across one cheek, the mark of Kallystine's razor ring, which had at first horrified Lyra. It occurred to her that she hadn't noticed it in a long time.

How odd, she thought, inconsequently, that it doesn't bother her at all. What must it be like, to care so little about one's personal appearance, much less need to?

A shout came from below: "Lyra! Where are you?"

"Here," Jame called back.

The Ardeth appeared on the stairs, wide-eyed and tousled in his night gear, arms clasped around his aching ribs.

On his heels came Brier, Rue, and several other Kendar, drawn by the uproar. Jame sent them off to bed except for Rue, who was dispatched to the kitchen to fetch warm cider and buttered bread.

"W-what happened?" Lyra asked. She couldn't stop shaking.

Jame glared at Timmon. "D'you want to explain?"

"Er . . . not really."

"Then I will. Lyra, Timmon can get into your dreams, at least when he's physically close to you. He tried it with me at Tentir, without much success."

"Is it my fault that your dreams are so weird? I still say that we could have had a lot of harmless fun."

"I can defend myself. Can this child?"

"From me, yes, as it turns out. Because she is a child."

"I am not . . ."

"Hush. But you were drawn deeper than that, weren't you? All the way down into the soulscape."

Now Timmon looked worried, even a little scared. "It was a terrible place, that hall. Those ghosts . . . I can still taste them in the back of my throat, all dust and ash. So bitter. And there was something else that didn't belong, that sucked us in . . ."

"I don't understand," said Lyra. "Why is the soulscape so much worse than the dreamscape?"

"Not worse. More dangerous, more . . . vital. Dreams can't hurt you—much—but much that happens on the level of the soul can. Look at your arm."

Lyra shook back her sleeve and stared at the bruises forming on her wrist, of four fingers and a thumb.

"She grabbed me. Oh, it was horrible!"

Jame put an arm around the girl's shoulders, which felt as fragile and tremulous as a bird's wing. "You're awake now, and safe. But never go to that place again."

Rue returned with a platter of fresh bread and an ewer of warm, spiced cider. Lyra ate, nibbling at first, then bolting down chunks of the crusty loaf. It wasn't only in a dream that she had missed supper.

Jame drew Timmon aside.

"You are here as my guest," she told him, speaking softly but with vehemence, "and so is Lyra, an innocent under my protection. It never occurred to me that you would try so underhanded a thing."

"I was bored," said Timmon, with a touch of defiance but not meeting her eyes. "I meant no harm. I'm sorry."

"I suppose you are. Nonetheless, you should leave. Tomorrow. Go home, Timmon. It won't be pleasant, but there are things you have to face, your lady mother not least. Don't tell anyone about Lyra, if you can help it. If you can't, well, in a day or two she won't be here any longer either."

Lyra heard this last bit and looked up, alarmed.

"Are you sending me home too?"

"No. Someplace else." Relenting, she smiled at the girl. "I think you will like it."

⚈⚈ CHAPTER VI ⚈⚈
Miming in the Hills
Summer 65—66

I

TIMMON left the next morning, looking so forlorn that Jame laughed in his face.

"Go home," she told him. "Grow up."

He pouted. "Where's the fun in that?"

"Survival is the issue, not fun. You may not have noticed, but the Kencyrath is starting to come apart at the seams. If Tori can't hold himself together, how can he maintain control over the rest of us?"

Timmon sobered. "You really think things are that bad?"

"They're headed that way. Right now, I try not to think at all, except about Tagmeth."

She wondered, though, as Timmon rode out the gate, if she should be doing more. Lyra and Timmon had somehow been drawn from the dreamscape down into her brother's soul-image. It had indeed been haunted, by Ganth their father, by the unhappy Kendar left in his power after Tori's escape, by someone else who shouldn't have been there, but not, strangely, by Torisen himself. Last night her brother must have dreamed about the Haunted Lands keep. She remembered snatches of that, before Lyra and Timmon had arrived. Something in it was restless, and hungry, and desperate. Something with cruel eyes and a horrible, soft voice.

Little, lost children, come play with me . . .

Dream-stalkers. Soul-walkers.

When she had shouted at Tori to wake up, for a moment she had found herself at Gothregor, in his bed, shaking him. She remembered the touch of his clammy skin and his wild, startled eyes, staring at her own from only inches away. So very close. Ah, the scent of his breath, the feel of muscles gliding under her fingertips, the taste of his sweat . . .

Twins, had come a gloating whisper out of the dark, with shining eyes behind it, *but always meant to be one. In each other's arms. In bed together. Deny that if you can, little girl.*

She had blinked, and found herself halfway down the stair to Lyra's apartment at Tagmeth. The moment's distraction had caused her to miss a step and nearly fall. This morning her twisted ankle still ached.

It was all very confusing.

"Is he gone?"

Lyra had come up behind her.

"Yes."

The Caineron girl studiously traced a line on the ground with her toe. "I'm glad . . . I think. He confused me. But he is very handsome, isn't he? And I don't think he meant to hurt me with his . . . his . . . whatever it was."

"Dream-stalking. He never means harm, but sometimes it happens anyway."

She had never stopped to wonder which face of their triune god Timmon as a Shanir was aligned to. So far he didn't create, he didn't preserve, but did he destroy? Narsa had hanged herself. Drie had joined the Eaten One in an aquatic love-death. The actions of Timmon's father, Pereden, had almost annihilated the Southern Host. Were any of these events Timmon's fault? Only what had happened to Narsa, and then only because Timmon had been too self-involved to pay attention.

Shanir didn't always mature at the same rate. She herself had committed acts both of creation and preservation in the past. Here she was now, trying to resurrect an entire keep. It wasn't a simple matter. What one did with one's nature had to be finely tuned to the situation in which one found oneself. So far, for the most part, Timmon hadn't done anything but please himself. Perhaps he would remain confused, ineffectual, until he took a side, until, in effect, he grew up. And maybe by then it would be too late.

Could the same be said about her?

"Where are you sending me?" Lyra asked.

"As I said, someplace I hope you will like. And I'm taking you there. Pack up. We leave as soon as you're ready."

II

IT HAD OCCURRED to Jame that one reason her people doubted her was because they didn't know where she went when she disappeared into the wilds. It really didn't have to be a secret anymore if, indeed, it ever had.

This was running though her mind as she waited in the courtyard for Lyra.

Char trudged through the inner gate, a heavy scowl tugging down the corners of his mouth.

"I'm worried about the cows," he said, without preamble. "Most of the pregnant ones are swelling fit to burst, and it's only been some forty days. They aren't due to calve until winter."

Jame hoped he was exaggerating, but still this was alarming news.

"What's our diminutive visitor up to these days?" she asked.

Char snorted. "Still hanging around, looking hopeful. The breeding season is past, though, with so many of the cows in calf. If he tries again, he'll get kicked to pieces."

"Hmm. I wonder if the Merikit have any experience with cross-breeds. Would you like to ask them?"

Char regarded her as if she had proposed a trip to the moon. "Well, of course, but . . ."

"Then gather your kit."

In the tower, Lyra could be heard to apostrophize whatever hapless Kendar had volunteered to help her: "No, no, no! That skirt is horrid! Can't you find anything better?"

Jame sighed. "We leave as soon as m'lady has sorted herself out, hopefully before sunset."

As it happened, Lyra was ready about noon, although then she insisted on luncheon as the previous late night's snack could only be expected to sustain her for so long. Jame gave her Bel-tairi to ride, with the Whinno-hir's reluctant consent. Char joined them on the road astride a stocky roan gelding. One of the cows lumbered after him. While not exactly bulging, she was clearly pregnant.

"This is Bene," he said, with a touch of embarrassed defiance. "Short for Beneficent. She's taken to following me everywhere. Why, I don't know."

Jame was still on foot, with Jorin trotting at her heels.

The River Road rose in steps beside the Silver as it spilled down over rocky ledges through the gorge above Tagmeth. The air was a cool haze of spray, and ferns hung dripping from the surrounding stone walls. Everything seemed to shiver with the roar of rushing water. Lyra talked on and on with animated gestures that jerked Bel's head back and forth, to the mare's evident irritation, but Jame couldn't make out what the girl was saying. At length they emerged from the ravine into a forest of gold-dappled leaves and lush undergrowth, still on the road, still beside the river as it curved northwestward.

"Are we really going to see the Merikit?" Lyra asked as soon as she could make herself heard. "Cousin Fash says that they're cannibals who eat their own babies. With salad greens for garnish."

Jame stopped Bel, took the reins out of Lyra's fidgeting hands, and slipped off the Whinno-hir's hackamore.

"Don't take anything Fash says too seriously," she said, draping the gear over a rock where it could be collected on the way back. Bel only wore tack as a courtesy to her rider. Off the road, in the wilderness, she did better without it. "I won't say that he's a liar, but he knows a lot less than he thinks he does."

He was also partly responsible for the flayed Merikit

skins that graced the floors of his lord's personal quarters. Lyra had been there. Jame wondered if she knew what she had been treading upon.

"It's over twenty miles to Kithorn," said Char, "and the Merikit village is beyond that. Are you going to walk all the way?"

"I hope not."

As the day progressed, however, she was still on foot and growing annoyed. Her ankle ached from the twist it had received the previous night. Jame wasn't used to being injured and didn't accept it gracefully.

Around midafternoon, Bel left the road. Lyra tried to get her back on course by kicking her sides and tugging her mane, but Jame stopped her.

"She knows where she's going. From now on, we follow her."

"No wonder you end up in strange places," said Char.

Soon they were beyond the sound of the Silver, picking their way through a trackless wilderness, lucky to know at least, judging from the sun, that they were still northward bound. Jewel-jaws danced around them on azure wings. Waterfalls spilled down the slopes of ravines through nodding ferns. The hills offered them turn after turn with no guarantee except that, eventually, a downward path would lead them back to the river.

Lyra continued to chatter without pause until her voice blended with the chittering birds in the trees under which they passed. Jame stopped listening. Char, however, kept shaking his head as if plagued by ringing ears.

Jorin butted Jame's knee in complaint. His paws were sore. He wanted to be carried. Jame declined. At forty pounds, he was too much of an armful for her, and she didn't intend to burden Bel with two riders. Char turned his head to hide a smirk. He clearly had no intention of accommodating his lady's spoiled pet. Besides, his attention kept turning to Bene, who repeatedly dropped behind to graze and then, just when they thought that they had lost her, lumbered up behind them, huffing through wet, red-rimmed nostrils.

In late afternoon they were overtaken by one of the Riverland's brief, hard showers, which made Jorin even more unhappy.

Finally, dusk fell.

Bel chose a campsite by stopping beside a stream, under a majestic horse-chestnut.

"How far d'you think we've come?" asked Char as he gathered what dry wood he could find and laid a fire.

"I have no idea."

"Huh."

Char glanced at Lyra, who had drifted off to regale Bel (again) with an account of everything she had seen that day and what she thought about it. The mare flicked an ear and continued to graze.

"Doesn't she ever shut up?" asked Char.

"This is extreme, even for her. She's nervous, though, and more than a bit afraid. After all, we're taking her to visit people whom she's been told are cannibals."

"And you're sure that they aren't?"

"Reasonably so. The problem is that we've never tried to understand them. Call folk savages and that seems to answer all questions about them."

"They did slaughter the garrison at Kithorn."

"Except for Marc. Yes, that was his home keep. What he thinks about being settled so close to that old tragedy, I haven't yet had the nerve to ask. However, I have since learned that the massacre was due to a misunderstanding, likewise to our ignorance about Merikit customs and beliefs."

"And that justifies them killing us?"

"Of course not. Nor does it justify the Caineron hunting them for their skins."

Char looked up, startled. "They do?"

"Yes. Some of them, anyway."

It was dark now. The crackling fire tossed sparks up into the boughs above where they landed like fireflies on fluttering seven-lobed leaves like flat, polydactyl hands. A glow spread through their veins, tracing their dance.

"Sssaaa . . ." they breathed as a breeze tossed them. "Ssssssssaaaa . . ."

Something beyond the campfire's light gave a harsh cough, and the flames leaped. The horses jerked up their heads in alarm. Jorin rolled off Jame's lap and crouched beside her, flat to the ground. The fur began to bristle up his back, down his tail. She jumped to her feet.

"Lyra. Come back to the fire. Now."

The girl rushed to her and clung, terrified, accidentally pinning her arms to her side.

Something huge moved through the forest, circling them. They saw it by the etched veins of fire that defined it against the sylvan darkness. Branches cracked as it passed. Saplings were shouldered impatiently aside. Massive paws made the ground shudder and left a smoldering trail even in the damp woods.

Bel crowded as close to the fire as she dared.

Bene glared myopically into the night, lowered her horns, and pawed the ground.

The gelding squealed and bolted into the woods.

Faster than seemed possible, the thing was upon him and he crashed down. His scream abruptly died, replaced by the muffled crunch of bones and a wet, slobbering snarl. The stench of charred flesh and burnt hair rolled out of the shadows in waves of heat.

Jame threw off Lyra's frantic grip. "Stop it!" she shouted into the darkness.

"Quiet!" hissed Char. "You'll anger it!"

"It's already quite mad, and then some. Dammit, stop!"

A low growl answered her: *"All things end, light, hope, and life. Come to judgment. Come!"*

That voice . . . it rasped on the nerves like a predator's tongue ripping flesh off bone. Something moved behind a screen of shattered boughs, of such vast power that it warped the very reality through which it trod.

Jame gulped. She could flee, screaming, or she could rouse her Shanir nature. Already anger thickened in her throat. Careful, careful . . .

She circled the fire, keeping the great beast before her, its potential prey behind. Her voice, when she spoke, emerged as a throaty purr.

"You tried to judge me once before, lord, and found no cause. Has that changed?"

"Huh."

Its snort sent embers flying. Leaves ignited overhead, throwing up their green, kindling hands in horror. Lyra squeaked and flung herself into Char's reluctant embrace.

"You were born guilty, girl, and yet . . . and yet . . ."

"If you condemn every Shanir born a nemesis, who will be left to fight the shadows? Think, cat, think."

"Arrr-HA!"

A hot wind roared past Jame, and the fire exploded sideways, into her face. In a confusion of whirling sparks, she heard Lyra shriek. By the time she had raked clear her eyes and stopped coughing, the girl was gone.

"Which way?" she snapped at Char.

He gripped her arm. "That was an Arrin-ken, wasn't it? *Wasn't it?*"

"Yes. Let go."

"And you're going to challenge him?"

"Not if I can help it."

She pinched a nerve in his arm. He released her with a curse, and she plunged into the darkness.

From ahead came the snapping twigs of Lyra's passage and the cracking branches of the Arrin-ken's pursuit. The Dark Judge had no reason to hunt her, Jame guessed. This was merely a cat's instinctive response to a fleeing mouse.

Still dazzled by the fire, she didn't see the ravine until she fell into it. The land dropped away and she rolled to the bottom through undergrowth, into a small stream. Before the cold ice-melt could penetrate her clothes, she was scrambling up the opposite slope.

At the top, something waited, glimmering in the murk.

"Huh," Death's-head snorted in her face.

At last.

The rathorn colt wheeled away, then charged back at

her, brandishing his horns. Jame stepped within his rush and swatted him on the nose. His skull mask bruised her hand, but he was startled into a lurching halt that nearly knocked her back down the gully. She grabbed his mane, first to regain her balance, then to swing up on to his back.

"Turn, you brute," she snarled at him, and kicked his ivory-clad sides. More bruises, but some instinct prevented her from using her claws. "Turn and follow."

They plunged through woods almost too dark for Jame's keen night-vision and emerged in a clearing, where the colt skidded to a halt on his haunches.

The Arrin-ken paced back and forth before them. It was hard to take in his size or shape since both seemed to spill outward, overwhelming the senses. His species was cat-like, certainly, but in this case raging madness added an extra dimension that frayed both nerves and reason. He reeked of the fire with which the changer Keral had burned out his eyes in the Master's House during the Fall. Smoldering cracks opened and closed in his flanks. Truly, he and the Burnt Man were well matched.

"Mine," he growled. *"Give me."*

As her sight adjusted, Jame made out Lyra huddling in the thick branches of a massive oak on the opposite side of the clearing. No, not branches. Arms, clad in warty, drooping flesh and brown, deeply fissured skin. They gathered up the girl with a great creaking of limbs and held her close to a broad, knobby bosom. High above, pale green eyes glowered down through the canopy of leaves.

"No," said the Earth Wife. "Mine."

The Arrin-ken advanced, snarling, under the oak's spread. A tremor ran through the tree's entire frame, and water captured in the earlier shower cascaded down. Where drops hit the great cat, clouds of rank smoke billowed from his overheated sides. He howled in pain and spun in a circle, tearing at his own flesh. A murky, stinking fog filled the clearing. Jame swung down from Death's-head. The rathorn backed up, snorting, shaking his armored head at the stench, and nearly ran over Char as the cadet emerged behind him from the woods.

The commotion at the heart of the miasma faded away as if into the distance.

"Here," called Lyra, like a distraught chick peeping. "Here, here, here!"

Jame waded into the smoke, batting at it with her hands. An indistinct figure emerged to meet her and flung itself into her arms.

Jame stroked Lyra's tangled hair, dislodging leaves and twigs.

"Thank you," she said to the presence that loomed over them.

"*Ha—hoom!* She is my old gossip Cattila's great-granddaughter. Rather, thank her. Fare you well, children."

The green eyes seemed to blink, and then fluttered off in opposite directions as wide-winged lunar moths. The oak settled back into its arboreal self. Somewhere in the forest, one cricket chirped, then another and another.

Jame and Lyra returned to the campsite, their way dimly lit by returning starlight and by the answering glimmer of the rathorn's ivory. Char was there before them, grimly rebuilding the fire. Jame settled the girl in her blankets among the chestnut's knobby knees, then rejoined the circle of light. Jorin flopped on the ground by her side with a sigh. Hearing a grunt behind her, she glanced over her shoulder to see that Bel had folded her legs at last to rest, as all equines must for at least two hours a day. The rathorn settled next to the Whinno-hir, his heavy chin resting protectively on her withers. He had lost his dam, slain by Jame, when still barely a yearling. In Bel, he had found the mother that he had lost. Relaxed he might seem, but his watchful eyes still flared red in the fire light.

"I've upset you, haven't I?" said Jame, to break Char's stubborn silence. "How and why?"

"You know."

"Truly, I don't."

Char chewed doggedly on a strip of dried venison. "That monster of yours . . ." He glared at Death's-head, who glared back.

"After all, he is the emblem of our house," said Jame, somewhat amused.

"That doesn't mean he should be in our house. Or here, for that matter. I mean, who actually rides a rathorn? All right, all right. You do, but you're a . . . a . . ."

"The word you want, perhaps, is 'Shanir.' One of the Old Blood."

"And what use are you? Your time passed long, long ago. The Kencyrath has moved on. I don't say that the present is better than the past. It isn't. In fact, lots of Kendar are pretty miserable with the way things are. But these days we face reality. Your kind stirs up memories of long ago. What is the past but a bad dream? Look at that . . . that . . ."

"Arrin-ken? Well, yes, the Dark Judge is a nightmare, and we in the Riverland are stuck with him. It isn't just being blinded that's driven him insane, either. It's his inability to punish the guilty unless they come within his range and break certain rules."

"You see? What good is the past? All the priests' talk, all these millennia, about our divine destiny . . . it doesn't work. It never did."

"And never will, you think."

Char jumped up and began to pace. "Why should we pin all of our hopes, our future, on fairytales, on failure?"

"But you wish with all of your heart that we could."

He stopped, glaring. "Haven't you been listening to me? All that mystery, all that glamour, the beauty of an old song, the banners of our honored dead . . . they are a trap, a snare. How dare you try to put our necks back into that noose?"

"I'm sorry," said Jame, and meant it. "It's very hard to keep faith when everything militates against it. I won't tell you what you should or shouldn't believe. Perhaps, after all, your reality is different from mine."

"But you exist! And . . . and . . . you shouldn't."

"Well, I'm not going to make a sound like a hoop and roll away."

Char kicked at a stone. "Now you're laughing at me."

"Truly, I'm not. Much. These are hard times in which to live, whatever one believes. Maybe you're right. Maybe I and the Dark Judge are both relics of the past, of no use today. But we are what we are."

"Ah," he said in disgust, and retreated to his bed-roll. "Be whatever you like."

Jame rolled up in her own blankets with a sigh, then unrolled enough for Jorin to burrow in beside her. She had brought Char with her in part so that he could bear news of her doings back to the keep, which had been kept too long in the dark. But she had also wanted to see his reaction.

So far, not good.

And they hadn't even gotten around to discussing the Earth Wife.

III

"WHAT IN PERIMAL'S NAME is that?" Char asked, breaking a long silence.

It was twilight on the next day, back on the River Road, which they had rejoined in the late afternoon. By the terrain, Jame guessed that they had made less progress than she had hoped, and wondered if the Dark Judge had somehow impeded them. Such spite would be like him. A subdued Lyra had maintained a welcome silence. Char, too, had been quiet. Bereft of his mount, unwilling to ride a cow, although Bene trod close behind him breathing wetly, affectionately, down the back of his neck, this time it was he who had been reduced to walking.

Ahead of them, a black figure hung from a tree, its feet just brushing the weeds sprung up between the stones of the River Road. A breeze caught it and it turned slowly, warily, as if only just aware of their presence.

"That's a watch-weirdling," said Jame. "One of the Merikit dead. Alive or otherwise, all members serve the community. This one detects alien metal, such as our tack and weapons."

"But it's . . . it's . . ."

"A corpse, yes. Sealed with wax in a suit of boiled leather. Note the mouth and nostrils, left open to catch our scent."

"I so note," said Char, looking rather sick. To him, of course, the unburnt dead were an abomination.

Jame touched the swinging figure to steady it.

"Kinsman," she said in Merikit. "I am your sister-brother, returned. Let us pass. There, now, Char. You see?"

"I do—although what, you tell me."

Jame snorted. "Such faith."

They continued. Kithorn's lower ward was contained by a hedge of overgrown cloud-of-thorn bushes, whose three-inch spikes reached out as if to detain those who passed. Here was the gatehouse. Up the road lay the keep itself, a desolate ruin. Blue flames flared in its courtyard.

Jame slowed, staring. She should have remembered.

"What?" said Char.

"Off the road. Now."

They moved into the undergrowth opposite Kithorn, except for Bene, who stopped to graze on the verge.

BOOM-Wah-wah . . .

Drums, coming down the road from the Merikit village. Torches cast light and dancing shadows in the darkening hollows of the hills.

BOOM-Wah-wah, BOOM!

"I'm a fool," said Jame.

Char gave her a sideways glance. "That I already knew. Why this time?"

"I was so preoccupied with Tagmeth that I forgot the Merikit calendar. This is the sixty-sixth of Summer. The solstice."

Ching . . .

Bells approached, many of them, jangling in unison.

An old, half-naked man trotted down the road toward them. Breasts made of goat udders swung under loose, gray hair, over tattooed skin smeared white with ash. The chimes strapped to his ankles rang shrilly with every step.

Ching, ching . . .

Behind him, in single file, came a strange procession: first, the padded parody of a woman, then another ash-smeared elder, then a youth festooned with dripping weeds, another elder, a hairy man aflutter with black feathers, another elder.

Ching, ching, ching . . . went the little bells attached to the old men's feet.

Others followed, lit by torch-bearers. Two were young men, one grim-faced, wearing red britches, the other bright-eyed and eager, clad in green. On their heels stalked a big figure muffled in a black cloak. After him came the rest of the Merikit males, men first, then boys hanging back as if to escape notice but chattering excitedly among themselves like a flock of sparrows.

Boom! went the drums that brought up the rear. *BOOM-Wah-wah, BOOM!*

Lyra fairly hopped with excitement, creating her own little storm of agitation among the leaves. "Oh, let's join them!"

Jame held her down. "Quiet."

They had seen Bene. A man separated from the others, cast a rope around her neck, and started to lead her back toward the village. This time, Char nearly jumped up.

"They're stealing her!" he protested as Jame restrained him.

"Of course they are, but we'll get her back. I promise."

When the procession had turned under the guardhouse and gone up the road to Kithorn, the travelers emerged. Frightened by the noise, Jorin kept close to Jame's heels. Death's-head and Bel, however, had slipped away, presumably until they were needed again.

The road led north, twisting between hillocks and hollows, until the Merikit village came into sight, perching on top of a hill between the confluence of the Silver and one of its tributaries. On the hill's summit was a large, round structure with a thatched roof. Below, a wooden palisade defended the settlement's lower margin. Firelight flared up against the sharpened posts under a dome of darkening sky, faintly freckled with stars. From within came the babble of many excited voices. It occurred to Jame that she had no idea what the women did while their menfolk were off prancing before their gods in Kithorn's courtyard. Perhaps tonight she would find out.

They crossed the Silver and climbed the hill to the village gate, which stood open. Inside, plank walks wound between many small hillocks on top of which were neat pocket gardens, or grazing goats, or sometimes, thanks to a broken fence, both. Smoke trickled up out of roof holes. Light welled out of the half-sunken doorways of lodges, and the savory smell of cooking rose. Lyra's stomach growled. Jorin's nose twitched.

Two girls bolted up onto the boardwalk from below.

"Favorite, Favorite!" they squealed with delight and threw themselves into Jame's arms.

Two adults followed them up the steps, one blonde and plump, the other dark and tall.

"Back at last, are you?" The latter gave her a gap-toothed grin and a clap on the shoulder. "It's about time."

"Hello, Da. I got tired of being hot."

"I hear it's always like that, down south," said the other, enveloping Jame in a cushiony hug. "And they have never seen snow? Amazing. Unnatural."

"What are they talking about?" hissed Char. Of course, he didn't understand Merikit.

"The weather. Hello, Ma. What's going on?"

Closer to the heart of the village, torches bobbed over figures bustling back and forth. A bonfire roared up toward the kindling stars, greeted by cheers.

"Women's mysteries," said Ma with a grin. "Even the boys are gone, some to Kithorn, others off to play games of their own in the hills."

"Where does that leave you and me?" Jame asked Da.

"On special occasions, Gran Cyd lets me turn my coat. You were the Favorite, but she may well grant you the same privilege."

Jame nodded toward Char. "And my friend?"

"Ask Gran. If she says no, though, expect to see him driven out in a hail of kitchenware."

Da and Ma set out down the walk, holding hands, their

twins bouncing before them. The three Kencyr followed, Lyra eagerly, Char with trepidation.

"The tall one is a woman, isn't she?" Char asked, speaking softly.

"She is, but a man by choice."

"And they have children?"

"Yes. Merikit mothers name the fathers of their babies as they please. The offspring and all other property belong to them. Ma is the lodge-wyf. Da is her housebond."

"Oh."

The village women were gathered around the clear space before Gran Cyd's lodge. Some stood on nearby hillocks for a better view. The rest crowded the walk and the margins of the open arc. The babble of cheerful voices broke off and everyone began to clap.

The lodge door had opened. A woman emerged from under the lintel, between posts glowing with gold and silver inlay. The mouths of the *imus* carved along the outer wall seemed to gape and sigh in welcome:

. . . ahhhh . . .

Firelight set embers aglow in her long red hair. Her face, when she turned it upward to smile at her audience, was broad and white across the forehead, set with smoky green eyes that smoldered even in shadow. As she mounted the steps, she seemed to rise out of the very earth, immortal in stature. Her mantle and tunic rustled with gold thread as she moved. More gold gleamed in torques twisted around her neck, bare arms, and waist.

Her smile deepened when she saw Jame. The women parted between them, still clapping and grinning. They embraced. The Merikit queen being a good head and a half taller than the Kencyr, Jame's face was pressed between the other's generous breasts. They smelt of sweet smoke and warm milk.

"Still skinny," said Gran Cyd, breaking off to regard her at arms' length. "You don't eat enough, child."

Jame grimaced. "Who has time? These are my companions, who seek your hospitality."

"Welcome, daughter," the Merikit queen said to Lyra, who was staring at her in open-mouthed awe. "Stay as long as you wish. As for you . . ."

Her gaze shifted to Char, who glared back. Jame guessed that he too was overwhelmed, as well he might be, but it wasn't in his nature to show it.

"Now, what shall we do with you? My women, what do you suggest?"

"He is a man," some called. "Drive him out!"

"A man, but no Merikit," cried someone else.

"Then turn his coat!" That, surely, was Da. "Make him a woman!"

"Yes, yes, yes!"

"So be it," said Gran Cyd with a smile.

They descended on Char, who flinched back, his hand dropping to his knife. Jame gripped his wrist. With an effort, he held himself still.

"It's all right," she said in his ear. "I think."

Various women divested themselves of whatever clothing they considered most feminine. One supplied a skirt spangled with silver beads, another a loose blouse, a third something fetching in pale pink leather. Char gritted his teeth as they stripped off his outer garments and re-clothed him. The deed done, they retreated. He glared down at his new finery and irritably tugged up the skirt, which had settled low on his narrow hips.

"You can't tell anyone anything about what happens here," Jame warned him.

He spat hair-ribbons out of his mouth and shot her a baleful glance. "D'you think that likely?"

"Hush. It's beginning."

Hands reached down and drew the Kencyr up onto a lodge roof. As they settled, someone started to tap a small drum, another to play the pipes. An eldritch skirl of music rose to greet the full moon, only just heaving itself over the shoulders of the eastern Snowthorns, pale against the fire's flare.

Flames leaped. A wizened, veiled figure now sat cross-legged before the conflagration, although no one had seen her arrive. Her eyes glowed like holes punched through her skull to the fire beyond.

"Now attend," she said in a thin, oddly familiar voice, "and I will tell you a tale of your gods, the Four, for I am Story-teller, and every hearth is my shrine."

Jame stirred.

"Do you know her?" Lyra whispered.

"Yes. That's Granny Sit-by-the-fire, from the Southern Wastes. Strange to find her here. Or perhaps not."

"Long, long ago, there was a great city, and in it lived a small girl."

Someone had handed Gran Cyr a sack. Out of it she drew rag dolls which she tossed at random into the crowd. Hands reached up to snatch them out of the air. Women scurried down into the open.

"Now, you may not know what a city is. Think of many,

many people living on top of each other. Oh, the noise! The confusion! Why, you might not even know who dwelt next to you, or her children, or her lovers."

Some younger women hesitated, but their elders had mimed this mystery many times before. They piled on top of each other while the audience improvised a babble of voices punctuated by made-up protests:

"Your elbow is in my ear!" "Who is that on top of me with a pole?" "Someone forgot to wear her drawers."

"*Hah'rum!*" Granny cleared her throat, spitting out live embers. "A small girl, I say."

To the right, the crowd parted and a tawny-haired figure was thrust into the open.

"That's Prid," Jame said to Lyra. "I hope you two will be friends."

"Oh, so pretty she was, so innocent."

The women hooted. Prid made a face. Jame wondered how the Merikit girl had been getting along with Hatch, the current reluctant Favorite, who had loved her since childhood. After all, he had been the male fertility figure for the entire village for the past year as she, Jame, had been before him.

"Many suitors had she, but scorned them all."

The women played up to Prid. Some spread hands as if offering her rich goods or lascivious attentions. Others rubbed against her like cats in heat until she slapped them away.

"At last one came, finer than all the rest."

Char sat up straight. "Those are my clothes!"

The woman wearing them swaggered across the clearing to cat-calls from the audience. It was Ma. Judging by her round, bulging bottom, Char would be lucky to get his pants back unsplit.

"He dazzled her, and she took him."

Prid and Ma disappeared down the steps to Gran Cyd's lodge. As the door closed, on-lookers began enthusiastically to groan and pant. Lyra looked puzzled. Char blushed.

The door opened again and Prid slipped out, greeted by applause. She threw her ragdoll to Gran Cyd. More poppets flew as the next round of celebrants was chosen. Prid wriggled through the crowd and threw herself into Jame's arms.

"Housebond! At last!"

"Hello, Prid. This is Lyra. Lyra, this is my lodge-wyf, Prid."

"Oh," said Lyra, staring.

"Believe it or not," said Jame, "I can explain."

"*Hah'rum!* Thereafter, many lovers she took and many housebonds, but the latter one at a time, as was the custom at that time, in that place."

Women passed before Gran Cyd, preening, flirting, while, one finger to her lips, she made a droll show of sizing them up.

"Observe my glorious clothes!" called someone on the sidelines, and several of the parading women flared their skirts.

"Observe my rich, fair hair!"

An elder ruffled her short, graying locks until they stood up like the down on a thistle.

"Look at my great big . . ."

"Oh, oh . . . !" others cried, convulsed with laughter.

One woman cupped her hands at her crotch as if supporting a considerable weight and swayed her hips. A second laced her fingers higher. A third made as if to cradle something thick and heavy to her bosom. Its supposed weight caused her to totter back and forth.

Char made a choking sound. When Jame glanced sideways at him, she saw that he was trying to swallow laughter, perhaps because Gran Cyd had produced an imaginary tape and was solemnly measuring each presented imaginary member. She had forgotten that the Kendar were matrilineal. Char had probably grown up with a healthy respect for large, strong women.

"Years passed. She grew rich, for each housebond gifted her with wealth and more she added by her own labors. Then one day in the market she saw a beautiful young man, and fell in love, and courted him."

Someone threw Jame a doll. She went down, unsure what to do, but the onlookers prompted her and Gran Cyd began to flirt. Jame's movements in response shifted into dance, miming curiosity and attraction, blending into courtship.

Careful, careful . . . she thought.

This wasn't the Res aB'tyrr and these no idle tavern-goers come in for an evening's entertainment, not guessing that they risked their souls. Much less was it the throbbing heart of a Kencyr temple, although, now that she was on sacred ground, she felt power stir around her.

She and Gran Cyd danced. For a large woman, the Merikit queen was surprisingly agile. She didn't know the Senetha, but followed Jame as if by instinct through many of its intricacies, bursting into laughter when her skills failed her. Drum and pipe began again to play.

Tap, tap, tap . . .

Feet hit the ground in time to the rhythm, both in the clearing and in its margins.

The pipes lifted in a swirl of sound that traced the fire's ascending sparks and the dancers spun to it, faster and faster, until suddenly they wound into each other's arms and stopped.

"Come down," the Merikit whispered in Jame's ear, her voice quivering with mirth or something else.

They descended the steps into the lodge.

"Of all her housebonds," said Granny behind them, "he was her Favorite."

The door closed. Jame found herself swept up into strong arms, her mouth pressed to sweet lips. The other's breath smelled of rich spices. Her tongue tasted like honey. Her full breasts buoyed up the world. She ran her hands down Jame's sides to cup her buttocks and draw her close. Jame melted into the embrace. Here and now, this was a goddess as much as a woman, the second face on the Ivory Knife, the passionate, fruitful mother.

"Awake," Gran Cyd breathed into her mouth. "You can not be your kind's Ice Maiden forever."

Granny Sit-by-the-fire stood beside them, her incandescent eyes barely level with the Merikit's elbow, leering but insistent.

"I said, 'He was her Favorite, but he died.'"

With a laugh, Gran Cyd released Jame and pushed her toward the steps. Jame stumbled up them, shoved open the door, and staggered into the clearing. By the fire,

Granny's smoldering eyes greeted her, as did a shout from the waiting women.

The drum quickened its beat. Stepping in time to it, she scrambled after her scattered wits. As she steadied, she moved into the wild music that prompted her to leap and spin. This was the delirium of fever, the death dance that seeks to transcend life.

Faster, faster . . .

The clearing spun around her as the drum thundered in a continual roar. Then, abruptly, it stopped. So did she, panting, but wound so tight that she thought she was about to fly apart. With a shout, she uncoiled in a leap that took her half way across the clearing, nearly into the fire. There she collapsed, panting. For a moment, there was a shocked silence. Then someone began to cheer, followed by the rest of the audience. Jame rose and gave them an unsteady bow, then rejoined her friends on the hillock. Lyra laughed at her, giddy with relief.

"Oh, you were so funny! Until . . . until . . . you weren't."

"And so she lost her only true love, but he left her with her only child, a son."

Jame removed the doll from her belt and dropped it into Lyra's lap.

"Your turn."

The other women had withdrawn from the clearing, leaving Gran Cyd alone. All eyes turned expectantly to the Kencyr girl.

"But, but . . ." Lyra stammered.

"Go on!" hissed Prid. "Just do what they tell you to. It's easy!"

When Jame had translated this, Lyra gulped and descended.

"Of course she spoiled him."

Gran Cyd stripped off her golden torques and loaded Lyra with them so that the girl swayed under their weight.

"Having much, he wanted more. 'All she possesses will be mine when she dies,' he said to himself. 'May that be soon!'

"But our lady was no fool. 'Alas,' she said, 'It breaks a mother's heart, but he must go or I.'"

Gran Cyd mimed energetically driving a spade into the earth next to the steps. The women grunted with each thrust. Cyd bent lower and lower, stopped to wipe her brow, and continued.

"'There was an old woman who dug her son's grave,'" Jame murmured, quoting something she had heard long, long ago.

The Merikit paused, as if to admire her handiwork.

"Go on, go on," breathed Prid, leaning forward, joined by others among the witnesses.

Lyra glanced at them, uncertain, but their urging was unmistakable. She stepped up behind Gran Cyd and gave her a tentative shove. The Merikit queen uttered an undignified squawk and jumped into the stair well.

"'And when it was done, he buried her in it.'" Of course. This indeed was a tale of the Four, how Mother Ragga became the Earth Wife.

Lyra scrambled back with a yelp. Under her feet, the ground heaved. Out of it came a claw-like hand with earth packed black beneath its ragged nails. A broad, mud-streaked face followed.

"Am I late?" the Earth Wife sputtered, spitting out dirt. "Tcha . . . men! They take forever to do anything, except in bed."

The bonfire flared. When it settled, Granny Sit-by-the-fire was gone. That, Jame supposed, marked the end of the women's mystery, or perhaps not quite. Half a dozen brought their babies down into the open space. Although no judge of such things, Jame guessed that these infants were some eighteen months old, already struggling free of their mothers' arms and toddling about with chortles of delight. Hands urged her to rise. She went down to join the milling miniature throng, stepping gingerly so as not to trample anyone.

What in Perimal's name . . . ?

Gran Cyd had emerged from her lodge, a child with hair the color of smoke in her arms. She smiled warmly at Jame.

"See, my Favorite? We have indeed been blessed."

"Oh," said Jame, staring. "These are . . ."

"Yes. Your daughters."

All of them had turned. Wobbling steps brought them to her knees where they clung, beaming up at her with luminous gray eyes. She stroked their hair. Their cheeks were warm under her fingertips, their upturned faces brimming with glee.

"Er . . ." Jame said. Children had never played much part in her life. "They . . . they're beautiful."

She touched the queen's child. It smiled at her with bright, silver-gray eyes, but it was something else, more subtle, more disturbing, that made her glance quickly at its mother.

"Cyd . . ."

"Hush. Not now."

BOOM-Wah-wah-wa-boomph . . .

The men were returning from Kithorn. Their torches wound up the darkling hill in a fiery stream and the open gates received them. Women scattered, dragging their daughters after them, stifling giggles. Chingetai burst into the open. His broad, bare chest was smeared with charcoal to represent the Burnt Man, whom he had played in the keep courtyard. As he slapped at it, intricate blue tattoos emerged through a cloud of dust.

"My consort and lodge-wyf!" He threw wide his brawny arms to embrace her, but let them drop when he saw what she held. She gave the child to Mother Ragga who retreated with it down into the lodge, glowering back over her shoulder.

"Housebond. Welcome."

Chingetai reached behind him and hauled forth a subdued Hatch with a bruised eye quickly turning black. "I present to you the Earth Wife's Favorite, returned to favor!"

"Oh." Prid's hands rose to cover her mouth. "Oh, no." Then anger sparked in her eyes. "Oh, Hatch, after I waited all year, do you relish your bed privileges as the Favorite so much? Then enjoy them, for you will have none of me!"

"Prid, wait . . ."

But she had stormed off into the night.

Hatch spread his hands in a helpless gesture. "I tried to lose," he said, looking from Jame to Gran Cyd and back. "But the Challenger hit me with a rock and then he insulted . . . well, what else could I do but smash in his face? I-I think I killed him."

Chingetai clapped him on the shoulder. "Then he was unworthy. Be proud, boy! Why, tonight you will be the envy of the entire village!"

"Not of all." His consort regarded him soberly. "We women sometimes see things . . . differently."

"And that, somehow, is our fault?"

"Have I said so? But still, think: Do you speak for the entire tribe?"

"For that of it which matters," he said, but would not meet her eyes.

Women bustled past, bound for the communal hall, carrying pots, pans, and trays heaped with steaming food.

"Now we feast!" said Chingetai, turning away to follow with evident relief.

"My housebond is a fool," Gran Cyd said sadly, watching him go. "Then again, his mother came from a neighboring tribe where women are held in less regard than they are here. Our customs do not always please him. Losing his little sister as Ice Maiden to the Eaten One didn't help."

Char emerged from the shadows, again in his own clothes. As Jame had feared, however, Ma had split his pants open down the back. Like most Kendar, he only wore a loincloth beneath and, by the way he kept tugging down the hem of his jacket, he was clearly feeling a draft.

"You said you would speak to someone about Bene."

"Oh. Yes, of course. Cyd . . ."

The Merikit queen smiled. Jame had forgotten that

she, like her consort, understood Kens. "Would this be about the stray cow that Chingetai brought back to our village? There, you must ask him. Cattle raids are his business."

Jame and Char caught up with Chingetai outside the hall, a curious Lyra and Jorin trailing after them at a safe distance. The Merikit still seemed shaken and disinclined to talk, but Char stepped around him, into his path.

"I want my cow," he said, glowering up at the big man.

For a moment, Jame thought that Chingetai would hit him. What should she do? Trip the hill-man? Catch his arm as he swung, hoping to throw him off balance? Step between them and risk getting her head knocked off?

But then Chingetai collected himself and gave a boisterous laugh.

"When cattle wander, boy, finders keepers."

"This cow is in calf to a yackcarn bull."

"Truly? Ah then, bad luck to us both. Have you ever seen a yackcarn female? Even new-born, they are huge. A domestic cow would burst, trying to birth one."

"And if the issue is male?"

"That would be very rare, and no doubt just as fatal. If young female yackcarn are big, think how enormous a male would be."

"But its sire isn't . . ."

Jame hastily cut in: "If what you say is true, why not give us back our cow and save yourself the trouble?"

Chingetai scratched his bearded chin. "Why not indeed. Very well. I return her to you."

As he turned to go, with barely suppressed fury Char

said, "That damn bull. If he's already in effect killed a third of our herd, we've got to kill or at least drive him off before he gets to the rest of it."

Chingetai swung back, staring. "You still have a yackcarn bull hanging around your cows?"

"Yes," said Char, ignoring Jame's effort to shut him up. "And a prime pest he is, too."

"But . . . but . . . this is wonderful! What a hunt it will be, worth a thousand songs for generations to come!"

"If we permit it," said Jame. "Remember, Tagmeth is on Kencyr land. Don't you dare launch a cattle raid on us."

Char cut in. "What will you give us in exchange for such a hunt?"

The Merikit looked at him with dawning respect. "What do you want?"

"Cows to replace all those that this menace of yours costs us. And a good bull—of proven potency, mind you."

"Done."

Chingetai spat on the ground and ground the spit in to seal the bargain. Char did likewise. With a nod, the Merikit turned and disappeared into the hall.

"Char . . ."

"What? D'you think you could have gotten a better deal?"

"No, but . . ."

Jame had just realized that she really didn't want the yackcarn bull killed. The memory of him being sat on by a cow was somehow endearing.

"When Chingetai finds out that his trophy male is a midget," she said instead, "will he keep his word?"

Char shrugged. "You know these people better than I do. We can only hope."

"Go with him," Jame told Lyra as the Kendar followed the Merikit inside. "Try not to let him pick any fights."

Lyra stared at her. "How?"

"I don't know. Faint?"

When they were gone, she stood listening to the cheerful clamor within, keeping her back to the door to preserve her night vision, although with the full moon now riding high that was hardly necessary. There. The pale oval of a face ducked back into the doorway of a nearby lodge. Jame crossed over to it.

"Prid," she called softly down into the darkness.

The Merikit girl emerged. Even by moonlight, Jame saw that her face was swollen with tears. She stumbled up the steps and threw herself into Jame's arms, sobbing. Jame held her.

"Being the Favorite isn't easy," she murmured into the other's tousled hair. "The village expects a lot, and so do the Four. Hatch did what he had to."

"S-some of the girls say I'm a fool for not w-wanting to share him. It isn't natural, they say, and n-neither am I."

"I doubt if Gran or Ma or Da would say so. Your beloved is quite handsome. It sounds to me as if your former friends are jealous."

"Does it?" said Prid doubtfully. "But he didn't have to win again. Oh, how could he, after I . . . after we waited so long?"

"You left before he could explain. The Challenger fought dirty. More than that, though—well, Hatch is a sensible boy. I've only seen him truly upset once, on our wedding night, when he thought I was going to hurt you."

Prid gave a shaky giggle.

"Yes, it was funny at the time, or would have been if I hadn't been so drunk on fermented fish piss. But tonight the Challenger insulted someone. I think it was you, probably for the same reason that you've been teased before. And Hatch lost his temper."

"Then . . . then it was all for my sake?" Prid drew back and wiped her nose on her sleeve. "Oh, what a fool!"

"Men can be like that when they fall in love."

"What are we going to do?"

"Wait another year, I suppose, if you still don't want to share your mate. There, there," she added as Prid burst into tears again. "You're both very young, although you might not think so. I'm told that anticipation makes some things sweeter."

"Would you wait?"

That was a good question. If she loved someone as much as Prid did Hatch, would she let anything stand in her way? Her situation was at least as complicated as the two young Merikits', more so if one considered the possible cosmic consequences. Jame thought of Bane, of Randiroc, of Torisen. Each had stirred her blood. A time might come when one of them struck sudden fire in her veins. What would she do then?

"Awake," Gran Cyd had told her. "You can not be your kind's Ice Maiden forever."

But why not? she thought now, defiantly. How much simpler it would be, how much safer. Then again, when had her life ever been either?

"Would I wait?" she said lightly, and reached out to chuck Prid under the chin. "I have you, sweet lodge-wyf. What more could I want?"

Prid stepped back, pouting. "Now you laugh at me, but you are never here. My lodge will be so empty with Hatch gone, for I see now that we can not share a hearth and not a bed."

"I may have a solution for that. Lyra needs to escape her own kin for awhile. Will you give her shelter?"

"Oh." Prid considered this. "That mask she wears—is she really so ugly beneath it?"

"Not at all. It's just that Highborn Kencyr women conceal their faces."

"You don't."

"I am something of a misfit, as you may have guessed."

"Even among your own kind?"

"Especially there."

"Well, she seems nice, and I have always wanted a sister. Yes. I would like that very much."

"Good. Now at last we can celebrate."

Jame paused at the hall's door while Prid eagerly went on ahead to join her new friend. The communal lodge lay mostly underground, a circular amphitheater with deep, earthen benches reaching down almost to water level and prone to flood in the spring when the Silver overleaped its banks. Wicker cages tucked back against each riser contained shadowy seated forms, the tribe's honored dead encased in leather and wax like the watch weirdling who guarded the southern approach. If they came out tonight, Char was in for a shock. Living Merikit crowded the benches, eating and drinking in a cheerful babble of voices. On the whole, Jame thought that Lyra would be happy here, and hopefully not get her young hostess into too much trouble.

Chingetai emerged near the fire-pit at the bottom of the hall and shouted to gain attention. When this failed, he put his fingers in his mouth and blew a piercing whistle. Folk shushed each other to listen, apparently expecting to hear something funny.

"My Merikit," he shouted up at them, "I bring great news! A yackcarn bull has been sighted in the Riverland, and we have been given permission to hunt him! Who among us has ever seen such a wonder? Surely, this generation is blessed. Give the word and I will lead you to glory!"

The men in the crowd stirred in excitement. "Yes!" cried someone.

"Yes!" "Yes!" "Yes!" others echoed.

By now they were all on their feet, cheering.

Chingetai strutted and preened before them.

Jame sighed.

⟨⟨⟨⟨ CHAPTER VII ⟩⟩⟩⟩
All Things Rampant
Summer 100—102

I

HE WOKE, or thought that he did, in the arms of
Kallystine. That, at least, was her perfume, musk with a
faint hint of corruption. She stretched out on top of him
as supple and seductive as a cat, her perfect breasts
pressing against his chest, her husky voice tickling his ear.

"See? Was that not good?"

"Yes," he said; then, with a shudder, "No."

She laughed. Only her eyes gleamed through the
heavy veil that she wore. The fabric drew taut, molding
itself to the features beneath. Sharp cheekbones, a
pointed chin, bared teeth . . . a skull, grinning down at
him.

"Someone else would like to say hello."

"W-what?"

"Shhh."

A fingertip touched his lips, then slid down to tease
his nipple. He shivered and cupped the heavy fullness of

her breasts as they swung before his face. They, at least, had always been sweet.

"Ah, Ganth, is this not what you have dreamed about? You could have had me."

"No." His voice grated, harsh and stammering in his own ears. "You wanted my older b-brother, Greshan. Father p-promised him to you."

"What Gerraint Highlord promised me was a half-Randir heir to his throne. I would have used Greshan, but someone better came to claim me. In your precious Moon Garden. Under your grandmother Kinzi's very window. Oh yes, I saw that ancient hag spying on us, may we have blasted her sight. But you, sweet boy, would you like to try again for a better heir than the one that you drove out of the Haunted Lands with curses? Shall I let you, Ganth G-grayling, dear little Gangrene? And you, standing there in the shadows, would you like to do more than watch? Once Kinzi said, 'We Knorth are a passionate house, and not always wise.' Not, indeed. Poor little lost children. Come play with me."

Feet sounded on the stair, rapidly descending.

"Whose dream is this?" said a sharp voice. "Ganth, Kindrie, Tori, wake up!"

Kindrie woke with a start. He was sitting in the apartment of the Jaran Matriarch Trishien, who was watching him with concern.

"Lady, how long was I asleep?"

"Only minutes. You dropped off in mid-sentence. Sleep again. Clearly, you are exhausted."

"No. There's too much to do." He started to rise, wavered, and abruptly sat again.

"At least rest a few moments longer. Tell me about your dream."

"How did you know . . ."

"You cried out."

Kindrie shivered, remembering, then tried to explain. "It was very peculiar," he concluded, giving up. "People kept turning into someone else, I among them, and they talked about things that I didn't understand." He felt his face heat, which in turn embarrassed him even more. "Some of it was . . . not meant to be seen."

"It sounds awful," Trishien agreed, although for a moment at this last bit her eyes flickered with amusement behind the lens sewn into her mask.

She picked up her knitting, a gaudy, amorphous piece full of dropped stitches, and made a tentative stab at it.

"Tsk!" she said in annoyance as her needle missed the loop. She gingerly probed for it again, as if into foreign entrails. "Have you dreamt such things before?"

"More often since I returned to Gothregor, but details change. It's never quite the same."

In truth, between exhaustion and all the time spent in other peoples' soul-images, much had become confused.

"What are we dealing with here?" he had asked the steward Rowan upon his arrival, in response to Trishien's summons as conveyed by Kirien, who had practically shoved him out Mount Alban's front door.

Rowan had been sneezing, her eyes and nose red.

"We call it the hay-cough or, if it gets really bad, lung-rot."

It had started with the midsummer Minor Harvest and

the discovery of a weed known as "false timothy" among the hay.

"It looks like true grass," Rowan had explained, "but it has a hollow stem and a chambered root. The latter collects moisture, and mold grows there. When a reaper cuts the stem, spores puff up into his face. A few days later, he begins to cough and wheeze. As you know—who better?—we Kencyr don't often get sick. This is usually a minor annoyance that lasts a few days at most. This time, though, more and more of us are falling ill, the young and old especially, who were never in the field with the harvesters to begin with. How did they catch it, too? We don't know. Then fluid collects in the lungs. The herbalist Kells might help, at least with the fever, but he's at Tagmeth. There have been several deaths already, with more to come if you can't stop it."

Trinity. Could he?

"Matriarch Trishien summoned me, not the Highlord."

"Blackie is sick too, and not thinking altogether clearly. He would welcome your help, if he had his wits fully about him."

Kindrie wondered about that. Since his arrival, he had barely seen his cousin at all, much less spoken to him.

"The odd thing," he said now to Trishien, "is that in each soul-image I enter, something is growing awry. One Kendar sees himself as covered with exploding boils. Another can't stop spewing gibberish instead of the lyrics to the song that defines her being. A third lives in a narrow room consumed by murals of ever-changing fungus."

He didn't add that, whenever he closed his own eyes, he was apt to find himself in a Moon Garden seething with weeds that spat white, stinging froth into his face. If he breathed it, it took root in his lungs, closed his throat, and sprouted out of his mouth. There was nothing for it but to keep pulling the beastly things up by their soggy, stinking roots. In short, sleep had become as exhausting as waking.

He rose again, this time keeping on his feet. So much to do . . .

At the door, however, he turned and blurted out what, even now, bothered him the most:

"Why does Kirien hate me?"

The Matriarch smiled at him. "She doesn't hate you, child."

"But she won't even speak to me!"

"Perhaps you aren't saying the right things to her."

Kindrie plucked at his blue robe, bewildered. "I was so happy when she gave me this and—and spoke so kindly to me."

Trishien put aside her tangled work, not without relief. "No, I don't suppose you have encountered much kindness in your life. Disowned by the Knorth as a baby, raised by the priests at Wilden in that foul subterranean school of theirs, tortured by Rawneth in her vile experiments, beaten by Caldane, used by Ardeth, rejected by your cousins, at least at first . . ."

"Torisen still doesn't like me."

"He fears what you are, the more so because he is beginning to see something similar in himself. And just now this illness preoccupies him. But regarding my great-niece, for whom I have high regard, is it like her to be so fickle?"

"No. Not at all."

"Then consider: perhaps she likes you very much, and all you have offered her in return is bashful friendship."

Kindrie gaped at her. "You mean . . . you mean . . . but that's impossible. Who could possibly love me?"

"Until you can answer that for yourself, expect to be miserable."

II

KINDRIE STUMBLED OUT of the Women's Halls and stopped on the edge of Gothregor's inner ward. The descending sun seemed to wobble in the sky, spitting fire into his dazed eyes.

Lady Trishien must have it wrong, he thought.

Like Kirien, however, she was no fool.

If there was such a one in this business, could it be he himself?

Yes. No. Yes.

Think about it later.

The inner ward spread out before him with its rows of bright green newly sprouted garden vegetables, the first crop having been pounded flat by the summer's eve hailstorm. Would these plants ripen in time to see the garrison through the next winter? Kindrie had heard that Gothregor might again have trouble feeding itself. The loss of the hay harvest was especially worrisome. While the false timothy had by no means outnumbered the true, the moisture it had contributed to the hay-ricks had caused many of them spontaneously to combust and others to rot. The other houses had little to spare. Thanks to Aerulan's dowry, Torisen should have been able to buy what he needed from the Central Lands, but word had it that the Seven Kings had raised the price to ruinous heights, hoping to force the Riverland lords into open contracts for Kencyr to fight in their spring campaigns. Truly, thought Kindrie, his cousin had much to worry him.

Shouts drew his attention, and the sound of many hasty feet. Both were converging on the bakehouse, which abutted the kitchens and the garrison's mess-hall. Kindrie found himself walking in that direction across the top of the ward, then trotting under the old keep, then running westward along the southern wall.

Ahead, he saw an anxious crowd milling outside the bakery. Something pallid, bloated, and quivering bulged out of its windows. Bubbles swelled and burst on its surface like gaseous pimples:

. . . *glub, glub . . . urp.*

"You don't understand," someone was saying as he approached. "Bake-master Nutley is still in there!"

This close, Kindrie couldn't see over the onlookers' heads. "What's happening?" he asked a Kendar on the edge of the crowd.

"A batch of sourdough has gone rogue. Stand back."

Other Kendar ran up brandishing clubs and bare fists.

"Beat it down! Beat it down!" cried voices closer to the action.

The dough collapsed grudgingly with many a yeasty belch, back into the bakery. Kendar emerged amid a babble of voices carrying a limp body.

"He was crushed against the wall." "He isn't

breathing." "Did someone say that the healer is here?" "Yes, yes!"

The crowd parted. Kindrie looked down at the burly baker, with his blue-tinged face, whom they had laid at his feet.

All of those eyes, watching him anxiously . . .

Kindrie pushed them out of his mind, knelt beside the man, and opened his shirt to touch his bare, hairy chest. Sometimes he simply fell into a patient's soul-image. On other occasions, it took him what seemed like forever to gain access, and even then some images were hard to recognize, being so personal to each individual. Here, at first he felt nothing, saw nothing, heard nothing.

I'm too late, he thought. *He's dead.*

Then a whisper reached him, rising as if out of a darkening void:

". . . I need . . . I need . . ."

Oh God, need what?

Then he understood: *I knead.*

Kindrie drove the heels of his palms into the man's chest. Never having made bread, he wasn't sure if he was doing this correctly. As he understood it, though, one pressed down with all of one's weight, folded the flattened dough, and pressed again to work out the air bubbles. Here, thick bands of muscle resisted him. His arms began to ache. Sweat dripped into his eyes. He seemed to be kneading the thick mat of hair inward while the skin turned smooth, white, and glistening.

The baker's mouth opened.

"Ahhh . . .!" the crowd breathed with him.

Kindrie sat back on his heels, panting. The baker

gasped again and opened his eyes. They were a startling periwinkle blue but, at first, clouded with confusion. Then they cleared.

"The second rise . . ." he croaked.

Most of those who heard him looked confused, but the bakery assistants exchanged horrified glances, turned as one, and plunged back inside. Chunks of hacked-up dough flew out the windows, already expanding again in midair as the yeast worked furiously within them.

Under cover of the ensuing uproar, Kindrie rose and tottered away unnoticed. There had been quite enough excitement for him already, thank you very much.

He had been bound for the garrison barracks that occupied the western wall of Gothregor. Once there, he climbed to the third floor where rooms were set aside for established duos, or trios, or (for the recklessly adventuresome) quartets. The Kendar Merry met him at the door. Looking past her, Kindrie saw that her child's cradle was empty. His heart caught in his throat.

"Oh, no," she said, seeing his expression. "The Highlord has only taken him up to the roof for some fresh air."

"Is he any better?"

Merry wrung her hands, saw what she was doing, and clasped them tightly behind her back.

"He coughed all night, just when we thought he was so much improved. It seems to go like that: good as gold one day with hardly a sniffle, sickening the next. If it should reach his lungs . . . Cron is beside himself, so soon after losing Ghill."

Ghill had been their first son, a sturdy, reckless boy who had tried to ride a new-born calf and been thrown, breaking his neck. That hadn't killed him, however. When his parents had seen that he was paralyzed, they had asked Torisen to give him an honorable death with the white knife. Kindrie could barely imagine how his cousin had felt about that. Later, he had given the couple permission to have this second child, Bo. Trishien thought that Torisen had come to see this small family as the symbol of his Kendars' well-being in general and of his success (or failure) as their lord. Only when the infant Bo had sickened with hay-cough and Trishien had seen the effect this had had on the Highlord had she sent for Kindrie.

"He's been so good with Bobo," Merry was saying, "stopping in to see how he is almost every day, sick as he has been himself. Go up and keep him company, lord, please do. Maybe . . . maybe you can tell him something cheerful."

Kindrie climbed to the roof, prey to dire forebodings. While he had seen his cousin (at a distance) since his arrival at Gothregor, he hadn't spoken to him. It occurred to him that Jame had said much the same about her time here, before she had set out for Tagmeth. True, Torisen had had problems accepting both of his Shanir blood-kin, but he had seemed to be getting over that. What had happened since the Feast of Fools to set him so far back?

The roof was some fifty feet wide, covering the inner and outer walls as well as the barracks crammed between them. Crenellated battlements lined both sides. Down the middle ran a raised herbal knot garden, now mostly taken over by plots of vegetables about as advanced as those in the ward below.

All of this Kindrie saw under a shielding hand as he

blinked the setting sun out of his eyes. The alternating tooth and gum of merlon and embrasure stood out black against the glare, with a patch of darkness between them backlit by flames. Torisen. Kindrie approached, cautiously.

"My lord."

"So you call me. Not cousin, as you might."

"I would, if I thought you would welcome such an address."

"Oh, so formal."

An ashen face haloed in black regarded him dully with tarnished silver gray eyes. Kindrie thought he had never seen Torisen look so haggard, or his hair so threaded with white. It was hard to remember that he was still a young man, not much older than Kindrie himself.

"What's wrong?" he blurted out.

"This child is dying."

Black-clad arms half-opened to reveal a small, still form—only asleep, Kindrie hoped. He wanted to snatch that morsel of life away from such encroaching shadows, but held himself still waiting, breathless, for the child to breathe. When he did, he began to cough, a wet, tearing sound. If fluid was gathering in his lungs . . . but what could Kindrie do? Children so young didn't yet have stable soul-images.

"I have failed him, them, everyone. Father said that I would. Father said . . ."

"What?"

"'Cursèd be and cast out. Blood and bone, you are no son of mine.' By what right, therefore, do I claim the Highlord's seat? But if I do not, what good am I to my people? Better, perhaps, we both should fall."

He moved as if to rise, while behind him space gaped. From this height, it was a long way to the foot of the outer wall. Kindrie spoke quickly to snag back his attention.

"You serve your people to the best of your ability. If not you, who?"

"I said that I wouldn't listen, but a voice whispers, gloating, that the true Highlord has yet to declare himself. I stand in the way. I should not. Is it only my pride that keeps me here? My people have suffered before because of me. Trinity, in the Haunted Lands Kendar ransomed me with their lives and I let them. I let them."

Kindrie wanted to say that his people today would suffer much more without Torisen, who at least cared about them. He had opened his mouth to speak when the other went into a sudden paroxysm of coughing. He sounded worse than the child had, and he was barking white phlegm directly into the boy's face.

Several things clicked together simultaneously in Kindrie's mind. Without thinking, he dashed forward and snatched the infant out of Torisen's arms.

"Don't!" he cried. "You're killing him!"

His sudden rush almost knocked Torisen out of the embrasure, but his hands leaped to catch the surrounding merlons. Before, he had seemed half in a sick daze. Now he was wide awake, and furious.

"What in Perimal's name d'you think you're doing?" he demanded.

Kindrie retreated, clutching the now wailing child, horrified at his own audacity and its near fatal consequences.

"I didn't mean . . ." he gasped. "I wasn't trying to . . . Tori! You must know me better than that!"

"I know that you almost killed me, and you're frightening Bo. Give him to me."

"No." Kindrie drew back. "You've got to promise not to see him again until you're entirely well yourself."

"Now see here . . ."

"I'm serious." And so Kindrie was. Even in his own ears, his voice had changed to a tone that he had never used before. "Swear it."

"I . . . swear. Now get out. Of my sight. Of my house. We will not speak of this again."

Kindrie stumbled down the steps to find Merry and Cron anxiously waiting below, where they had undoubtedly heard the uproar overhead. He dropped the infant into their arms.

"Is he . . . are you . . ."

"Fine, fine." Kindrie wiped cold sweat from his brow with a shaking hand. Not so fine, really.

Cursèd be and cast out . . .

If he had used a special voice on Torisen, so Tori had on him.

Get out. Of my sight. Of my house.

"I made him promise not to see Bo again while they're both still sick. Don't you see? When a person has hay-cough, they can pass it on as if . . . as if they were a stalk of false timothy with mold in their lungs instead of in their roots. When the stalk is cut, when they cough, the spores spread. That's how people who never attended the harvest can still come down with the disease, and why Tori and Bo keep re-infecting each other. Trust me! I'm a healer!"

Torisen wouldn't stay on the battlements forever. Kindrie fled to his apartment in the northwest drum tower and began throwing his meager possessions into a saddle bag.

Rowan came to the door.

"It's already getting dark," she said. "You can't leave tonight."

Kindrie hesitated, a boot in one hand, an inside-out shirt in the other. She would hold him here—by force, if necessary—until dawn, but he couldn't stay.

"It would be foolish to run off so late," he said, carefully.

Some tension went out of the steward's shoulders. "I heard what happened at the bakery."

"How is the bake-master?"

"Recovering, if somewhat bemused. Everyone thought at first that you had bruised his ribs with all of that pummeling, but the swellings have risen into a pair of quite respectable female breasts. His assistants always did say that he had yeast in his blood. Maybe that's so. Temporary or permanent, though, it's too soon to be sure. And no, they don't go 'glub, glub, urp' and collapse when squeezed. I tried."

"Er . . . how does he feel about such a development?"

"Rather pleased, I think. His partner, on the other hand, is delighted." She cleared her throat. "I also heard, in part, what happened on the roof. You really think that's how hay-cough spreads?"

Kindrie shrugged. "We Kencyr don't have much experience with communicable diseases. Nothing much a Rathillien native can catch affects us. Why here with such a severe bout of harvest-cough and why now, I'm not sure, but when the Highlord is vulnerable, so are his Kendar."

"At least this gives us a way to fight it. We owe that to you, too, whatever Blackie said."

"Blackie—Torisen—is confused just now, and no, I'm not sure what the problem is there either. But he will sort himself out eventually. He always does."

Rowan almost smiled, stopped by the tightened skin on her scarred forehead. "I'm glad that you understand him so well."

Not well at all, Kindrie thought sadly as the door closed behind her. If only he did. But then, according to Lady Trishien, he had barely begun to understand himself.

Night fell. The garrison clattered around itself, in the mess-hall, in the dormitories, finally, bit by bit, settling down. Kindrie waited until the sentry passed. Then, taking his bag, he slipped out into the hall and out of the fortress.

Down by the Silver, the post station had also quieted for the night, although a candle still burned in the duty-officer's room, in case a vital message should suddenly arrive as might be the case at any hour, day or night. The remount herd stood shot-hip, half-asleep, in their corral. Some stirred as Kindrie moved among them. While he could ride, he was no expert and had no idea what sort of a mount to select. Presumably any here would do. He chose a quiet-looking piebald and led it to the tack shed. Kindrie had never rigged out a horse before, but he had seen it done. He hoisted up a saddle and, after some fumbling, secured it with various straps. Closer observation revealed that the horse was not an "it" but a "he." When he presented him with a bridle, he roused and looked askance at the bit.

"Come on, come on . . ." Kindrie muttered.

Get out of my house.

He had to go. Therefore, this horse had to take him. Kindrie jammed his fingers into the hinge of the animal's jaws and forced them open. The bit slid in over the tongue. Yellow teeth chewed irritably on the metal, a harsh, grinding sound.

Quiet, quiet . . .

Kindrie led the beast down to the River Road where, with difficulty, he mounted.

"Your name is Spot," he said, as if naming him increased his rider's control. "Now go."

Spot snorted. The next moment, he had launched at a dead gallop with Kindrie clinging desperately to his mane.

III

ROWAN GROPED HER WAY into the benighted bedroom, and swore as she tripped over a pair of discarded boots.

"Can't you put anything where it belongs?" she hissed into the darkness.

Bed-leathers creaked under a shifting weight.

"Is all well?"

"You tell me." Rowan found the edge of the pallet and sat down on it, as usual misjudging its height and landing with a thump. A muffled snort of laughter greeted her.

"It's as you feared," she said, pulling off her own boots

one by one, then struggling out of her other clothes. "They fought. Why do those three have to rub each other the wrong way all of the time? You'd think they had enough in common to make common cause."

"Perhaps they're too much alike, in ways that please none of them."

"Maybe. I'm just a simple randon. What do I know?"

"You know them. Blackie in particular."

She slid under the blanket and punched him lightly in the side. "Jealous?"

"Should I be?"

"Only if you're a fool. Which you aren't. But how is it with you? This has been quite a day."

He turned and slid an arm around her. "My ribs ache. No worse, though, than after preparing for the midsummer feast. All of those meat pies, all that holiday bread!"

She rolled into his embrace.

"Good. Want to play bouncy-bouncy?"

Bake-master Nutley lay back, drawing her on top of him, and grinned up into the shadowy planes of her face, where scars meant nothing. "At your service, m'lady."

IV

A GIBBOUS MOON ROSE and, after a time, set, leaving the sky awash with stars. Clouds of them drifted past overhead with speckled chasms between, then familiar constellations like the Frog and the Three-leggéd Wolf, then a curtain of silent, wavering lights that danced for awhile, apparently for its own amusement, before disappearing. It was a mild, late-summer night, with a sweet breeze from the south, perfect riding weather.

If he bounced one more time, though, Kindrie thought he would split in half.

He had heard that it took a post rider some two hours to get from keep to keep. By that reckoning, he had hoped to reach Mount Alban by early the next morning. However, he hadn't counted on what so much riding would do to unaccustomed muscles. Barely an hour north of Gothregor, he was obliged to break from a canter to a trot, which hurt even more. Without spurs to urge him on, Spot soon shifted to a sedate jog. At least they had the River Road mostly to themselves. Only twice did Kindrie have to draw off it, dismount, and hold his mount's muzzle lest he whinny to a passing messenger, bearing what message he shuddered to guess. Getting back into the saddle was harder each time.

Toward dawn, they drew near the Brandan keep of Falkirr. Spot tried to turn into the post station there, which was just beginning to stir, but Kindrie whipped him on with a stripped willow withy. Their progress thereafter was slow and grudging. It occurred to Kindrie that perhaps post riders made such good time because they changed mounts often, but he could hardly present himself to Brandan's ostlers without facing a flood of questions and, probably, detention.

North of Falkirr he drew off the road into a grove of trees, dismounted, and hobbled Spot. Not thinking the trip would take so long, he hadn't bothered to bring any food. Now, despite a growling stomach, he rolled up in his cloak and slept while his disgruntled mount cropped grass nearby. In his dreams, he labored in the Moon Garden to prop up bruised stalks, the leg muscles pulled in his long ride throbbing with every move. The piebald was there too, wandering about. Only the white patches of his hide showed, the black melting into the shadow of deep grass.

On waking near dusk, Kindrie realized that he had lost sight of the Silver. He had heard Jame speak of the dangers of leaving the road, but hadn't quite understood what she meant. After all, the Riverland was bracketed with mountains. Down was down. From the east bank, turn toward the setting sun and, sooner or later, you would find yourself by a descending stream or back on a beaten path.

However, like others before him, he hadn't counted on an evening haze of low, drifting clouds. The ground rose and fell. Trees leaned this way and that. Streams babbled, but out of sight. Perhaps, if he had been on foot, he could have told by the pull on his still sore muscles which way he was going, but on horseback he lost even that advantage. Spot seemed to know the way, however, so Kindrie gave him a loose rein, which he promptly abused by snatching bites of every bush he passed.

They began to pass between tree stumps. Here there was no forest, only the rotting remnants of one, dotted by shrubs and boulders.

Finally the haze kindled sunset red to the left, by which he knew that they were still traveling north. Soon after, in a dip below the clouds, he saw the River Road below, and a post station, and the lights of a fortress across the river, going out one by one.

Could that possibly be . . . yes, it was: Shadow Rock. Somehow, they had come a good twenty miles in less than an hour, at an amble. Kindrie had heard of the folds in the land that one might encounter off the road, but had never understood them. If that was truly the Danior keep, though, then they had emerged from the wilderness almost on top of Wilden.

In burst of panic Kindrie tried to turn his mount back toward the heights. Spot fought him. Below were the shelter and food that he had sought, also hands to rub him down before a well-deserved rest. Then he shied violently as a figure in black rose up from behind a boulder and rushed at him.

"You aren't taking us back!" it cried.

Kindrie hit the ground before he even realized that he had been thrown. His first instinct, after he caught his breath, was to check for damage. No broken bones. No ruptured organs. Good. Not that he couldn't heal either, but that would have taken time.

He heard Spot plunge off down hill.

Then someone landed on top of him and a pair of hands scrabbled at his throat.

". . . you aren't . . . you aren't . . ." a broken, stinking voice panted into his face.

This was more serious, perhaps imminently fatal.

Before he could properly register the threat, however, the slight weight was knocked off. He rose on an elbow, gasping, to see a figure in mottled green hunting leathers grappling with his black-clad assailant.

"Don't!" he croaked.

Green rose like water flowing backward and stepped away.

Kindrie scrambled over to his erstwhile foe. When he raised the man, his bones felt as light as a bird's, shifting under loose flesh. Healer's hands futilely cupped a skull wrapped in skin that crinkled like paper. His fingertips traced brand scars on the back of the other's neck, the swooping lines of the rathorn sigil.

"I know you," he said, sounding stupid even to himself.

"And I know you too, lord."

The man relaxed with a sigh that was half laugh, half groan. "Take care of them. They have no one else." The sigh turned into a rattle. Flesh crumbled from bone, bone into dust.

Kindrie wiped grit and hair off of his shaking hands. The latter clung, as hard to shake off as guilt.

"He was dead before I even touched him. What in Perimal's name is going on?"

He became aware of the green man standing over him, watching. A hood shaded his eyes against the dying light. White braids hung over his shoulders, reaching almost to his waist. Kindrie nearly called him by name, but this close to Wilden, that would be dangerous.

The other turned. "Come out," he said, in a voice rusty with disuse.

Four gray and brown clad figures hesitantly emerged from behind scraggly bushes and boulders—two young acolytes and two younger novices of the Priests' College.

"He said he would protect us," one of the former whined. "Now what do we do?"

It took awhile to sort things out, to the extent that was possible.

"Things have been bad at the college since early spring," said the senior acolyte, who was all of twelve or thirteen years old. His name, he had told them, was Oreq. "There are . . . were . . . former Knorth there—you know, Oath-breakers like . . . like . . ."

Nervously hugging his knees, he glanced at the pitiful pile of ash, still smoldering, around which they sat. Kindrie had barely whispered the pyric rune, but his throat still felt scorched. Not that he begrudged that. His only fear was that someone in the darkened Randir keep might have seen that brief flare of light that marked a brave passing.

"She took away his name," Oreq blurted out, horror in his voice. "Lady Rawneth. And now we can't remember . . . remember . . ."

"Who he was," Kindrie finished for him.

He himself had never known the man's name, only that during Kindrie's imprisonment at the college two years ago, this priest had risked much to warn him that the Witch of Wilden had her claws hooked in his soul-image. Names, souls, and shadows were interlinked, as were all three to bodies. What happened to one affected the others. Only great willpower must have held the priest together until he had been able to pass along his charges.

"Anyway," continued Oreq, "Lady Rawneth suddenly decided that all the Knorth at Wilden were traitors to her house, never mind that most of us actually belonged to the College and were her guests. We here are the last left, and only quarter-bloods, at best."

"Why did she turn on you?" asked Kindrie.

"Ancestors only know."

Kindrie looked around the circle of frightened faces. There was no question of returning these boys to the Randir fortress. If they hadn't caught Rawneth's attention before, they surely would now.

"Now what?" he asked the man in green who stood back from the light, gravely listening.

"Shadow Rock?"

Consternation rippled through the fugitives. The Danior keep was too close. Rawneth would hear that they were there and demand their return. Kindrie agreed. Cousin Holly was in no position to defend such visitors, although he might well feel honor-bound to try.

"Gothregor?"

That, no doubt, was where the nameless priest had meant to take them, but Kindrie couldn't return. Not now. Not yet.

"If you go there, it will have to be without me."

Twin, white-haired novices huddled on either side of him, no older than five or six. Their small hands clutched anxiously at his sleeves. "Don't leave us!"

Kindrie felt pangs both of sympathy and obligation, drawn by their drop of Knorth blood, even more by their helpless appeal.

"Mount Alban?" he suggested.

The younger acolyte gave a half-strangled yelp of protest. "I can't walk that far! And why should I? I . . . we haven't done anything wrong. We should go back to Wilden and beg M'lady's forgiveness."

The older boy jabbed an elbow into his ribs to shut

him up. "Mercy? Don't be a fool, Loof. You know perfectly well that she has none."

The man in mottled leathers had apparently made up his mind. "Follow," he said, and strode away down the hill. Not a blade of grass whispered as he passed.

They descended through the ruin of great trees. Over the past century, Wilden had cut down everything within two miles of their fortress to enlarge its inner structure. When land had crumbled, the Silver had changed course. When Wilden had lost the rich bottom lands, it had largely been due to erosion.

Kindrie walked with a twin holding tightly to each hand. When he had asked their names, one had answered "Timtom" and the other, "Tomtim." Someone, obviously, had had a cruel sense of humor, but not about their Shanir nature in abandoning them to the Priests' College. He didn't know to which face of their god they were aligned or how their abilities might manifest themselves, assuming they did yet. Many Shanir only showed themselves at puberty.

The mist turned to mizzle. It was a very light rain, but Loof began to whine again and tried to lag behind. Part Knorth or not, Kindrie would gladly have left him, except that his return would probably rouse the garrison. He caught the eye of Oreq, who took the boy in charge.

The night was very quiet except for their progress and muffled protests that "You're hurting me!"

The man in green had ghosted ahead of them. They caught up to him at the post station. Light shone around the shuttered window, but flickered out when he knocked on the door.

The corral held a dozen remounts, all steadily munching hay, while Spot tried to reach through the bars from the outside to snatch a mouthful.

A saddled mare stood beside him. Mirah, Kindrie supposed, she of the leaf green eyes and the pearl-gray coat dyed all the shades of the passing season, although it was too dark by now to make out any details. She whickered softly at the approach of her master.

They caught and saddled two horses ("But I can't ride!") while the ostlers continued to hide. Kindrie took one twin up behind him on Spot, the green man the other on Mirah, and they set out northward.

The River Road seemed to stretch out forever at the foot of brooding Wilden. The clop of hooves rang so loudly in the silence that Kindrie winced at each one. He didn't even want to look at the Randir fortress, that cruel prison where he had spent so much of his life. His memory was already too full:

. . . the stench of the subterranean school, compounded of damp, mold, and unwashed boys . . .

. . . a scream in the night, down in the priests' quarters where a novice had been summoned . . .

. . . the sting of a teacher's rod: "Half-wit, moron, bastard, you aren't paying attention!"

. . . blue-tinged milk, moldy bread, green-veined cheese swarming with mites . . .

. . . bullying, brutality, boredom . . .

That bitter catechism:

"Who is our patron?"

"Lady Rawneth."

"Whom do we serve?"

"The high priests."

"Who is our family?"

"Each other."

"On whom do we spit?"

"On our cruel god, who has forsaken us."

And Rawneth again, with that chill, caressing smile and behind her mask those glittering eyes that never seemed to blink.

"Let me see you, infant. Come close. Closer. Close enough. They say that no one can do you lasting harm. How . . . intriguing. Shall we see?"

Yes, he had survived, but his flesh remembered what had followed, many a day, many a night, when only soft laughter answered his cries.

The thin arms of Timtom (or was it Tomtim?) tightened, trembling, around his waist. No doubt the child had memories of his own. Kindrie laid a hand on small, cold fingers, only too aware that he himself had little warmth or comfort to give.

Mirah stopped suddenly, the other horses behind her.

"Go on, go on," Kindrie urged under his breath, frantic to be gone, but then he too sat still, listening.

The Silver chuckled. Streams descending from Wilden's overflowing moat slyly gurgled past them. One horse snorted, its breath a white plume in the growing chill of night. Another stomped.

Then from somewhere the faint sound of distant knocking . . . *tap, tap, tap* . . . and a voice that cried out urgent but barely recognizable words.

The moon, near full, had risen, and cast its silver light down Wilden's winding streets, which were so steep that one could see most of them over the outer wall, all the way up to the high terrace and the Witch's Tower.

A small clot of darkness marked a figure standing on the main way, outside a family compound. Like all the rest in the fortress, its door was shut, the courtyard and house behind it dark. There was a slight movement, as if of a pale fist rising and falling.

. . . *tap, tap, tap* . . .

Was that cry "Let me in," or "Let me out"?

Kindrie glanced at Oreq, who shrugged. As an inmate of the college, he probably knew very little about what happened outside of it.

A point of candlelight appeared in the courtyard. The street door opened a crack. The slight figure was pushed aside by a rush of men who had been concealed by shadows on the other side of the street. The candle jerked back and fell, extinguishing. Someone cried in protest or pain, perhaps both, a sound as quickly subdued as the light. The men emerged and shut the door softly behind them. Already, the first figure had drifted on like a sleepwalker to another door and was again raising its fist.

. . . *tap, tap, tap* . . .

That nightmare summons.

The man in green stared up at this mysterious performance. Wilden was in trouble, and he was Randiroc, the absent Randir Heir, driven out by Rawneth, who had chosen after randon training at Tentir to live his life as a solitary in the wilderness, migrating as the seasons decreed with a flight of carnivorous butterflies. Still, this had been his home, and he was still, at some level, responsible for its inhabitants. No wonder he had been drawn here at this time. Then too, however, he was also responsible for these children who had been the guests of his fickle house.

Everyone held his breath.

Randiroc sighed, turned Mirah back to the road, and cantered off. The others followed.

V

AFTER THAT, it was a long, slowly traveled night. By himself, even Kindrie could have made better time, but confinement in the college without exercise had weakened the boys, and Loof complained at every jolt. All that had saved them from pursuit so far was that the ostlers had probably spent the night quaking behind their door, as had every other surviving inhabitant of Wilden.

Birds began to chirp as false dawn lightened the eastern sky. Across the Silver, the randon college of Tentir came into view.

"I'm tired," whined Loof, "and hungry."

So was Kindrie. No doubt, everyone else among the fugitives felt the same, although no one else complained.

"Would Tentir give us sanctuary?" he asked Randiroc.

The Randir Lordan regarded the college, only just visible in the growing light. He had trained there. He was one of the elite who had earned his randon's collar on his own merits, before the growing peculiarities of his Shanir blood and Rawneth's ambition had made him an outcast.

"A Coman is commandant there now," he said.

Kindrie didn't understand the intricacies of randon politics. Jame had told him that house alliances weren't supposed to matter at the college, but they did. The Coman were aligned to the Caineron, who in turn were allies of the Randir. The current commandant might well convince himself that these runaways were Wilden's problem, to be held until reclaimed.

"Wait here," said the green man, and rode off across the bridge.

"Aren't we going, too?" asked Loof, his lower lip beginning to tremble.

"You said you were tired," Kindrie told him. "Rest while you can."

They had all dismounted. Kindrie sat down and slumped against a tree trunk with Spot's reins looped around his wrist and the twins curled up in warm lumps on either side of him. He only meant to rest his eyes and jolted bones. It seemed mere moments later that he woke with a start to find Randiroc standing over him. The Heir had brought back baskets full of food. He must have bypassed the commandant altogether, Kindrie thought fuzzily, and gone straight to the kitchens where the staff would have denied him nothing.

Oreq sat up, rubbed his eyes, and looked around.

"Where's Loof?" he asked sharply.

True enough, the younger acolyte and his horse were gone, probably on their way back to Wilden. They might meet Rawneth's agents on the road. If not, their arrival back at the Randir keep would surely spread the alarm.

"Eat as you ride," said Randiroc, distributing loaves of fresh bread, cold meat pies, and creamy cheese.

He put Timtom (or was it Tomtim?) in the saddle before him while Kindrie did the same with his twin, and the three horses set off at a fast trot. Most of the food either jounced out of the riders' hands or smashed against their lips—a messy feast, but the best Kindrie thought he had ever tasted. The growling in his stomach subsided and new strength began to flow into his tired limbs. It was a race now. What might happen to the boys if they were caught was probably nothing compared to his fate, much less that of Randiroc, whom Rawneth had so long pursued.

The River Road wound back and forth, sometimes following the course of the Silver, sometimes cutting across a meadow when the river wandered off absentmindedly into convoluted meander-loops as it had between Shadow Rock and Wilden. The weather had turned clear and bright again. Early color daubed some of the foliage and a few host-trees launched their leaves into the air as they passed. Kindrie thought at first that the latter explained the sudden dapples on Mirah's rump, then realized that the Heir's attendant flight of jewel jaws had caught up with him. These were a special breed called "crown jewels," whose wings took the hue of any surface upon which they rested. Mirah was stained a mottled green with a touch of harvest gold and dashes of scarlet. The carrion butterflies chose this last to imitate, spangling her flanks as if with fluttering spots of blood.

Toward midday, Kindrie shared the fragments of a pigeon pie with the little boy sharing his saddle. No one suggested that they stop. Even so, they weren't going as fast as they should. In bypassing the Tentir post station,

they had foregone fresh mounts. These would run until
they dropped, but no one wanted that, nor to be caught
on foot.

Late afternoon brought them under a range of cliffs
with foothills that ran down almost to the river. Kindrie
recognized the approach to Mount Alban, which itself was
carved out of the cliff face. That, even, might be the
college's square observation deck, barely peeking over the
intervening hills.

"Horses," said Randiroc.

From the sound of them, they were coming fast up
the road, already too close to out-ride. Then they
rounded a curve. There were eight of them, seven
mounted on black mares with wicked red-eyes and red
rimmed, flaring nostrils. Cruel bits forced their jaws
wide open so that they bared sharp, white teeth against
the slanting light and each other. Jame had told Kindrie
about such creatures, the vicious offsprings of mares and
rathorn stallions. Thorns, she had called them. They
were the favorite mounts of the Karnids in the Southern
Wastes. What were these doing here, in Rawneth's
possession?

The eighth equine was a stumbling, lathered post
horse with Loof clinging to its back.

"But I am loyal to our lady," he was protesting. "I only
want to go home!"

The oncomers slowed, seeing their prey at bay before
them.

The Heir handed Kindrie the other twin. "Run," he
said, and rode forward to meet them.

Their leader advanced a few steps and stopped. Her

smile was as white and sharp as that of the beast on which she rode, it being the practice of Rawneth's favored servants to file their teeth to cannibal points.

"Well, well," she said. "The Pretender. Lady Rawneth will be so pleased to see you." Her eyes raised to Kindrie, her smile deepening. "And her favorite plaything, too. Tell me, little priestling, do you still scream in the night? Do you still cry? Shall we see?"

Kindrie fidgeted with the reins, then gave up. It was stupid perhaps—probably—but he couldn't leave Randiroc to face these people on his own. He slid down off Spot, leaving the twins astride, wobbling as his saddle-sore legs took the strain.

"Take them to Mount Alban," he told Oreq. "Send back help."

"You still finger paint, I see," remarked the Randir, regarding Mirah's colorful coat. "And keep company with those winged vermin. A man of such talents, all of them worthless. What would your father say?"

It occurred to Kindrie that he had no idea who the Heir's father was. Presumably the previous Lord Randir. How, then, had Rawneth shoehorned her own son into power?

Small, cold fingers gripped his hands to the left, to the right. Looking down on the twins' white shocks of hair, he realized that while he had heard two horses clatter away, he hadn't checked to see who rode them.

Despair gripped him, followed by a spasm of nausea. Superb fighter though he was, Randiroc couldn't defeat so many enemies on such mounts before help came, if it did. He was about to trade his life and the future of his house for a straggle of Knorth, three barely of the blood, the fourth widely considered to be a bastard.

Kindrie's gut convulsed again.

Oh no, he thought. *Not now.*

It look him a moment to correct the situation. When he looked up again, it was to see the thorns shifting uneasily. Tail after tail jerked up and liquid filth poured down. Their riders hardly looked more comfortable, but with no such convenient way to relieve themselves. Then Kindrie saw that the paving stones of the River Road were breaking up and sinking as the ground liquefied under the thorns' hooves.

The twins' fingers trembled in his grip. Somehow, they were doing this . . . with his help?

Purge, he remembered a old healer telling him, with that smug smile of an elder imparting divine wisdom on a junior, who probably wouldn't have the sense to profit from it. *It's good for the body as well as for the soul.*

The Randir leader spurred forward with a hoarse cry, breaking free of the soil's hold, bearing down on Mirah. The mare wheeled out of the way. She and her rider seemed to be exempt from the general scourge, and lucky for them that they were as the thorn turned with frightening speed and launched herself back at them, fangs bared. She ran into a rising cloud of jewel-jaws. Blinded, maddened, the thorn bucketed off across the adjacent meadow, throwing her rider in the process.

The others had sunk up to their necks in what was fast becoming a quivering midden.

"Now that," said a rough voice behind Kindrie, "is something . . . one doesn't often see."

The haunt singer Ashe stood there leaning on her iron-shod staff while other scrollsmen and women, former randon all, panted up behind her.

"You should go on . . . to the college," said Ashe. "It seems that we . . . are still needed here."

"Take me with you!" Loof cried. He appeared to be standing on his saddle, his poor post horse having sunk completely beneath him.

Randiroc looked down at him. "No," he said, with the flicker of a smile. "You stink."

VI

"ASHE HAS THREATENED to make a song about it," said Kirien, refilling Kindrie's wine glass. She laughed at his horrified expression. "She was joking. Probably."

They were sharing a late supper in her Mount Alban quarters. It had taken some time and much debate (all loud, meant to be overheard) as to whether the Randir intruders should be rescued or left to stew in their own excrement. Then it had taken even longer to extricate them. The thorns had fought like demons and terrorized the draft horses brought to haul them out of the muck, admittedly at the risk of throttling them. Meanwhile, the lead Randir's mount had escaped into the hills, a promise of future trouble. Relationships between the Jaran and the Randir would not be . . . er . . . fragrant for some time to come, as Ashe put it, although she was probably the only one who hadn't suffered from the stench.

So far, it had been a somewhat prickly meal.

"You ran away again?" Kirien had asked, on hearing of his hasty departure from Gothregor. As he had blurted out his story, however, she had become intrigued by the bake-master's tale and by the technique Kindrie had used to deduce how hay-cough had spread to so much of the fortress.

"It never occurred to me that the physical frame could be so altered by soul manipulation," she said thoughtfully about the former. "That presents all sorts of interesting possibilities. If you explained it to Rowan, though, I trust that she will repeat your reasoning to Torisen. You can see, however, why he was upset. 'You're killing him!' That was hardly tactful, given his state of mind."

"I know that," said Kindrie, exasperated. "I was upset too, at the time."

"No doubt you were."

She put down the ewer and returned to her seat opposite him, across the table. Candlelight threw shadows under her fine, gray eyes and high cheekbones. He wondered if she too had been losing sleep, and why.

"As for the hay-cough," she continued, "I believe that I have read similar speculations in a native manuscript about the transmission of lung-warts among Rathillienites. I wonder if Index knows anything about that."

"Index may be a scrollsman, but he isn't a healer."

"I never said that he was. However, herbs are his field, when he isn't trying to wheedle Merikit lore out of your cousin Jame. Even then, he doesn't heal the body through the soul. Neither do surgeons. There are reasons why your craft is valued above theirs."

Kindrie throttled back irritation at the mention of

Index, who tended to assume superior airs with everyone, let alone with such a rag-tail, escaped priestling as he had at first been. After all, she had just paid him a compliment. It had been a hard few days, he reminded himself, to excuse his short temper, and his innards still didn't feel quite right after the twins' tweaking. Or maybe for some other reason.

Ashe entered with a bowl of porridge. "This always . . . settles me," she said, plunking it down on the table.

"Thank you," said Kirien. "I think, though, that the chicken was sufficiently bland."

"I didn't know that she ate at all," Kindrie said as the haunt singer left. "I mean, wouldn't it just fall out?"

"Ashe is . . . trying to be helpful," said Kirien, with an exasperated look at the not-quite-closed door. "Now, about these boys from the Priests' College . . ."

"Will Mount Alban return them if Rawneth demands it?"

"Of course not, unless they wish to go. We can always use new apprentices, especially ones with good memories. D'you realize how many ancient texts are apt to be lost, for lack of the will to remember them? And yes, some scrollsmen are finally coming to the admission, grudgingly, that some things need to be written down. Or, if that doesn't suit your boys, Valantir and other opportunities await just across the river. In particular, we need to watch those twins. They show signs of an uncommon Shanir trait—although, come to think of it, one of your cousin's ten-commanders has shown skills along similar lines."

Kindrie sipped his wine. He wondered if the flutter in his stomach was truly due to the twins or to general nerves.

How many times had he imagined this scene, usually to a fractious end? He allowed the drink to untie his tongue although, he assured himself, he was by no means drunk.

"When I was at Gothregor," he said, carefully, "I talked to Lady Trishien, or rather she talked to me. In her opinion, I've been a fool. About you. About us."

Kirien set down her wine glass. Although her tone was light, her glance was keen. "She said much the same to me. What do you think?"

Kindrie made a helpless gesture. *Speak the truth and shame the shadows,* he told himself. "All of my life, people have called me an idiot. As a novice, as an acolyte, as an escaped priestling. It appears to be a congenital weakness. That must seem odd to you. After all, no one has ever suggested that you are stupid."

Kirien gave a most unladylike snort. "According to the other matriarchs, Highborn girls aren't supposed to be intelligent. It complicates their plans. Then too, my Randir mother died bearing me, so that makes me suspect breeding stock."

"Mine died too. Most people still consider me to be a bastard, although I'm not."

"I know. Then they dropped you into that foul pit of a Priests' College. I at least had Father, Great-aunt Trishien, and a host of other kinfolk, all eager to spoil me."

"Well, they didn't succeed. In spoiling you, that is. I've never met anyone more unselfish."

She turned her head so that a silk curtain of hair concealed her face, but not before he had seen her blush.

"Maybe you don't know me so well after all," she muttered. "When I want something, I usually get it."

Kindrie fought the urge to scramble back to safe ground.

"Does it bother you?" he blurted out.

"What?"

"That you, that we both aren't considered marriageable material?"

"If we belonged to different houses, it would ruin us both. Nonetheless . . ."

"'Nonetheless' nothing, and contracts be damned. Everyone here knows that you are a brilliant scholar and someday will be a fine leader, as much as you may not relish the prospect. People value you. The rest are . . . are just stupid."

Ashe reappeared at the door.

"Go away," said Kirien.

She turned back to Kindrie. "You do see, though, why I might feel a bit unsure about . . . about, well, us. According to the Matriarchs, I can't be trusted to breed true, even if I should want to, which I don't. Breed, that is. Not now, at least. I was taught a thing or two by Aunt Trishien. The rest of the Council doesn't even recognize me as female, nor will they sanction anything that I do, although they may well condemn it." Her voice broke into a shaky laugh. "After all, this is hardly my area of expertise."

Kindrie felt his throat tighten. "And you think that it's mine?"

The conversation, he felt, was getting muddled, as was he. Too much wine. Too much . . . everything. He looked at his glass, which was somehow full again.

"Are you trying to get me drunk?" he asked, more curious than upset.

"Ashe suggested it."

Kindrie burst out laughing. "How many people d'you suppose are listening out in the hall, ready to . . . er . . . help?"

"Me," rasped Ashe.

"And me," piped up Index.

"And me," said a deep voice with a chuckle in it—the Director of Mount Alban himself.

Kirien marched over to the door and firmly closed it.

"You're welcome," came a chorus of voices from outside, followed by the sound of retreating laughter.

Kirien's hand twitched. "T'cha," she said, exasperated, and drew out her chalkboard. "Now Aunt Trishien is trying to send me a message."

"Don't answer her."

Kirien threw the tablet across the room, where it shattered against the opposite wall.

"Well," she said, rather helplessly, leaning back against the door. "Hopefully our well-wishers are out of earshot or they'll think that we've resorted to chucking crockery at each other. What now?"

Kindrie rose, pleased to find that he was still relatively steady on his feet. He touched her face, felt her breath and lips warm against the palm of his hand. So beautiful . . .

"You're the scholar," he said, with a catch in his voice. "You tell me."

They tried to kiss, and bumped noses.

"Obviously, this requires more experimentation," said Kirien, with a tremulous laugh. "Let us be fools together, then, in the name of research."

❧❧ CHAPTER VIII ❧❧
Autumn's Eve
Summer 120

I

THE FIRST FURROW for the sowing of the winter wheat wasn't ready to plough until the last afternoon of summer.

Of all the relatively clear patches near Tagmeth, this slope down to the Silver south of the keep on the east bank had seemed the most promising, and even then it had taken most of the season to prepare. First, they had had to clear the saplings and bush; then, the stones; then the weeds, helped by a rooting herd of young swine. Even now, it looked a poor thing, thinly covered with soil and a top-dressing of manure.

Not for the first time, Jame wondered how the original settlers at Tagmeth had sustained themselves. Perhaps, like the later Caineron colonists, they had depended on supplies from keeps downstream or even from the Central Lands. Still, they must have suffered shortages as the Kencyrath now did, the rare rich water meadows and bottom lands notwithstanding. Tagmeth still had its mysteries, and she was running out of time to solve them.

Farmer Fen and his helpers were assembled at the north end of the field behind the keep's only plough and a team of oxen. For some reason, they had asked Jame to stand in the turning space or headland at the southern end of the first proposed furrow. How odd, she thought. As if Fen needed her to mark where he should go. As if she knew where to direct him. For that matter, why launch the sowing of the winter wheat so late in the day? True, only now after feverish last-minute activity had they managed to prepare the ground. It had something to do, she supposed, with this being the last day of summer and tonight being Autumn's Eve, when the dead were remembered. Perhaps traditional Kendar considered it an ill omen to cross from one season to the next with this work not even begun. Then too, how long could it wait?

Stray, drifting snowflakes dusted her eyelashes and melted like cold kisses on her lips. Uphill, some trees were already bare while others blazed crimson and gold or even still stood green. The weather had turned frosty early this year. True, the chill might not last unbroken until winter, but what if the field froze before it could be sown?

Fen seemed to be making a speech to the assembled farmhands. He gestured to the field, then apparently to her, then raised his whip. The Kendar cheered.

Crack.

The oxen leaned into their yoke, set their great, flat hooves, and trudged forward. The metal blade bit into the earth. The first furrow-slice curled away to the plough's right toward the River Road and the Silver. Fen was steering carefully: all subsequent furrows would be guided by this one. In time, soil washing down the hillside would level this field somewhat, but it would never be ideal.

Halfway to her, some fifty feet away, the oxen faltered. Fen flicked his whip over their heads, without effect. They stopped. Now they were trying to turn in opposite directions at that glacial pace common to their kind, with all of its corresponding massive strength. The yoke groaned and snapped.

What in Perimal's name . . . ?

Something snorted down the back of Jame's neck. She turned to find herself nose to nose with Death's-head. The rathorn colt was a mess, his coat clotted with burrs as if he had rolled in an acre of weeds. More clustered on his barrel behind the elbows and in front of the stifles, where they must prick him every time he moved. When he irritably twitched his matted tail, it scourged his muddy sides below the ivory plates like a flail.

He snorted again, impatiently, as if to say, "*Do something.*"

"What have you done to yourself?" she demanded of him.

The fragment of a previous night's dream returned to her: the yackcarn bull romping ahead with his tail straight up, swerving, the burdock-choked gulley opening up under her hooves . . . no, under his . . . falling, rolling, tangling . . .

"He tricked you, didn't he? God's claws, where is Chingetai with his host of avid hunters?"

That was a good question. The summer solstice was long past, the season on the turn toward the autumnal equinox. Earlier on, she had expected the Merikit virtually any day and had wondered how she would explain their advent to her own people. She still didn't know what she would say when they did at last arrive.

A rider from the keep had pulled up next to Fen and now bent from the saddle to speak to him. The farm-master listened, then threw up his hands in exasperation or despair, impossible to tell which. He waved the rider away and came trudging across the unbroken field toward her.

"Sorry about that," Jame said as he neared, indicating the truculent rathorn.

The colt bared his fangs and hissed through them.

Go away.

Fen stopped at a wary distance.

"I didn't catch his scent," Jame added, "but obviously the oxen did. Can the yoke be repaired?"

"More like replaced, lady, and, as it turns out, we'll have all winter to accomplish that. Someone has tampered with the seed wheat."

"Oh no. More thistles mixed in, as with the rye?"

"This time, the bastard pissed on them. Repeatedly. The entire batch is stinking and moldy."

Jame swore under her breath. She had hoped against hope that all of the previous misfortunes had been accidents, however unlikely, all the way back to those at Gothregor. However, one didn't urinate by chance with such accuracy, over and over. Someone wanted Tagmeth, wanted her, to fail.

"And," continued Fen mercilessly, "the storage room is hopping with those wretched mice."

This was a separate issue, or so Jame hoped. The rodents had first appeared one night near midsummer or that, at least, was when they had first come to her attention by invading her bedchamber. She had woken to repeated thuds and had seen Jorin bounding around the room in soaring leaps. That he was trying to catch something became evident when a morsel of gray fur landed on her stomach and stared at her with dark, beseeching eyes. Above that were a pair of startlingly large ears, below, twitching whiskers, tiny forelimbs, elongated hind ones, and a tail longer than its entire body. Then it was gone and Jorin had landed in its place, all forty pounds of him. While she struggled to regain her breath, she had seen the mouse spring around the room—six feet high, ten feet at a jump—while the ounce scrambled to catch up.

. . . bounce, pounce, bounce, pounce . . .

So on and on until this tiny invader had leaped through the doorway, down the stairs, and Jorin had bounded after it, missing his footing as soon as he was out of her sight and tumbling all the way down.

Hopping mice were native to the Southern Wastes.

And now they had spread to Tagmeth's larder.

Fen looked up the hillside, so painstakingly prepared, and sighed. He began to fish things out of his capacious pockets: a ball of twine, bent nails, half a sandwich, a live, protesting dormouse, and finally an iron curry comb, which he tossed to her.

"Here. You'll need this."

As he plodded off, Jame turned back to Death's-head, who snarled at the comb.

"What, d'you expect me to groom you with my teeth?"

At first the rathorn twitched and grumbled with each freed burr. Then he began to relax.

Jame worked methodically from his head to his tail, teasing out the sticklers and tangled hair first with the comb, then with her own extended claws. With the arrival of cold weather, she had started to wear gloves again, which gave her fingers some protection but not at the tips, which had been slit open. In a way, she welcomed the punishing sting under her nails. It seemed to her that it was her fault so much had gone wrong at Tagmeth. If she hadn't dragged everyone so far north into this wilderness, they would have had friendly neighbors and help, if needed. But no: she had deliberately chosen isolation the better to prove herself to her brother and to the Randon Council. Now all of her people were about to pay the price for that arrogance. She remembered Marc telling her about that terrible winter of famine in his home keep, when he had tried to sustain his little sister on a gruel made of melted, dirty snow, bugs, and worm-ends. That had been at Kithorn, only some twenty miles north of where she now stood. Then, the Caineron had blocked any supplies sent to the stricken garrison. So they would surely do again.

"Fair warning," Sheth Sharp-tongue had told her. "M'lord won't give up Tagmeth easily."

That was why they were still here, on this of all days, facing this of all nights.

Autumn's Eve was when the lord of each house visited its death-banner hall and named all of the dead staring back at him through the weave of their mortality. Most would be Highborn, with a few notable Kendar mixed in.

The rest of each Kendar family would gather together in remembrance of their own dead. Names linked each to his or her house. To be forgotten, even in death, was to crumble away from the only immortality that the Kencyrath craved.

Jame had walked the Gray Lands where such lost souls lingered, decaying shells of their former selves. The blood on a banner flakes away. A lord stumbles, unable to remember a face, a name long passed, and a soul is set wandering, roofless and rootless, thinly keening even after it forgets what it has lost. Truly, dumb neglect could strike as deep as any living curse.

Certain Kendar had petitioned her to return to Gothregor and their families, just for one night of remembrance. She had consulted with Brier and Marc, who had both agreed: if they weakened the garrison even by so few, Caldane would take notice and Tagmeth would fall. Jame wanted them to regard this keep as their home. Perhaps some did, but many still wavered, or so she believed. Their lord dwelt far to the south. How much strain would their bond to him take before it broke, and what could their so-called lady offer them in return? Jame had overheard the grumbles. Brier Iron-thorn and Marcarn Long-shanks had thrown in their lots with her, even if only the former was bound to her. Other Kendar apparently clung to them, in a chain that she previously hadn't recognized. As for the rest, why should they suffer? That must be how the trickster had felt, unleashing his sordid flood on the winter wheat.

Sun and moon had both set, the latter a thin crescent waning to the dark. Stars began to wink overhead, a great spangle of them like diamonds cast into a blue velvet bowl. Death's-head glimmered in the gathering dusk. His ivory-crowned head drooped almost to his knees. Jame freed the last burr. She stood for a long time, her hand on the rathorn's warm shoulder, watching the jewels turn above them.

Against that, why did any of this matter? she wondered. Then again, how could it not?

Too much rested on her. On them. The end of all things, or at least their change into something ghastly. Did their ancestors ask for this? Did they know what it involved? Probably not. Words from an unseen mouth. Promises, implied. Weapons withheld . . .

Unless they are us, Tori, Kindrie and me, she thought. *But we are only mortal. A breath of wind could kill us— unless the Arrin-ken are right that that would take another Kencyr. So. Death from the hand of a friend, a relative, a lover. Enemies will have to stand in line. But what can I do about it? Only take one step at a time and hope that I tread true, for the sake of those whom I love.*

She slapped the rathorn's neck. Death's-head woke from his doze with a startled snort and nearly fell over.

"Silly boy," she told him, and started the long walk back to Tagmeth.

II

IT WAS FULL DARK and snowing hard by the time Jame reached the keep. The guard at the river gate informed her that everyone else was at dinner in the mess hall. When she thanked him by name, he seemed startled, which amused her.

She crossed the upper end of the pasture and passed through the second gatehouse into the inner ward where the Caineron *yondri* still had their camp. To her surprise, however, the site was empty. She wondered if the first snowfall had finally convinced them to leave, then, more doubtfully, if Marc had invited them in to share the Autumn's Eve feast, now in progress.

The campfire at the center of the encampment had gone out, but smoke still rose from its ashes, or rather from under them, and the surrounding snow had melted. Jame squatted to look more closely. The remains of logs lay across a metal grill, which in turn was positioned over a hole in the ground. Smoke ascended from below, mixed with flickers of light, a muffled murmur of voices, and the tantalizing smell of roast pork.

How very curious.

A ramp just within the shell keep led down to the cellar, now converted into a small subterranean stable against harsher weather to come. Jame had been here before, making sure that Bel-tairi's winter quarters were fit to receive her. However, the stalls only underlay the keep, so they weren't the source of the smoke. Brier had said something about a second, half-flooded level that extended beneath the ward and the pasture. The entrance should be just about here. Yes. Set against the southern wall of the stable, behind a bale of hay, was a small, round door. It opened inward—silently, on greased hinges— onto a short flight of shallow stone steps. Halfway down, Jame bent to peer into the cavity beyond. It appeared to be a long, low-ceilinged natural cave. The walls ran with water. So did the floor, except where a section of the roof had fallen to create an island in the midst of the flood. In the middle of this relatively dry space was a framework of branches with leaping flames at its heart and a suckling pig suspended above them. Smoke rose to a ragged hole in the ceiling above which, no doubt, were the remains of the campfire in the inner ward.

Half a dozen people or more sat around the fire below, frozen, their faces turned toward her. As quiet as the door had been, she guessed that they had felt the tell-tale draft when she had opened it.

"Hello, Must," she said.

The young Caineron *yondri* stood, fists clenched at her sides.

"We didn't steal the pig," she said, and stifled a cough. It was warmer here than above, but still perniciously damp. "Your steward gave it to us to honor Benj."

"Who . . . oh."

That, presumably, was the Kendar whom Fash had speared in the back.

"I'm sure Marc did," she said. After all, that was exactly the sort of thing her old friend would do. She herself had completely forgot about the only death so far suffered at Tagmeth. "Does he know, though, that you're roasting his gift underground?"

"No one does—except, now, you."

"I'm surprised you could get a fire to burn in such a wet place."

Must shrugged, still wary. In her experience, Highborn who began by speaking quietly often ended up shouting abuse. "Sometimes when we gather firewood on the upper slopes, we find fallen ironwood branches. It took weeks above ground to kindle even the smallest of these. Down here, they won't burn as long as an ironwood trunk—"

Hardly, thought Jame, given that a prime fire timber took centuries to consume.

"—but we reckon they'll at least get us through the winter. If you don't drive us out."

There, again, was the dilemma. Unwilling to expel them when they had nowhere else to go, she had given them tacit permission to camp in the inner ward, and kind-hearted Marc had provided them with the means to do so. Now they had crept even deeper into the fabric of the keep, like foxes going to earth. What did it hurt, though, that they were here? She hadn't offered them the bond. As things stood, that might never lie in her power. But, if so, was it fair to give them even so much encouragement as this? Her own people wanted them gone. At least one of her people wanted her gone too— unless the trickster was here below, a Caineron agent posing as a *yondri*, set on Tagmeth's destruction. It would be a relief to think so (not one of us), but if so, he (or she) hadn't been at Gothregor when the trouble had started— unless those earliest incidents had truly been accidents.

G'ah. It all made her head hurt.

Shapes shifted. Shadows moved. Jame realized that there were more people here than she had thought.

"Everyone, come out," she said sharply, unconsciously shifting into the voice of command.

(First quiet words, then abuse . . .)

Pebbles rattled down. Somewhere farther back, a stalactite fell with a great splash. After the tense pause that followed, Kendar emerged from the shadows of the rough island as if its very rocks had come to life. Ten, twelve, eighteen at least.

"Must . . ." Jame said, in a warning tone.

Must braced herself and swallowed. "Some are from Restormir. The rest come from Wilden."

Jame scrambled to make sense of this sudden invasion. "Randir *yondri*?"

One stepped forward, a boy as nervous as Must, although better at hiding it. "Lordan, we were bound to a Randir Highborn, a good man. But then the trouble started. Lady Rawneth . . . we think she's gone mad. By day life is much the same as always, but by night . . . She walks through the streets of Wilden, knocking on doors. If one opens, her men rush in and kill whomever they find. That was what happened to our master, all because he couldn't resist her summons."

"But why kill him for that?"

"We think . . . we think she wants no witnesses to her compulsion, to her . . . her weakness, as she would see it. Why does she knock? We don't know. Wilden lives in terror of the night. Then, the next morning, her men came back. Our master was a traitor, they said, so we must all be too. His family chose the White Knife rather than exile. So did many others. The rest of us fled. On the road, we met Caineron fleeing north. They said they hoped to find refuge here with the Knorth at a new, cadet keep, so we came with them. Please, lordan . . ."

He stopped short as Jame raised a hand.

"Enough. I won't drive you out of the undercroft, at least not here and now. As for the future . . . well, good night."

She fled up the stairs to the stable, shut the door behind her, and leaned against it. Her head and heart pounded.

Nothing had been resolved. Instead, her problem with the refugees had tripled. And what if more came? God's claws, what was going on at Wilden and Restormir? Was the entire Riverland falling apart? What would Tori do? What was he doing right now?

Autumn's Eve. The death-banner hall at Gothregor with so many faces crumbling between warp and weft, so many names lost in time. Would he remember them all? In his place, she wouldn't, but then she had never been formally introduced to most of the Knorth dead.

The randon wanted her to learn leadership. Obviously, so far she hadn't, or she would know what to do with these unwelcome guests. Again, what would Tori do? She had no idea. She was no leader. Perhaps she never would be.

Footsteps sounded on the stable ceiling, under the mess-hall. They would all be there, more people whom she was failing. Nonetheless, she ought to get some dinner, even though she had lost her appetite. With that thought in mind, reluctantly, she mounted the stairs through drifting snow into Tagmeth's courtyard.

III

JAME PAUSED outside the mess-hall. With the exception of the guards, her entire one-hundred command sat within, their platters piled high with roast pork, baked apples, and buttered yams. What conversation reached her was muffled and subdued, this usually being a somber feast. She had wondered if she should cancel it altogether in the face of the potential famine to come, but had refrained, sensing that these people needed familiar rituals to feel that they were part of a community.

Niall's ten-command sat at the table nearest to the door, so on her way in Jame stopped to ask him about his day's work. A nervous boy who had seen too much at the Cataracts and tended toward nightmares, he had nonetheless settled down considerably since coming to Tagmeth. Jame suspected that he was grateful for the new duties that kept him preoccupied. Assigning him solid, patient Erim as a five-commander also seemed to have been a good idea. Since the other eight had stopped eating to listen, she spoke briefly to each of them in turn, pleased to find that she remembered their names.

Corvine's table came next.

"I wish Quirl were here," Jame said to the big Kendar.

Corvine looked momentarily confused, but as if with minds of their own her fingertips traced the name carved into her forearm and she gave a heavy sigh.

"I did have a son, didn't I? A randon cadet, too. Until that witch bitch took away his name and he died. That was at Tentir?"

"Yes."

It was frightening how much harm Rawneth could do, through names, shadows, and soul-images, even if Quirl had actually died at the teeth of a direhound after his unsuccessful assassination attempt on the Randir Heir. If she had truly run mad—*Why*? nagged that tiny voice at the back of her mind—it bloody well served her right.

"But the flesh remembers," she said, touching Corvine's self-inflicted scars.

Their interchange had disturbed the ten-command, who clearly knew nothing about the unfortunate Quirl. Consequently, it seemed even more appropriate than before to address them individually, by name.

Three more tables. Thirty more names. Berry's ten-command, dour Talbet's, absent Jerr's, who were on guard duty with his squad of second year cadets. The game was getting harder. Jame had a good memory, as did most Kencyr in a society that traditionally depended more on recall than on writing, but here there was an element of strain, a growing fear that she would forget someone.

What should that matter, though? These people weren't bound to her, except for Brier, nor would remembering their names make them so. Unlike Torisen, she wasn't responsible for their souls. That required a true leader.

But, somehow, this was still important. She had already considered that, so far from home, they needed rituals, a sense of belonging, or Tagmeth would fail. Now she began to draw on the memory of Kindrie's chart that listed all the Knorth Kendar and their relationships to each other. Many of the dead were listed there as well as the living, and she named them where she could. The hall had become more and more quiet. Everyone was listening. Marc had come to the kitchen door to watch.

"Go on," he mouthed.

Jame came up behind Damson. Short, stocky, and

unprepossessing as the Shanir cadet was, the more sensible of her command regarded her with wary respect not unmixed with fear. Perhaps they sensed how different she was, how potentially dangerous. From the foot of the table her Five Quill gave Jame a quick, rueful smile. Seeing it, Damson turned to scowl at her.

"I wanted to talk to you earlier," she said, as ever brusque, "but you were off somewhere."

"Was there a problem?"

"So you might say." She pointed her knife, a chunk of meat impaled on it, at two second year cadets, a boy and a girl, sitting on opposite sides of the table, ignoring each other. "Wort and Dens. They've been quarreling over a particularly fine horse ever since Gothregor. I told them that the remount herd belongs to our lord, not to us, but they wouldn't shut up."

Jame regarded the cadets, who refused to meet her eyes. In the normal course of events, they would be at Kothifir now, training with their peers, instead of here, thrust into what amounted to a third-year field assignment but without the benefit of rank. The regular Kendar tended to indulge them as if they were children which, actually, they were. How strange to think that at the start of the previous year her own ten had been much the same. She didn't include herself in that estimate. Her childhood had passed in the Master's House, under the shadows of Perimal Darkling, and she was glad to have forgotten most of it.

"So," continued Damson, "I couldn't find you. Then Quill told me an old story and that gave me an idea."

Jame glanced down the table at Quill, so named

because his parents had wanted him to become a scrollsman. While his ambitions had taken him elsewhere, he still loved a good story, the older the better.

"Which one?" she asked, already feeling qualms.

"The Judgment of Sully."

"Let me guess. You said that you would split the horse between them."

Damson gave her a suspicious look. "That's right. Head or tail. Their choice."

"And one of them said, 'Oh no, not that. Give it to him.' So instead you gave it to her. Or vice versa."

The girl Wort regarded her plate with a slight smirk. Jame realized that she also knew the story and had guessed that by appearing to value the horse's life over its possession, she would win it.

Damson had thought she was being clever. So had Wort. On the other hand, Damson may have meant exactly what she had said. Head or tail.

"In future, Quill, be careful what stories you tell your poor ten-commander. She tends to be quite literal minded."

Damson glowered. "What does that mean?"

"Quill will explain it to you. And you, Wort, no more games."

The other cadet looked up, confused. "What?"

"The rest of you—" and here Jame named each one— "take heed."

Dar and Mint had shoved their tables together, a sign, Jame guessed, that their relationship was still strong.

"Playing mother and father?" she asked.

Dar grinned. Mint blushed. Their joint commands

laughed indulgently. It was easy to remember all of their names.

"How did you escape Beneficent?" she asked Char at the next to last table.

"Gave her an extra helping of feed. Ran away while she was eating it."

His ten-command had settled in to care for Tagmeth's assorted livestock. There were more attractive jobs, certainly, but this one was important, too, and Jame hoped that they had learned to take an interest in it. As her eyes swept around the table, they met only one sulky stare, and her heart sank. She knew that face. The cadet was one of her original ten, for Trinity's sake, and now Char's five-commander. But she couldn't remember his name.

This is ridiculous, she thought as she stumbled through the others. *I know him perfectly well, better than most in this room. Why can't I remember?*

All that came to mind was Mullen, whose name her brother had forgotten. The poor Kendar had virtually flayed himself alive to reclaim Torisen's attention. Not another Mullen. No. Never.

Some of her strain communicated itself to the rest of the hall, which bit by bit grew quiet again. The unnamed cadet lost his truculent air and began to look frightened as he realized that, so far, he had been passed over.

Jame dug her claws into her palms. With pain came sudden enlightenment.

"Killy," she said. "Dodged any falling trees lately?"

Everyone laughed at this feeble joke—except for Killy, who still looked shaken—and the babble of conversation resumed.

"Well done, lass," said Marc as she joined him at what passed for the high table. "Master Rackny, come out here and be thanked for this splendid feast."

With a jolt, Jame remembered the little Southron cook, whom she had previously remembered only by his title.

Rackny bustled out of the kitchen, beaming, followed by Buckle and her ten-command who were currently serving as the cook's helpers. He introduced them to Jame and they good-naturedly received her praise for a meal that she had not yet tasted. When they had trooped back to their work, shooed by a grinning Buckle, Marc pulled out a chair for her.

"Sit. Eat. You look a little pale."

Jame managed a half-smile. "I'm not really hungry, and my head hurts, a bit. I think I'll just go to bed. Marc, Brier, Rue, Kells . . . er . . . Swar, Tiens, Cheva, thank you."

IV

SOME TIME LATER she awoke in her apartment, in a tangle of blankets, still fully clothed. Jorin sprawled on top of her, snoring in her ear. Otherwise, except for the eternal roar of the falls, the keep was silent. She had dreamed . . . what? Something confused and distressing, something to do with Torisen.

Not another Mullen. No. Never.

Between the play of torchlight and shadow in the death-banner hall, had her brother had trouble remembering the names of their ancestors? Something occluded his soul-image, to the extent that even thinking about it choked her breath. There was a shut door there, or perhaps more than one, and the muffled sound of fists beating on it.

Let me out, let me in.

What did that mean?

She sensed, however, that he had called on brute memory to recall every face, albeit without the connection to them he should have had both as Lord Knorth and as the Highlord of the Kencyrath. Something distracted him.

Oh, Tori, what's gone wrong with you? How can you lead our people without full access to your own soul?

Rue had left a tray of bread and honey beside her pallet, also a mug of milk, but Jorin had already dealt with that. Jame's stomach growled. She ate, then lay back, cuddling the ounce, to stare out the window at the midnight sky. It had stopped snowing. The last crust of the moon had long since fallen. There might have been stars, but her view was to the north, toward the darkness that towered beyond the Barrier like a cliff about to fall across an entire world.

Near dawn her eyelids at last drooped and she slept, without dreams, until daybreak.

CHAPTER IX

A Lather of Yackcarn
Autumn 1—36

I

THE SNOW SOON MELTED and warmer weather returned in one last glorious burst of summer. The hillsides blazed as if splashed with sunset fire. Host trees cast their leaves up, veins flashing, to begin their southward migration. Above them honking gray geese and black swans spread their wings. Leaves already fallen rustled underfoot. Blades of cooler air slid through the moist, rich atmosphere, a promise of things to come.

Early on the morning of the autumnal equinox, Jame went out in search of Char. As she had expected, he was on the long slope opposite the keep, surrounded by cows, with Bene grazing nearby.

"Just look at them!" he said as she gingerly maneuvered through their ranks, around horns and haunches, between redolent cow-pies abuzz with flies. "I've seen stock about to calve who were smaller."

A third of the herd did indeed look uncomfortably swollen, including Bene.

"I suppose it's too late to ask Kells for an abortifacient," said Jame.

"I should have thought of that earlier," muttered Char, "but then I didn't know what to expect until that blasted Merikit told us. Where is he, anyhow?"

"With Chingetai, who knows."

Around them, one after another of the cows raised her head and stared toward the gorge above Tagmeth. Something huge was lumbering down the stairs that constituted the River Road at that level. It emerged from the mist as the foot of the cascades and paused to shake itself. Matted cords of black hair flew in a spray of diamond droplets.

"HUH," it said, brandishing a four-foot span of horns and gnashing upper tusks against lower ones, all four as long as scimitars.

Then it trotted on, grunting with every stride.

The cows swung to follow the brute's progress.

Someone on the other side of the keep gave a startled yelp, followed by a splash.

The cows swung back as another monster emerged from the spray. Trinity, it must be at least nine feet high at the shoulder. This one crossed the bridge to the New Road and lumbered down it.

"Squeee . . . huh!"

The yackcarn bull bolted out of the forest and galloped down toward the road, tail up, scrotum swinging so that he nearly tripped over it. He collided with the much larger newcomer, who knocked him down and plodded over him without missing a step.

"Poor bully," said Jame. "They aren't in season either."

"What in Perimal's name are those things?"

"Yackcarn cows. The fall migration must have started, late again. Quick. Run back to the keep and rouse our hunters, also horses, dogs, spears, bows . . ."

"Why?"

"More are probably coming. With luck—a lot of it— that's our winter larder on the hoof."

They both ran, Char turning right on the other side of the bridge, Jame left. Luckily, she didn't encounter another yackcarn on the stair. It was odd, she thought, bounding up the slick steps, that the herd had made it so far south without scattering into the hills. Usually that happened between Kithorn and Tagmeth, so that most Riverland keeps weren't even aware of it.

At the head of the ravine she stopped, panting, peering into the cliff top grove of trees. Morning light glinted through golden leaves, some still part of a lacy canopy, others drifting down in slow arabesques. Below, the undergrowth glowed red, orange, and russet with a lingering touch here and there of green. So calm, so beautiful . . .

From behind her came the hollow roar of the falls in the throat of the gorge. The Silver rushed past, now risen in its bed nearly to the top of its banks. A faint breeze swirled leaves in her face and rustled them underfoot.

If I'm wrong, she thought, *I'm going to look pretty foolish when the entire keep arrives at my summons, armed for battle.*

Then she felt a slight tremor through the soles of her boots and, kneeling, pressed her palms flat on the ground. Yes. Something was coming. Darkness moved through the falling leaves, shouldering them aside. A rank smell breathed in her face, growing stronger by the second.

She rose, nervously wiping mold off her hands. It occurred to her that unconsciously she had been expecting Death's-head to swoop down to her rescue as he had so often before, but a belated touch of her sixth sense told her that the rathorn was far afield, hunting. Now here she stood, alone, in the face of an impending yackcarn charge. Foolish indeed.

Voices sounded behind her. Horses, riders, bowmen and dogs boiled up from the smoking ravine. Sunlight glittered on spear points and armor, on bows and helmets and swords. Even with so little time to prepare, they had done a thorough job of it. Even the direhounds and the Molocar wore quilted coats with spiked collars.

Cheva drew up next to Jame on an agile courser and stood in the stirrups to survey the oncoming tide.

"Yes," she said, as if checking off items on a mental list. "Char said that they were tusked like boars and horned like bulls. He didn't quite manage to convey their size, though. So those are yackcarn cows."

"Such is the mystery and grandeur of the female."

The towering black shapes were close enough now to show the white glimmers of horn and oversized tooth. Corded hair swung from shaggy shoulders. Cloven hooves tore up the forest floor. There were too many of them to count, with more coming.

The Kencyr horses watched their approach with bright eyes and pricked ears; the direhounds strained whining at their leashes; the keep's matched pair of Molocar leaned forward. However, other dogs already bounded through the forest, snapping at those hirsute heels.

At first Jame didn't recognize them. The canines she had last seen ambling happily about the Merikit village had looked half-asleep. Now, however, they were working.

So were the unkempt ponies who darted after them, bearing riders, both men and women, so big that their feet nearly tangled in the undergrowth.

A hound leaped, caught a yackcarn by the ear, and brought it crashing down. The ponies swarmed amid flailing hooves, flying dirt, and bellows of rage.

One rider gave a gleeful whoop: "It goes, it goes!" That, surely, was Gran Cyd, a moment later unmistakable with her long red hair flowing in tangled braids and her strong, white arm upraised, brandishing a bloody spear.

"Hold, hold, hold!" cried others, apparently to encourage the hound who still had the beast's head pinned to the ground as much with pain as with its slight weight.

A man jumped onto the black, bristling back. With a falchion-thrust, he severed its spine at the base of the neck. The monster jerked and made a whining sound that was its last breath escaping. Then it lay still. The Merikit cheered.

"That's one down, at least," murmured Cheva.

Jame saw that it was Chingetai who had made the kill. Looking up, he saw the Kencyr and shouted to them, "Don't let any pass!"

"And now we have our instructions. Lady, stay here."

"But . . ."

"You have neither horse nor weapon. Besides, you are Tagmeth. Stay."

So spoke the master of the hunt, whom even the lord of the keep must obey in the field.

"Tiens, loose!"

Direhounds leaped forward, the two Molocar roaring on their heels like an avalanche. Horses backed a step as if to cock themselves, then launched after them. The hunters' cries rang through the woods, and battle was joined.

Jame had been left standing on the river bank, next to what seemed to be the only dead tree in the entire forest. Behind her, archers and other folk on foot blocked the road at the mouth of the gorge. The Caineron *yondri* were there, as well as the Randir refugees. Some, like Must, had gotten their hands on bows. Others wielded pitchforks or scythes fixed to the end of stout poles. All looked determined and purposeful. Jame shivered. As the only person stranded in the middle ground, unarmed, on foot, she felt both vulnerable and useless.

Fool, fool, fool, as if you have to be at the heart of everything . . .

From here, she could only see the forefront of the clash. The dead tree leaned out over the water, providing an easy path upward. Jame settled in a fork some fifteen feet up. From here, she could see that above the falls the Riverland did indeed present a bottleneck into which the Merikit had driven their intended prey.

Not all could fit. The bulk of the herd milled about at its northern end, hacking at each other in a frenzy of irritation. Dust boiled above them, and uprooted trees crashed over. Enough had entered, however, to fully occupy the hunters.

It was a melee, involving one yackcarn to five or more combatants with dogs, ponies, and horses assisting. The cows made short charges, slashing with tusks and horns, then, unable to break through, reared back on their hocks and tried again. One caught a pony and slit it open from groin to chest. It fell, tangled in its own bowels, further ripping them out with its dying kicks. A dog yelped in pain. Someone screamed. Jame anxiously followed Cyd's flaming hair as she threaded between conflicts, lending her spear where needed. Her housebond Chingetai was there somewhere too, no doubt where the battle raged the fiercest. The man might be an idiot, but here he was in his element. As for the Kencyr, although they had never fought such foes before, they were quick learners and fearless in their attacks. Dust eddied around more and more black mounds as the yackcarn fell, and blood trickled between the torn gold of fallen leaves to pool in the forest's hollows. The rest of the herd began to withdraw. Some charged up the valley's slopes, either achieving the heights or falling back. Others retreated the way that they had come, no doubt to find more accessible inclines. Most would find their way south into the high mountain pastures, but they left behind enough dead.

One fight continued. Jame climbed higher to watch as a massive cow held off a growing horde of hunters with shrewd swipes of tusk and horn. The dead and dying lay trampled under her hooves, mostly dogs but some hunters as well. One Merikit, slashed open and tossed, hung from the branch of a nearby tree, drizzling gore on the combat below.

The beast's calculated moves suggested that she was older and wiser than her comrades—a true matriarch of the herd—but she was also more stubborn than they and more thoroughly enraged to find her way blocked. A Molocar lunged for her throat. She knocked it aside, nearly impaling it. Its mate seized her haunch. She squealed and spun in a circle, swinging the huge dog as if it were a pup. Horses reared. Hunters scrambled back. The Molocar flew off, a chunk of her flank still gripped in its jaws. For a moment, the circle of predators broke, and the yackcarn plunged through their ranks.

She was charging straight at Jame.

No time to jump down and run. Jame scrambled farther up, dead branches snapping underfoot. The cow hit the trunk and the tree swayed. Jame looked down into those small, red-rimmed, canny eyes, and realized that this was no accident: one queen had sighted another across the battlefield.

"Now, now . . ." she said.

The cow shook her head, backed up, and charged again. The tree tipped. Its roots began to tear free from the bank, slowly at first, then with a groaning rush. One moment Jame was in the air, the next underwater. Branches held her down like so many dead, brittle fingers. She thrashed, snapping them, desperate for air, and surfaced, only to be hit in the face by the Silver's rushing water. The swift current was bearing her downstream, toward the falls and the drowning cauldron that seethed at their base. Something smashed into her side. She scrabbled at it with her claws as the current tore her past and found herself clinging, breathless, to a boulder.

Water spilled over it as something enormous surged up its far side. Once again her eyes met that mad, porcine stare: the yackcarn had followed her into the river.

"*Huh,*" it said, and began to haul itself up over the rock.

Jame noted in passing that its breath was unbelievably foul and that its upper tusks sharpened the lower, while both were backed by strong, grinding molars. This beast could bite off her head with one snap. Moreover, she couldn't let go of the boulder to defend herself without being hurtled down over the cataracts.

An arrow sprouted from the beast's shoulder, then another one. Blood trickled down through the matted hair and was borne on in streamers by the current. On the bank Jame saw the Caineron and the Randir, those who could with bows raised. Must drew and shot. A red-fletched arrow pierced the yackcarn's left eye. The right blinked, as if in surprise, then widened, and that fearsome mouth gaped. The next moment, its entire black mass seemed to melt down into the river and tumble past, revolving, with its hooves in the air.

Jame continued to cling. The water was very cold and had numbed her fingers. It also rushed into her mouth, eyes, and nose whenever she raised her face, so that she felt half-drowned. Hands plucked at her clothing. The boulder, she dimly realized, was on the tip of a spit of land that thrust out into the river. Now she was being dragged, then carried over rocks, and finally lain down on the shore. Swallowed river water surged up her throat. Gagging, she turned on her side to vomit.

When she lay back, it was to observe a circle of concerned faces staring down at her.

"Did we fill the larder?" she croaked.

"I think so," said one, not sounding very sure.

"Good," Jame said, and fainted.

II

RUE PAUSED IN THE DOORWAY. "You have a visitor," she said, almost making it a question: *D'you want another one?*

Over the course of a busy morning, it had seemed as if everyone in the keep had made an excuse to see Jame, as if needing to reassure themselves that she was neither dead nor dying.

"No, just bruised and battered," she had told Brier, and then had gone off into a spasm of coughing that felt as if she was trying to disgorge her lungs. That, in turn, had loosened Kells' poultice so that he had had to come back with a fresh pad of comfrey leaves.

"Bruise-wort, we call it, as well as knit-bone."

Jame had looked down as her blackening side disappeared under Kells' deft touch and a fresh bandage.

"D'you think I cracked a rib?"

"It wouldn't surprise me, nor that you may have also punctured a lung. I'll bring you something for that later, just in case. Hold still."

Jame tried not to fidget. The comfrey leaves might smell nice, like freshly cut cucumbers, but they were also studded with short hairs that prickled.

"Serves you right," Kells grumbled, addressing her side and his task. "Good little girls do not get themselves chased by berserk cows roughly the size of small continents, much less scare everybody else half to death in the process."

"With me, things tend to happen all at once. I didn't mean to fall out of a tree, into a river, onto a rock either."

"I should hope not," he had said sternly, and taken his leave.

Now Jame heard footsteps on the stair behind Rue, who belatedly, reluctantly stepped aside.

"Cyd!" Now, here was a guest whom she was pleased to greet. "Come in."

The Merikit queen ducked under the low mantle and entered, smiling. She had washed off the muck of the hunt, re-dressed her glowing hair, and donned a golden doeskin tunic beaded with amber.

"So this is Tagmeth," she said, looking around curiously. "I have never been here before. Granny Sit-by-the-fire tells an old story about this place, how that in our ancestors' time a race of small, gray people traded magical fruits for the right to live here. Those are said to be their runes carved over the arches below, though none can read them now. Then one day they simply disappeared."

"How peculiar," said Jame, remembering Granny's tales of the desert gods, told at a campfire in the Southern Wastes.

"I tell truth you'll remember," she had said with her skull's-head grin, "even if I have to lie to do it. My lies carry truths that fact's spindly legs cannot."

Most people seemed to have stories of other unearthly

races occupying their land before they came to it. If so, the remote past must have been a very strange time indeed.

"Have a seat," she now told her guest. "Tell me what everyone is doing."

"Oh, a lovely time we're having of it," Cyd said with a chuckle, settling down into a chair and stretching out her long legs. The soles of her boots still bore traces of blood and mud. "First, we had to sort out who owned what carcass. My dear housebond at first was tedious about it, as you may well imagine, but then he suddenly turned generous. Perhaps he realized that he was surrounded by heavily armed Kencyr, on their own ground. Perhaps he remembered how much meat we already have to dress and carry back to the village. We've been hunting and killing all down the River Road as it is."

"And I was thinking of the larder when I should have remembered the size of our smokehouse," said Jame ruefully. "Also, we have a limited supply of salt."

Cyd produced a packet. "That occurred to me. These spices and herbs will help preserve your meat. Add them sparingly to your salt; they are quite potent."

Jame accepted the gift gratefully. Such ingredients must be virtually priceless.

"As for what everyone is doing now, unmaking the yackcarn. Unless the meat is field-dressed immediately, it goes bad. The dogs have been given such a feast of entrails that some can barely walk."

Jame fiddled with the packet, then looked up. "Cyd, I have to ask: is Chingetai still determined to hunt our bull?"

"Alas, yes."

"Then why has he waited so long?"

The Merikit sighed and fingered an amber bead. Jame had never seen her look so troubled.

"We have fought, he and I," she said softly. "You may remember that his mother came from a different tribe and taught him different ways. He thinks that men should lead in all things. We laughed at him at first, but some of our men, especially the young ones, have started to listen. It creates discord. The yackcarn bull has become the symbol of their would-be power and the hunt the expression of their will. I confess, I have hindered him. Not without reason, however. Do you remember the equinox you spent with us in the hills? That year the yackcarn were so late in their migration that we feared we could face starvation that winter. I sent Chingetai out to find the herd. Instead, he raided southward into Caineron lands."

"But the yackcarn were still to the north, blocked in a valley by a pit of volcanic ash."

"As we now know. And when rain solidified the dust, they came south in a rush. Well, you were there. You know how close the village came to destruction. Could Chingetai have prevented that? Perhaps not, but he could have warned us. Instead, you did, barely in time."

"What did you do this year?"

"I shamed him. His arrogance and neglect had nearly destroyed us once. It must never happen again. So I told him in front of the entire tribe. The women hissed him down when he protested that, then, the yackcarn stampede might be more than half a season away. Time enough, he said, to hunt the bull first. Perhaps there was. However, I gave him no choice but, this time, to go north early. Two moon cycles has he been cooling his heels on the edge of a glacier, waiting. To be fair, it gave him time to devise this drive, with the result that we have more than enough meat to last the winter. But never forget: I have rubbed his nose in the fact that you saved the village instead of him. Even before that, that the Earth Wife should choose a female favorite at all was, to him, nothing but a joke."

"This is a nice mess," said Jame, "but about that bull . . ."

"More company," said Rue, sticking her head in the door, then dodging out of the way as Lyra and Prid charged into the room, the latter carrying a toddler.

Lyra threw herself into Jame's arms, ignoring her grunt of pain.

"Oh, they said that you were dead . . . or maybe that you ought to be . . . but I'm so glad to see that you aren't!"

Jame detached herself. "I'm glad to see you too, Lyra, and you, my lodge-wyf. And this is . . . ?"

Cyd took the child from Prid. "Have you forgotten our daughter so soon?"

"Of course not. It's just that you never told me her name."

"Tirresian. It means 'between' in Merikit."

More confusion ensued on the stair, this time as Rue tried to stop someone. Hatch burst into the room, wearing a jacket, the red pants of the Earth Wife's Favorite, and a thunderous expression.

"There you are," he said roughly to Prid, who recoiled

a step. "Didn't I tell you not to make a nuisance of yourself?"

Prid rallied. "You are not my housebond. Even if you were, by what right do you give me such orders?"

"Chingetai says . . ."

"Ching, ching, ching," chanted Lyra.

Jame noted that she had used her time in the hills to learn passable Merikit, as Prid had Kens.

"What is he but this lady's lodge-wyf?" Lyra continued. "Ah, I meant housebond. Anyway, who is he to give orders?"

Hatch turned red in the face. "He is a man."

"Ha!" said Prid. "A thing with three legs, only two of which are useful."

Lyra tugged her sleeve. "Come, I have something wonderful to show you. It has been my secret, but now it shall be yours too."

They departed, whispering and giggling, leaving Hatch still asputter.

"This is all your fault!" he shouted at Jame. "You brought that unnatural chit into our midst. Now she and Prid goad each other to become war maids together. Prid should have long since been my wyf."

"Not, however, while you still wear those pants. I'm sorry, Hatch, but you are the Earth Wife's Favorite with duties of your own."

He glared at her. "Then I'll go exercise them, shall I?" And with that he stormed out.

"Small luck he will have with the war maids who accompany us," Cyd noted. "Worse with your women folk, I should think."

"So I should hope. Still, poor Hatch. No wonder he listens to Chingetai."

The Merikit sighed. "Others do too, with less cause. But here, see how your daughter yearns toward you."

The child with hair the color of pale smoke was indeed leaning out of her mother's arms, reaching for Jame. Jame took her gingerly. Silver eyes laughed up into her own and small arms tightened around her neck.

"Sit," said Cyd. "It will be easier, given your injuries."

Jame sank gratefully into a chair. The child cuddled in her arms and began to suck her thumb while keeping her heels away from Jame's bruised side.

"Look there, now," said Cyd softly. "She knows that you are hurt and would not cause you further pain."

Jame regarded the infant, feeling an unaccustomed sensation as if their bodies were melting together. She didn't want ever to let go.

"Is such sensitivity usual at such a young age?"

Cyd laughed. "Hardly, but then much about this child is unexpected. You felt it when you first saw her, did you not?"

"I was startled that I couldn't tell if she was a boy or a girl."

"I still have my doubts and an opinion that alters from day to day—yes, even I, her mother. I call her 'she' because I have always wanted a daughter. Such changelings are sometimes born to us. We call them Tirres and value them highly."

"But not Chingetai."

"No. He sees her as a freak, a . . . a monster. I watch him closely when he is around her, which is not often."

"Cyd, if you mistrust the man so much, why don't you divorce him?"

The Merikit queen smiled sadly. "He is not always so . . . unpleasing. Perhaps one day you will understand."

Jame shrugged this off. It probably had something to do with love, or lust, or both, neither of much interest to her.

"What about her sisters?" she asked.

"Ah, definitely girls, but special nonetheless."

Some slight sound made Jame turn, then start as she saw Must standing in the doorway, staring at her and Tirresian.

"That child has your eyes," said the Caineron *yondri*.

"So I'm told." Jame got her nerves back in order. After all, this guest she had summoned.

"The Merikit consider her my daughter. I suppose I do too. Anyway, I wanted to thank you for saving my life this morning. That was a fine shot."

"I do have some worthwhile skills."

Jame frowned, wondering why the girl was being so prickly. What she feared, of course, was that Must would use the occasion to press her demand for a place at Tagmeth. Pleading obviously didn't suit her. As for this new note of defiant arrogance . . . For the first time, Jame wondered if the Caineron might have some Highborn blood.

Sensing the tension between them, Gran Cyd gave the girl a warm smile. "I, too, thank you for saving the father of my baby. And when is your own babe due?"

Must went white.

Jame stared at her. "You're pregnant? When did that happen?"

Cyd spoke encouragingly, still not understanding. "Almost six months ago, was it not? By wearing such loose clothing, you make it hard to guess."

Jame felt her own face flush while Tirresian stirred uneasily in her arms. "If so, you were with child ever before I came north, and now you are here, intending to force my hand by any means available. When were you going to tell me? What is this, if not another attempt at blackmail?"

Must looked ghastly. Unset as she was herself, Jame noted how thin the other's face was in contrast to her bulky clothing.

"I would never so demean myself nor offer such an insult to you. Accept your life at my hands as a gift. Good morning."

She departed stiffly, then, by the clatter of her boots on the stair, ran as soon as she was out of sight.

Jame leaned back with a tired sigh. Tirresian was tapping at her face with minute fists. "Yes, yes, I know that that was wrong. Please stop hitting me."

"I do not understand," said Gran Cyd, looking worried. "That young woman did you a great service. Is it not fitting to reward her?"

"It's not that simple." Jame trapped Tirresian's hands in her own, at which the child turned to glare up at her. "Kendar don't even get pregnant without their lord's permission. When a lord accepts a baby into his household, it has his protection and a place there for life. I can't do that without my brother's permission, and he probably already regrets giving me so much freedom in the first place. I hold Tagmeth at his pleasure. His displeasure can drive us all out and . . . and I think most of these people want to stay. It wasn't so at first. They look to me, y'see, for their security. Can I risk that for one desperate girl who wants her own way, at whatever cost to others?"

"Then it would not serve her either, to see you stripped of command."

"I know, I know, and so must she, but the need to belong drives her, all the more powerfully with a child on the way. The devil of it is that Kendar can't control conception with Highborn. Whatever her latter plans, this wasn't it in the beginning. Truly, I would help her if I could, and so many others as well."

Cyd regarded her with sympathy. "I see that many cords pull at your life, one way and the other. How can you behave as you ought, caught in such a weaver's tangle?"

Jame laughed, an unhappy bark that made Tirresian twitch. "It occurs to me that this is my form of honor's paradox. I must obey my brother for the greater good, even when it forces me to act against my own instincts, perhaps even against my honor."

"Would he wish it so?"

"Tori? Not if he knew. However, he is caught in his own snarl, and we don't talk."

"Then you should. I tell you this, queen to queen: unless you do right by that girl, your efforts here are doomed."

Rue appeared at the door. "I was only gone a minute. Did that Caineron sneak up here?"

"She isn't a sneak, Rue. I invited her. And I shouldn't have dismissed her with insults."

Rue snorted, as if to say There's no accounting for tastes. "Well, here's someone you will want to see."

Marc bent almost double to enter the room, the balding dome of his head first. He straightened, and his face lit up when he saw Tirresian. "Now, who is this little . . . lady?"

"Here." Jame rose, off balance as the bandage pulled at her side, and hastily gave him the child. "You decide."

The Kendar held his sudden charge gingerly, big hands almost engulfing it. "I haven't cuddled one of these since Brier was a tot." He turned Tirresian this way and that, too polite to probe. She giggled and reached out to seize his nose. "Oh-ho! Now there's a strong grip!"

Movement caused both Kencyr to turn their heads. Gran Cyd had dropped to one knee in a bow.

"Cyd . . ." Jame said, uncomfortable.

"I crave your pardon, Marcarn of Kithorn. My great-grandfather was one of those who slaughtered your family. All I can say in excuse is that it was unplanned and afterward deeply regretted."

Not least, Jame supposed, because Marc had come back to claim the blood price in full—a necessary thing but not to his liking. He had been slow to shed blood ever since.

"Well, now." He let Tirresian settle into the crook of his arm. "I haven't rightly spoken to a Merikit since I was a boy, and then only to explain myself before I killed him. It was an unhappy time." He drew a deep breath, as if pausing to consult with his slain ancestors. "Still, the price was paid. That should be the end of it."

"And will you let it be so?"

Jame waited, her own breath baited. She still hadn't asked him how he felt to be living so close to that old tragedy. As he said, a fulfilled blood price should lay to rest all debts, but he had lost so much and had continued to pay for it the rest of his life as a wandering *yondri*.

"Ah well," he said at last, bouncing Tirresian gently, to her crowing delight. "Let it go."

Cyd jumped up and stood on tip-toe to kiss him on both cheeks while he hastily juggled the child to prevent her from being crushed. He emerged from this embrace blushing furiously, and gave Cyd a bobbing salute.

"Lady, you honor me." Then, to Jame, "I came to ask what we should do about dinner, given that we have that monstrous great beast of yours to roast. Shall I also tell Rackny that the Merikit will be our guests?"

"That would be a kind gesture," Jame said, with a warm smile at him. Of course, she could count on her old friend to be generous. When he ever been anything else? "Gran Cyd, do you accept?"

"With pleasure. That brings me to my original reason for playing this visit, other than to see how you fared. This is the equinox, and we are far from home. What say you that we celebrate it here, in your courtyard, before we dine?"

Marc scratched his chin through his beard, looking dubious. "Truth be told, the garrison has been leery of letting Merikit into Tagmeth at all. They remember Kithorn too."

"But if you gave it your blessing?" asked Jame.

"Well, then, I suppose they would agree. After all, if *I* don't protest, why should they?"

Cyd scooped Tirresian out of his arms and beamed up at him. "I knew coming here was a good idea, Chingetai's hunt aside. Who knows: maybe the equinox and his role in it will satisfy him."

With that, she bustled off, Tirresian waving a tiny starfish of a hand over her shoulder.

"Drat," said Jame as her footsteps receded down the stair. "I never got a chance to explain about that wretched bull."

III

BY NOW IT WAS AFTERNOON and most of the field-dressing was done. Their work completed, people began to stream back into Tagmeth, Kencyr and Merikit alike. The former looked a bit dubious as the latter took over the courtyard, but no one hindered them. The word, apparently, had gone out.

Jame climbed up onto the tower's flat roof and observed the preparations below through the parapet's crenellations. Except for the kitchen staff, already hard at work, the garrison had retreated into the barracks and were also watching curiously through the windows that overlooked the courtyard, like spectators about to witness a play, which was partly true.

First came the cleansing as brooms swished clean flags cleaner still. Then a square was painted on the stones with yackcarn blood, the keep's well at its center. Tagmeth had no sockets for the ritual torches along the square's sides, so the Merikit used brackets already set in the surrounding circle of walls between the sealed arches. Jame wondered if that would expand sacred space, if they chose to invoke it. Here, before so many curious eyes, how authentic did they mean to be? The ceremony seemed adaptable, if only judging by the Merikit war maids beginning to fill the space between square and circle. Perhaps they had been allowed to turn their coats and become honorary men for this ritual usually reserved for a male audience.

Boom-wah-wah! came the thunder of the drums.

Some of the garrison made an instinctive grab for their weapons. On realizing that this wasn't an attack, the rest laughed at them and craned out the windows to watch the approaching procession.

Ching-ching-ching, rang the bells strapped to the shamans' ankles.

Tungit trotted into the courtyard wearing the feathered cape of the Falling Man. His was the southern corner of the square. A colleague followed him clad in silvery scales: The Eaten One, bound to the west. Next came Chingetai, naked except for tattoos, soot, and a good deal of hair, to the north. The last of the Four entered in her own clatter of hooves upon the pavement—Mother Ragga, the Earth Wife herself, wearing her doe-skin cape with its split skull crowning her own head and its feet tumbling at her heels. Everything beneath swayed and jiggled inside a voluminous dress. She waved to the audience as she passed, including the watching Kencyr at their window. Some of the latter hesitantly returned the gesture.

Hatch followed in his red britches and vest, looking grim.

Then came the four servants of the Four, wearing high leather caps a-flutter with black feathers and carrying long-handled forks.

When all had entered the square, Chingetai raised his hands and everyone was quiet.

"Hail, equinox!" he boomed.

Around the walls, the torches ignited one by one with bursts of blue flame. Some hardly showed, but the afternoon sun had begun to decline and those in the growing shadow of the walls cast a faint, eerie light.

"Balance bright day with long night," roared Chingetai, waving his arms, shedding little clouds of soot. "Courage we crave to face the coming dark. Faith we have in the strength of our arms, in the favor of our gods. The harvest is done!"

Above, Kencyr murmured. They couldn't but remember that their own harvest hadn't amounted to much.

"Now the hunt begins! Days of daring deeds, nights of drunken song. Blood we crave, rich fat on the bone. Fire, bring us warmth and light. Air, carry to us the black swans of winter. Water, bring us your teeming young. Earth, yield your bountiful beasts. All hail the Earth's Favorite, the Lord of the Hunt!"

Boom-wah went the drums.

Hatch stepped forth, holding a weighted net. The servants of air began to weave around him, flicking their spear points like beaks to draw him out. He cast his web but they dodged aside with jeering whistles. In passing, one slyly poked him in the butt. He whipped around and cast again. The net flew clean, spread, and wrapped itself about a bird-man, bringing him down. The others swarmed in, pecking Hatch with their forks. He caught one spear under his arm, turned, and threw its wielder into his mates, three of whom fell. The fourth staggered back to totter on the edge of the well which, unlike its equivalent at Kithorn, had no cover.

"Our water supply," said someone above, plaintively.

Hatch jerked the man back to safety, and tripped over his flailing fork. All five of them ended up entangled on the ground, to laughter from outside the square.

Hatch fought clear and rose, also laughing, his ill temper forgotten. The others likewise hastily sorted themselves out in a great scramble after hats and spears and dignity.

Standing in the kitchen door, Marc began to clap.

Hatch glanced at him, nodded, and picked up the rhythm with a skip and a kick.

In a moment, they were all up, dancing.

Clap, clap, clap . . . clap, clap, clap . . .

Bird-men wove back and forth. Their spears clashed in patterns, tine to tine, while the net swirled over their heads. Back came Hatch through their midst, spin and jump, spin and jump. They retreated. He advanced. Flourished spears drove him back again. To and fro, to and fro.

The upper windows took up the beat.

Clap, clap, clap, stomp . . . clap, clap, clap, stomp . . .

In his northern corner, Chingetai began to twitch. Jame leaned over the parapet, peering down. It seemed to her that she caught the hint of glowing threads where veins ran close to the surface of his skin. He might well be irritated that the rite was falling in farce. As for its deeper truth, it had never been clear to her whether the Merikit chief believed in the Four or not. She only knew that he couldn't see them in their full truth. Ignorance, however, was no protection.

Clap, clap, CLAP.

As one, the bird-men fell down, leaving Hatch triumphant.

Loud applause greeted this finale, below and above.

A scramble followed: there was no backstage here. Off came the feathered hoods. Underneath were the upper halves of big fishes, hollowed out to fit as caps. It was the Eaten One's turn.

Hatch grabbed an abandoned fork and wove warily between the fish-men as they circled, going *"Glub, glub, glub."* The hunter had unexpectedly become the hunted. Jame thought of Timmon's half-brother Drie, who had joined the Eaten One as her chosen, but for how long? Hers was a carnivorous love, and he was only mortal. Were those pallid arms reaching out again, that eager mouth with its sharp teeth gaping for new prey?

The courtyard began to fill with pale blue smoke as sacred space spread from wall to wall. From above, it was like staring down into hazy water. Those below tried unsuccessfully to wave it away from their faces and some began to cough.

A cry rose from the sidelines. Chingetai had snatched Tirresian out of Gran Cyd's arms and thrust the child into the square. There was a scuffle as others restrained the Merikit queen from following. The fish-men turned toward this new bait thrown into their midst. Their caps had slipped down to their shoulders so that they groped blindly forward with outstretched hands.

"*Glub,*" said the gaping fish mouths that topped their heads. "*Glub, glub.*"

After a startled cry, Tirresian remained silent, watching their stumbling approach with wide eyes. She, at least, could see only too well.

Hatch dodged through the piscine ranks and scooped her up. Then he didn't seem to know where to turn. Perhaps, from within the square, the outside had disappeared. He bumped into one of the Eaten One's servants, who swiped at him with nails sharpened into spines, drawing blood. The others turned toward its scent. Hatch backed into the middle of the square, where he came up with a jolt against the wall that surrounded the well.

The air seemed to breathe with a hoarse, smoky overtone: "The Eaten One's mouth. Throw her in."

From far beneath the earth, in the depths of the well, came the resonant answer: "BLOOP."

Hatch tightened his grip, at which Tirresian whimpered but didn't cry out. The fish-men groped toward them with webbed fingers.

Something sailed through the air—a half-roasted bustard trailing a stream of its own juices—and plunged into the well. There was a disconcerting pause. Jame remembered, belatedly, that the actual water level lay below the subterranean stable, a drop of at least thirty feet.

Splash. Gloop.

The Eaten One, at least, had been fed.

As if a cork had been drawn, the smoke spiraled down the well with a swoosh.

On the far side of the square, at the kitchen door, Marc stood wiping greasy hands on his pants. Trust him to know what to do.

The servants fumbled off their fish heads, panting, looking dazed. *What did we almost do?*

Cyd rushed into the square to retrieve her baby from Hatch, casting a baleful glance at Chingetai as she passed. He also seemed dazed, as if to say, *Whatever happened, it wasn't my fault.*

Then it was his turn as the Burnt Man.

Everyone else scrambled out of the square, except for Cyd, Hatch, and the Earth Wife, Tirresian having been entrusted to one of the war maids.

Chingetai paced around the well swinging his arms and shaking his head as if to rouse himself from deep sleep. Jame noted, however, that these efforts only fanned his glowing blue veins to red. He made as if to grab Gran Cyd and embrace her. She held him off with a raised, warning finger.

Three things we ask of fire, thought Jame: *Light, warmth, and companionship. But woe to those over whom it seeks mastery.*

Cyd turned her back on Chingetai, and continued to turn as he circled her. His gestures spoke for him.

Listen to me, said his big, eloquent hands. *Be reasonable.*

He touched her shoulder. She spun to face him. They began to stride back and forth, back and forth, faces turned toward each other, glaring. Veins like threads of lava pulsed between the smattering of soot and tattoos down Chingetai's heavy arms.

A murmur of unease passed through the spectators.

Mother Ragga emerged from her corner. She flounced over to Hatch, waved a knobby finger in his face, and slapped him. He looked startled, then fell in with her performance to a nervous ripple of laughter from outside the square. As their principals paced, so did they, but stomping with exaggerated force, and with each turn they exchanged resounding blows, one two, one two.

Jame was reminded of puppet shows she had seen in the streets of Kothifir and Tai-tastigon. Often they used exaggerated violence to ridicule their rulers, but in such a way that made their audiences laugh rather than look for stones to throw. More than one riot had been forestalled by a hasty display of puppetry, so that it was rumored King Krothen always kept a troupe ready to send out in case of domestic unrest. She wondered if it would work here.

Chingetai and Cyd, at least, paid no attention to their mimics, nor to anything but each other. Their conflict resolved itself into a kind of angry dance, one trying to outdo the other. Cyd spun and swept her finger across the flagstones, drawing a line. Her housebond attempted to cross it but faltered, boot in midair. He drew his foot back and pawed the stones with it. Sparks flew.

Not fair, thought Jame. He was drawing on the Burnt Man's power, whereas Gran Cyd only had her own, considerable as it was. In doing so, however, he was opening himself to that elemental's madness.

Cracks broke Cyd's line, and he passed through.

She drew back a pace, but only that. They circled again, chest to chest. Tall as she was, he overtopped her like a smoking mountain. Her doeskin tunic was spotted with soot and burning embers.

Behind them, Mother Ragga and Hatch had their hands at each other's throats, one reaching up, the other down, due to their disparate heights. Trinity, were they infected too? But Ragga was the Earth Wife, herself a force to be reckoned with. She broke Hatch's grip and retreated to the well. One on either side of it, grimacing at each other across its mouth, they wound the winch to bring up a bucket of water.

Cyd's face flushed with more than rage. The tips of her long red hair, already flowing down her back like a river of fire, began to singe. She didn't give ground, however, until Mother Ragga shouted a warning.

The Earth Wife emptied the bucket on Chingetai. Given how short she was, the water slapped no higher than his waist, but below that the molten veins also ran. A great cloud of steam rose off of his buttocks and he bolted forward with a yelp, nearly running over his consort. It was a wonder, between fire and ice water, that the offended parts didn't shatter and fall off. As it was, the Merikit chieftain charged around the square trailing smoke, howling, and clutching his bottom.

"Serves you right, Chingely!" the Earth Wife shouted after him. "Don't mess with what you can't control!"

Someone threw him a jacket. He wrapped its arms around his waist and smothered his haunches with its folds. As ebbing stream seeped out around the edges, he stood dripping sweat, shuddering like an overwrought stallion.

Jame wondered how much he remembered of what had just happened. Most of it, she guessed, judging from the apprehensive sidelong glance he shot at his consort.

Cyd was brushing herself off and frowning at the holes burnt in her clothing. Some of the amber had melted, drizzling resin down her front. A fly trapped in one lump of it emerged, fiddled its legs experimentally, and flew away.

"Well," she said to her mate. "Are you quite finished?"

Chingetai shook himself.

"Not quite," he said, making a supreme effort to compose himself, "and neither are you. We have honored air, water, and fire. Have you forgotten the Earth Wife's turn?"

Gran Cyd's lip twitched. "I supposed that she had just taken it."

Mother Ragga made a rude sound.

Ignoring her, the Merikit chieftain assumed an injured look. "How can you say so, beloved? We still have a yackcarn bull to hunt, for her honor and for that of the tribe."

"By which you mean for yourself."

By now, Chingetai had regained his aplomb. He removed the jacket from his waist and shrugged himself into it, a tight fit. "For me, for us all. Friends! Warriors of renown! Join me—or rather the Earth Wife's Favorite—in this great hunt! Forward!"

Boom-wah-wah-boom! went the drums as the Merikit streamed out of Tagmeth, snatching up their weapons at the gate. Failing to catch Chingetai, who had set off almost at a run, Cyd seized Hatch.

"If you can, please tell my dear consort to put on some pants."

As one, the garrison craned to look up at Jame.

She sighed and called down to them, "Oh, all right. Go, if you must,"

The barracks emptied.

Jame descended more slowly. She was beginning to feel more herself, less shivery and shaken. Her side still hurt abominably, though, and she didn't intend to ride after the hounds, assuming they weren't all still too stuffed from their morning's gorge to hunt at all.

By now it was late afternoon. The sun had set and long shadows stretched across the courtyard. The square had been scuffled virtually out of existence by all of the hasty feet passing over it, but a few torches still feebly flared against the walls and blue smoke drifted. A clatter rose from the kitchen where the cooks were dealing with the yackcarn cow's monstrous carcass as well as with other dishes. Jame worried briefly about the outlay for fifty-odd extra mouths. With potential famine coming, Tagmeth seemed to be feasting a lot. On the other hand, Marc was right that not all this flood of fresh meat would fit into their modest smokehouse. Besides, it was important to show their guests fit hospitality.

Her steps slowed. By now nearly all of the torches had guttered out. Where the last one still burned, its flickering light fell between the arches. There was the tracery of stone, but it seemed oddly insubstantial, like a screen of gauze, and something moved behind it. Two figures approached through hints of a glimmering landscape. Stone muted the colors, but surely that was the flash of blue water, and beyond it sand golden under slanting beams of afternoon sunlight. The figures neared. Now they were walking forward down what seemed to be a short tunnel. Just as the torch flared out, they stepped into the courtyard. It was Lyra and Prid, their arms full of small brown and purple fruits.

"You see?" the former was saying to the latter. "Wasn't that wonderful?"

Jame cleared her throat.

The girls jumped, spilling figs and dates across the flagstones.

"W-we didn't mean . . ." stammered Lyra. "I didn't t-think . . ."

"Do you ever? I take it that this has something to do with all of the times you disappeared when you were a guest here."

Despite the shadows into which she had stepped, Lyra could be seen to blush furiously.

"It was my secret," she mumbled, not meeting Jame's eyes. "You all thought that I was so silly, so . . . so worthless. But I can't have been, could I, when I knew about this?"

Jame sighed.

"We'll talk later. For now, take this fruit to the kitchen. Rackny will find some use for it."

Chastened, the girls gathered up what they had dropped and scurried away.

Jame regarded what appeared to be a solid stone wall. This development was indeed peculiar, and interesting. But there would be an opportunity later to consider its implications.

Out in the hills, the hounds were hallooing and voices shouted. Time to see what Chingetai was up to now.

IV

JAME SAT ON the close-cropped hillside in the deepening twilight, surrounded by dancing fireflies. The western sky glowed cobalt while the eastern shaded into black velvet. As if in imitation of the earth, stars spangled the whole moonless vault above, winking brighter and brighter as the light faded.

Below, on the lush grass of the island's lower pasture, tables and benches were being set out. Marc had apparently decided that everyone had seen enough of the courtyard for one day. The garrison and its guests would dine by torchlight under a sparkling canopy of stars—if anyone got a chance to eat, that was.

Hunters called to each other in the darkening hills. Hounds belled, sounding baffled and, sometimes, frightened, those that still gave voice at all. Fruitless hours had passed, not that the hunt seemed to range far a field.

Someone sat down beside Jame.

"They've lost the scent again," said Char.

"Why do they keep doing that? I'd swear that he hasn't traveled far, and that mostly in circles. Trinity, he's passed by here on the road twice already."

Char snorted. "Myself, I think it's that white brute of yours. Whenever they find the track, he muddles it with his own cursed scent and the dogs go mad with fear. Most of them have run off by now. I hear that our own direhounds are cowering in the kennel."

"Death's-head probably doesn't want to lose his playmate. Are you disappointed that they haven't caught our visitor yet?"

Char stirred restlessly. "Yes. No. Dammit, I'm not sure. I want that pest gone, but do I want him dead? I thought I did. Look at what he's done to the herd. To Bene." With a whoof and a sigh, the cow settled behind them. Char leaned back against her bulging belly. "Still, he only acted according to his nature, and so did they."

A contingent of Merikit appeared on top of the facing cliff, one almost falling off in his forward plunge. Jame remembered, from experience, how suddenly one came to the edge. They withdrew, their grumbles audible across the valley.

More Kencyr settled onto the hillside to watch the show, Char's ten among them.

Torchlight flared over the shoulder of a hill downstream. A dog yelped with panic, but the sound was drowned by many eager shouts.

Char sat up. "They're on the track again. Look."

Up the New Road trotted the yackcarn bull, making his third pass, a bobbing dab of darkness all but swallowed by the valley's growing shadows.

". . . *huh, huh, huh* . . ."

Panting, nearly done, he turned aside and staggered up the slope toward the herd, which scattered at his approach. Bene lumbered to her feet. Horns and tusks bowed his head nearly to the ground. He stumbled over his dangling scrotum but kept going, up to Jame and past her, with a desperate look askance. The cows lowed as he passed. The garrison rose and turned as one to watch him go.

The Merikit rounded the bend and surged forward, still shouting. They followed the only dogs still on the scent, Tagmeth's matched pair of Molocar all but dragging Tiens on their heels. After him came Chingetai brandishing a boar spear. Jame noted that he had found a pair of pants somewhere, although they fit him as tightly as a casing did a sausage.

More torches glared through the trees upslope and more shouts sounded. Another company of hunters. The bull was surrounded. He turned at bay just short of the forest. The oncoming light cast his shadow gigantic against the lowered boughs as the Merikit surged up after him past the Kencyr.

"*Squeeee . . . !*"

At this desperate challenge, his pursuers slowed. Even the Molocar hesitated, looking puzzled. The light behind emerged from the trees, banishing that enormous shadow, leaving a diminutive figure roughly the size of a donkey but much heavier, with huge genitalia. As if to stress the latter, the bull extended his arm-length penis and pissed on the ground—in defiance or fear, it was impossible to tell which.

If anyone had laughed at that moment, especially Gran Cyd, who had just come up behind the Merikit chieftain with her baby strapped to her back, the entire hillside would have roared and Chingetai would have been destroyed.

Instead, Tirresian said, quite clearly, "Poor bully."

Those might have been her first words.

"He . . . ah . . . is very well endowed," said her mother, no doubt biting her lip.

After a moment's flabbergasted silence, Chingetai took the hint.

"What a magnificent male," he exclaimed. "Just look at him! Should we destroy such an exemplar of our tribe's virility? I think not. Behold the Merikits' new totem!"

That roused a cheer, ironic from the war maids, hesitant from the Merikit men, heartfelt from the Kencyr. Someone produced a rope and slung a loop over the bull's neck. He fought a bit, but on the whole seemed relieved at his fate. Jame imagined that if the lodge-wyves of the village had the last laugh, they would be wise to keep it behind their teeth.

Chingetai swung wide his brawny arms. "And now," he bellowed to the hillside and all who stood there, listening, "we feast! To neighbors!"

"To neighbors," Jame echoed the toast, raising an open hand instead of a cup. They would all have sufficient to drink soon enough, and well earned at that.

CHAPTER X

The Gates of Tagmeth
Autumn 37—Winter's Eve

I

LYRA SCUFFED A BOOT on the floor, refusing to meet Jame's eyes.

"Why are you blaming me?"

"I'm not. You didn't tell me this story before. Very well. I'd like to hear it now. How did you discover Tagmeth's gates?"

"You told me to leave you alone," the girl burst out. "You know you did! And no one else would talk to me— at least, no one interesting. I was lonely. I was bored. So I crept around this rotten old keep trying to keep out of the way so that no one else would tell me to get lost."

Jame sighed. "That's not what I said, or meant. Lyra, sometimes people have work to do and no time to play. I've told you that before."

Lyra regarded her boot. Scrape, scrape. "He wanted to play," she mumbled. "Timmon. The Ardeth Lordan. He smiled at me and I felt . . . I felt . . ."

"I know. He does that to people."

"He doesn't to you," the girl muttered, "and I know that he's tried. Am I so much more foolish?"

How to answer that honestly?

"No, just young. Timmon is heady stuff. He doesn't mean harm, but he doesn't always consider consequences."

Lyra blushed. "Neither do I—sometimes—but I do try."

"I know," said Jame again, wondering if she did. However, scolding Lyra was like slapping a kitten. After all, she was growing up as fast as she could, in a house that required nothing from its ladies but beauty and mindless compliance, Kallystine and Cattila notwithstanding.

"How did it happen?" she pressed.

"It was after you told me to go away. Then Timmon teased me. I was in the courtyard. Cooks were clattering about the kitchen and oh, I was so hungry, but there were too many of them and I couldn't sneak in to grab a bite to eat. That big Kendar Marc came to the door. He would have been kind, but he didn't see me. Then he went back inside. Shadows were growing against the walls. I thought, oh, if only I could walk through them into someplace far away. And I did."

Jame curbed her impatience. "Again, how?"

Lyra smiled to herself. "It isn't so hard when you know the trick. Look for an arch where the mortar has cracked. The shadows grow there, you see, and you stick your fingers into them, sideways. The stones seem to move but don't, really. Then, suddenly, a light shines through. I crept inside, and found myself in another place. There were funny skinny trees and water and sand and all the figs I could eat. You didn't even notice when I was sick afterward, did you?"

"Sorry. No, I didn't."

"You see? No one cares about me. I might as well be d-dead."

"Don't say that. I care. So does your great-grandmother Cattila, the Earth Wife, and even Timmon."

Lyra brightened. "Really? Oh, he's so handsome. . .!"

"Er . . . yes. He is that. So you found another land beyond the arch. More than one, or so I gather, beyond other arches."

Lyra nodded, proud. "Also a peach orchard." Then she looked uneasy. "There was another place that wasn't at all nice. The grass was gray and whined and—and something was charging down on me. I didn't stay to find out what."

Jame wasn't sure either, although the description tapped some memory that she couldn't quite recall.

"I take it that your great-granduncle didn't discover any such thing when he was in residence here."

Lyra looked scornful. "Of course not. You have to be clever to make such a discovery. He wasn't. I was."

Prid appeared in the doorway. "Lyra, we're leaving. Or—or do you want to stay here?"

The plea in her voice was obvious. Jame sensed that she still wanted someone to stand between her and Hatch, perhaps even more so after the equinox rites where his good performance may have caused her to question her dismissive attitude toward him. Ah, young love, as far as she knew what that was.

Lyra all but ran to her friend and seized her arm.

"Of course I want to go. Come on!"

Jame struggled up from her chair. "Lyra, wait . . . !"

"Good-bye, housebond!" Prid called back to her as Lyra tugged her down the stair.

Jame followed more slowly. Kells' poultices and a night of deep sleep had gone a long way toward setting her right, but there was still a savage stitch in her side.

Below in the courtyard, Gran Cyd and Chingetai waited on their ponies, ready to leave. Lyra had already scrambled into her saddle and taken off with Prid rushing to catch up.

Dammit, Jame still had questions to ask the Caineron. Her hasty departure perhaps was a sign that she didn't want to answer. Secrets were power, of which Lyra had precious little. Just the same. . .

Chingetai sat tall in the saddle, an impression of grandeur somewhat limited by his feet nearly touching the ground. Jame wondered if he had convinced himself that he had a genuine prize in the captured bull or if he was putting on a show. Gran Cyd kept a straight face, but her eyes twinkled. So did those of Tirresian, who peered over her shoulder from a back harness.

"We are neighbors and allies," Chingetai proclaimed. "Perhaps in future we will also be trading partners."

Jame smiled wryly. He must have seen that they had precious little to spare.

Cyd corrected him gently. "As allies and neighbors, and as the father of my baby, you have the right to ask for anything within the Merikits' power to give."

Marc emerged from the kitchen bearing tankards of

cider on a tray—a stirrup cup for friends. All toasted each other and drank.

With that, the Merikit turned and rode out of the courtyard.

In the outer ward, Jame saw Cyd pause and bend down to speak kindly to Must. That made her uneasy, remembering the Merikit queen's prophecy that the venture at Tagmeth would fail if she did not somehow help the Caineron fugitive. Well enough, and so she wished, but how?

The procession met with the other hillsmen on the road and climbed the steps beside the descending Silver. Most of them walked beside ponies laden with the spoils of the hunt. The yackcarn bull trudged at rope's end between two mounts, who regarded him warily askance. Jame wondered about his fate. He was probably doomed to become the village pet.

On their departure, the keep settled down to its usual morning routine with Kendar scattering this way and that to their assigned tasks.

Jame regarded the arch through which Lyra and Prid had walked the night before. It looked and felt perfectly solid. Meanwhile, passing Kendar regarded her curiously.

Somewhat abashed, she retreated to her quarters to write a report to Tori.

Then Brier arrived to discuss how each ten command would be employed over the next ten days. It was decided that Char would have his command back to help shift the cows and horses to fresh pasturage down stream.

"I don't like having them out of sight," said Brier,

frowning, "but they've cropped the hillside down to the roots."

"What are you afraid of?"

"Lord Caineron. He's left us alone so far, perhaps because he expects us to fail on our own, but that won't last. Sooner or later he's going to try to push us out of Tagmeth, and a raid on our herds would be a logical first step."

"Agreed. Can we afford to leave Char's command out in the field? They can't oppose a strong attack, but they can give us warning and, in the meantime, prevent the stock from wandering."

"Yes. That's practical. Killy will have a fit, though. He's already complaining that he's no cowherd and that 'his' command should be severed from Char's."

"Who's . . . oh yes, Char's five."

That was already an irregular situation. By rights, Char should have had the rank of an independent master ten, as did Farmer Fen, Cook Rackny, herbalist Kells, hounds' master Tiens, and horse-woman Cheva. If so, that would give Killy the independent command that he clearly craved. Was he ready for it, though? Nothing Jame had heard or seen suggested that he was.

"We'll leave Killy in place for the time being," she said. "He can herd with Char and like it. After all, everyone here is subordinate to someone else."

That made her think of her latest letter to Tori. She had been sending them regularly since her arrival, detailing their progress, but had not yet received an answer. There had been no demands either, which was something, but still. . .

She wondered what was going on in the Riverland proper and at Gothregor in particular. When her messengers returned, all they reported was unrest, whatever that meant.

That in turn reminded her of a recent dream.

These days she and Tori seldom encountered each other in the dreamscape, but sometimes something trickled through, as this had. She had found herself in the Haunted Lands keep, in the circular great hall where the garrison had once met, where now only nine-legged spiders spun lopsided webs from the rafters, in which to catch nightmares. Someone, her father presumably, was banging on the door that led to the ramparts.

. . . oh, his bloody fists, the fletching of the arrows in his chest that scraped against the wood as he leaned into it . . .

"I will tell them," he had shouted, in that hoarse voice just short of a stammer as he struggled for control. "I will tell them all! You left me without my permission. I died cursing you. And now you dare to call yourself highlord?"

Another muffled, sullen voice answered from outside the closed front door:

" . . . leave me alone, leave me alone, leave me alone . . ."

"Heh," thin, gloating voices had chortled over her shoulder. "Heh, heh, heh."

Yet, when she turned, there had only been the spiders watching through a myriad of hungry, faceted eyes.

Rue arrived with a tray.

"Porridge," she said, plumping it down before Jame. "With milk and honey. You missed breakfast. Again."

"Huh. You won't be happy until I weigh as much as Brier."

Rue eyed the tall Kendar askance and snorted. "Maybe by spreading out sideways. That I'd like to see."

Brier picked up her much corrected, heavily misspelled notes and rose to leave. "If that's all . . ."

"Not quite. Something odd happened today."

With that, she told her Lyra's story.

Brier sat down again, staring. "That girl. How d'you know that she didn't dream it?"

"Then so did I."

"She and the Merikit actually walked out of a wall? Humph."

Jame could see that she disapproved of a place where such irregular things happened. After more than two years with Jame, she should have been over that by now.

"So." The Kendar squared her shoulders, as if taking on an unwelcome weight. "What do we do now?"

"Wait until the shadows gather. Then I'll try my luck."

Brier considered this. "Set in the southern wall, isn't it? There won't be strong shadows there, but late afternoon before sunset is our best chance."

"'Our'?"

Brier snorted. "D'you think I'm letting you go on your own?"

II

THE DAY PASSED as most did at Tagmeth, full of minor triumphs and disasters.

Char and his ten moved the herds southward. What Killy thought about this didn't reach Jame's ears.

She attended Marc and Master Rackny in the larder and storage rooms, where they went over what supplies remained, surrounded by bouncing mice and Jorin practically air-borne in pursuit.

The *yondri* reported on the firewood that they had gathered—an impressive stash—although Must hung back, not meeting Jame's eyes. Now that she knew that the Caineron was pregnant, she couldn't help glancing askance at her muffled figure. Cyd was right: no one could tell. Trinity, what to do . . .

The masons reported on the rebuilding of the earthquake-damaged outer wall, now nearly complete.

Farmer Fen suggested that they at least plant their small supply of rye in the field prepared for the winter wheat.

Kells appeared with a fresh poultice and made grudging sounds of approval over her improved condition.

Tiens reported that half the dogs were still sick after their gorge the previous day.

Mid-afternoon, Brier returned, apparently intent that Jame not do anything stupid without her, and they descended to the courtyard with Jorin bouncing on their heels.

The timing was good: Most Kendar were still at work and the kitchen hadn't yet started preparations for dinner. Watched by Brier and, in his way, by Jorin, Jame prodded the stones of the southern arch. They felt, again, perfectly solid.

"You should have borrowed one of the Merikits' special torches," said Brier.

Jame glowered at her over her shoulder. "Now you're being sarcastic. Besides, opening sacred space takes a whole range of rituals that neither I nor Lyra have access to. There's got to be some other trick."

She looked more closely at the blurred runes carved on the lintel, but could make nothing of them except that they seemed to be punctuated by grinning *imus*. It wasn't usual to see these primitive, stylized faces so overtly cheerful, yet who would make a joke of them?

Remembering Lyra's comment about approaching sideways, Jame moved to the left edge of the arch. To her surprise, the stones seemed to shift as her perspective did, standing farther out from the wall.

"Did you see that?" she asked Brier.

Still positioned squarely in front, the Kendar frowned. "See what?"

Jame flattened her back against the wall and peered aslant.

"I can see light between the stones. Lyra must have left the gate ajar."

"It's probably from the mess-hall on the other side."

"I don't think so. And there's a hot breeze."

"Probably from the kitchen."

She tried to move the stones farther out, but they didn't budge. Lyra had spoken instead of widening the shadow. Jame inserted her fingertips into the crack. The stones still didn't shift, but the space between them and the framing arch increased. The light was now blinding.

"Here we go," she said, and wriggled through.

III

JORIN SQUIRMED through on her heels, and tripped her on the far side. Face down on the ground, she spat out sand and blinked. The glare still filled her eyes. She was looking into the sun as it hovered over a western bluff. Even as she averted her gaze, the lower rim of fire kissed the rocks and began to sink. Here, as at Tagmeth, the day was declining. That she was somewhere else was obvious. For one thing, the Riverland didn't have white sand of this nature. For another, at this season it wasn't this warm, although the creeping shadow of the bluff brought a hint of the evening's approaching cool.

Before she could rise, Brier came through after her and stumbled over her prone body, accidentally kicking her in her sore ribs.

"Argh. Why doesn't someone just kill me outright?"

"Sorry. You completely disappeared from the courtyard. I panicked."

Jame rolled over to look up at her habitually expressionless face. "You?"

"Me. Did you think that I couldn't?"

Jame reflected that the big Kendar had been increasingly on edge since she had nearly gotten trampled in the yackcarn stampede. The event had evidently brought home to Brier as nothing quite had before that her liege lady was prone to dangerous situations. That in turn was bringing out a stubborn protective streak that Jame found annoying.

Brier surveyed their surroundings. She, apparently, had had the good sense to come through with her eyes closed. Besides, the sun had almost set.

"It looks like a garden," she said.

Jame got to her feet, dusting herself off. Behind them was a stone wall pierced by the short tunnel down which they had come. At its end were the blocks that partly sealed off the gate, now edged with fading light from the courtyard beyond. Over the top of the wall, however, there was no sign of the keep. They appeared to be in a depression surrounded by worn cliffs. Ahead of them stood a grove of short trees with smooth, white bark, large, lobbed leaves, and small, plump, purple fruits. Jame picked one and broke it open. The inside was as red as a fresh wound and dotted with seeds.

"Figs," she said, tasting it. "We only see them dried in the Riverland, even in Kothifir, but in the Southern Wastes. . ."

Brier looked at her as if she had lost her senses. "That's more than a thousand leagues away."

"Nonetheless, we're here. Look at those date palms."

Sure enough, Lyra's "funny, skinny trees" swayed in the distance over the figs, each one crowned with a tuft of fronds and bunches of brown fruit.

"Yes, but how?"

That was a good, although not altogether unfamiliar, question.

"Rathillien is a strange world. One thing I know about it—besides the fact that much of it is alive, and moving—is that there are lots of peculiar ways to get around. Weirding, soft patches, folds in the land, even arboreal drift if you catch a passing tree. . . Beyond those, have you ever heard of step-forward stones? Tunnels lined with them run between the Builders' city in the Anarchies and the nine temples. Step on one and you're transported miles ahead to the stone's original geological site."

Brier looked dubious. "Is that possible?"

"It must be. I've done it, and so has Marc. My guess is that these gates are something similar. What puzzles me more is why they're at Tagmeth. I mean, here we are—were—in the middle of nowhere. The Riverland keeps do each seem to have something odd about them related to the hill fort ruins, but this is new, at least to me. By the way, where's Jorin?"

The ounce had disappeared.

They went looking for him, through groves of olives and apricots, mangoes and guavas, oranges and lemons. Most of the trees were dwarf, and set out in formations surely not natural. Water glinted through leaves, leading them to a spring fed lake reflecting a sunset sky. On the far side, set in the encircling wall, was another gate.

"Probably to the desert," Brier said, regarding it distrustfully.

"Or perhaps to another part of Rathillien."

"You and your blasted shortcuts. Unnatural, I call them."

"Then so is this entire world."

On the shore near at hand was a white, mud brick hut with a molded frieze of happy *imus*. Jame bent to peer under its low lintel.

"Hello? Is anyone there?"

No answer, not even an echo, although several mice bounced out.

One of the questions Jame had dearly wanted to ask Lyra was whether she had encountered any people during her explorations. Here seemed to be at least one answer, if the building wasn't long abandoned.

A flicker of movement caught the corner of her eye. When she turned to look, however, all she saw were leaves beginning to dance in the evening breeze. Still, the sense had definitely been there of being watched.

"Look," said Brier, pointing.

Down the darkening shore, a small bonfire leaped in the growing shadows. Approaching it, Jame first saw Jorin stretched out on the sand, apparently intent on the blaze. Then she saw that someone was turning a spitted mouse over it. Skinny arms, legs like sticks of kindling under the tattered folds of a skirt, a half veiled face. . .

Eyes rose aglow with reflected flames. Ragged teeth grinned at her.

"Took your time, didn't you, girl?"

"I didn't know that you were expecting me. What if I had gone through a different gate?"

"Then I would have been waiting for you there."

Jame lowered herself to sit cross-legged on the sand. "Granny, this is Brier Iron-thorn. Brier, meet Granny Sit-by-the-fire, also known as the Story-teller."

The Kendar nodded and sank to her heels, a wary pose.

"Well," said Jame, "now that I'm here, what do you want with me?"

The half-veiled grin turned almost carnivorous. "Why,

to tell you a story, of course, and to ask a question." She cleared her throat and spat into the fire, almost hitting her dinner. "D'you remember the desert gods?"

"Some. Stone, that tells truths hard to bear. Dune, that reveals with one hand and covers with the other. Mirage, that always lies and lies without purpose. And Salt the Soulless."

"Very good! There are also gods of the mountains, the plains, and the oceans, of course, or were in the old days. Some have since lost their voices; others, themselves. Man came, you see, and big truths like Stone and Dune and especially Salt—they frighten him. He has to recast everything in his own image, so he took what he found and made it look more like himself. A new pantheon arose. You call it 'old' now, given what followed."

"Is this making any sense to you?" Brier asked Jame.

"Yes. Granny is saying that the Old Pantheon brought divinity down a peg by adding the human element. Remember the healer Vedia, sometimes woman, sometimes statue, wreathed in all of those snakes? In Kothifir, her kind were banished to the Undercliff. I hope Kroaky has kept his word and let them out. Gods in the basement are never a good idea."

"Heh, heh, heh. So they aren't, pretty-pretty, as you well know. But the story I have to tell starts in the days when the so-called Old Pantheon reigned. Before the tribes of the middle plains built their cities and then their empires—"

"Bashti and Hathir?"

"Yes, yes. Don't interrupt. Before them, I say, a clever

people lived in the land. Did you never wonder where the ruins in the Riverland came from? Perhaps they were the distant ancestors of the hill-tribes, but oh, they were so much more cunning. Among many other things, these folk discovered the use of stepping stones, and that allowed them to settle wherever they pleased, with their fields and gardens half a world away—always depending on the presence of the right stones, of course, and they tend to show up where this world is most itself. But nothing lasts forever. In time, their wisdom faded. Maybe it was war, or sickness, or religion, but one by one they wandered off and their keeps fell into ruin. However, that's not the story I meant to tell, either."

Brier snorted. "Does she ever get to the point?"

Granny pointed her skewered mouse at the Kendar and shook it with a stink of burning fur, its whiskers and tufted tail alight. Jame saw that she had neither skinned nor boned it.

"Silly girl. What do you know? Your mother swims under the sand and your great-grandfather tortures cranberries."

Brier stiffened, but Jame put a calming hand on her knee.

"After all," she said, "Granny is right."

"*Hah'rum*! In the days after those of which I speak, not long before the wheel of the gods turned yet again, a strange folk came to us. They were no bigger than children and their skin was gray, laced with blue veins, but oh, they were smart. Your home, Tagmeth, was one of the last keeps with a nearly intact step-forward ring. They learned from it, and used it, and built one of their own in their new city. Heh, but one not as good as ours. These were native stones, y'see, and these people, they were as alien as . . . as you yourself are, and the rest of your kind. They may not have meant harm, but they caused it. Mother Rathillien had her revenge on them for their arrogance, oh, yes she did."

Granny slid the mouse off the skewer. Holding it by its tail, she ate it as a snake might, head first, whole. More disappeared down her skinny throat with each swallow.

Glup, glup . . .

She nipped off its tail with her snaggle teeth and threw it to Jorin, who snatched it out of midair.

"Ah . . ."

With that, she fixed her firelit glare on Jame.

"You know what I'm talking about, girl, don't you? Mother Rathillien is patient, but nothing lasts forever. You and your temples and your god—as if three faces could out-face many."

"Then you disown the New Pantheon and the Four?"

Granny grimaced. "Your lot changed much, but not everything. As I am the daughter of Stone and Wind, so Mother Ragga is my granddaughter. This is her time, hers and those other three. I only watch, and warn, and tell my tales. For now, farewell."

The fire leaped sideways. In a moment, she was wrapped in flames, then ash, then gone.

Brier had jumped to her feet, aghast.

"Don't worry," said Jame, also rising. "She often leaves that way."

IV

SAFELY BACK IN TAGMETH, the next day Jame took Farmer Fen through the barrier, although he nearly got stuck in the process. In his opinion, while not all of the trees were in season, enough should ripen in time to see them through the winter.

"Mind you," he added, "we'll need more than fruit unless you want rampant diarrhea."

This led to the next expedition, through the gate to Lyra's peach orchard. Here they found no peaches, their time being past in this clime. In a neighboring field, however, apples ripened on the bough. Beyond that, Jame wasn't sure where they were. High, rugged mountains rose to the east above a thick belt of trees over which gray, eyeless birds circled. To the west, the land descended steeply toward the distant glint of a river. It could be the eastern slope of the Ebonbane bordering on the Anarchies, she supposed, or even the other side of the Snowthorns, although that would put them in the Western Lands, which might not even still exist.

While the peach orchard was done for the year, there were still the apples and farther sweeping fields of tall wheat and other grains growing wild.

So far, so good.

Which gate should they open next?

There remained Lyra's third expedition to the "dark place," but here Jame hesitated to follow her lead. Something about that description still bothered her, and gave her bad dreams that she couldn't remember in the morning, except for the trickle of mortar dust.

Most of the remaining gates also had cracked seals, damaged in an earthquake perhaps as recent as three years ago when she had escaped from Restormir in Caldane's boat down the ravaged Silver, fleeing the weirdingstrom. Trinity, what a long time ago that seemed, given everything that had happened since.

But she wondered most of all about the last part of the Storyteller's tale. Had Granny really meant to suggest that ancient Tagmeth had given the Builders their model to construct the nexus under their city in the Anarchies? True, mysterious ruins and relics were scattered throughout Rathillien, hints of times long since lost. Everywhere, civilizations rose and fell, each with its own secrets. It wouldn't be surprising if the Builders, coming across a particularly clever trick, would try to adapt it. If so, their step-forward roads were indeed more clumsy and long-winding than Tagmeth's short tunnels, but she could see them still wanting to use Tagmeth for access to provisions. Ancestors knew, anything they could find to eat in the Anarchies would probably bite them back.

Her own only contact with that mysterious, diminutive people had been with one of their ghosts wearing a gray hooded robe and subsequently with his skeleton, which had crumbled to dust at her touch. For their careless arrogance in sealing off sacred land, the rathorns had screamed them to pieces. What a fate after millennia of faithful service to the Three-Faced God, even if they hadn't actually been counted as members of the Kencyrath.

While she was pondering all of this one afternoon

some days later, the watch in the hills sounded his horn. Tagmeth was about to have visitors.

Jame put on a coat against the crisp autumn weather and went down to the courtyard where Kendar were scurrying about hiding the two opened gates, not that that made them look much different. Rue came up to her, panting: She had run out to see for herself.

"It's two Caineron and three horses," she reported. "Coming openly."

"Well then, let them in."

A short while later, two mounted men crossed the bridge, the second leading a pack-horse. The Caineron *yondri* in the outer ward either stood defiantly, watching them pass, or ducked aside. Must seemed of two minds, but in the end stood her ground, glaring. The lead rider looked down sharply at her, then away with a grunt. Something odd sat upright in the saddle before him, not unlike a short roll of fur.

"You forgot to mention the pook," Jame said to Rue, then stepped forward to greet her guests as they entered the courtyard. "Hello, Gorbel. Hello, Bark. Hello, Twizzle. What brings you three so far north?"

The Caineron lordan swung down, his hunting leathers creaking. Jame remembered the latter gear from both Tagmeth and Kothifir, but now it barely fit. Gorbel had grown a considerable paunch. He lapped it with both hands, looking disgusted.

"I got sick of eating all day long, half through sheer boredom. They say that some keeps are like to starve this winter, but you'd never guess that at Restormir. Good, hard hunting, that's what I need. So here I am."

Jame laughed. "You missed the real fun. Come up to my quarters and I'll tell you all about it."

When Gorbel had heard, he snorted.

"I envy the first hunt, but not the second," he said. "Chingetai struck me as a fool the first time I saw him, but all in all he made a good recovery. I'll be curious to hear how Bully works out as the village pet."

"So will I," said Jame, smiling.

Rue entered carrying a tray burdened with tankards of cider and a plate of figs.

"I haven't seen these since Kothifir," said the Caineron, popping one of the latter into his mouth. "Where did you get them?"

Jame shot Rue a dirty look, at which the Kendar cadet turned dusky red under her thatch of tow-colored hair.

"Oh ho, a secret."

And some people thought that Gorbel was stupid.

"Restormir has mysteries of its own," she said with a tight smile. "But seriously, have you any news to share about the Riverland? For all I hear, we might as well be a border keep three hundred leagues away."

Gorbel accepted this change of topic with a grimace.

"Things are pretty much as they were," he said. "A mess. More Kendar are coming back from Kothifir, bringing more mouths to feed. The harvest has been poor, and the Central Lands have raised their prices on everything. Meanwhile emissaries from the Seven Kings haunt every keep, dangling contracts for mercenaries. The Highlord ordered that no one was to negotiate with them."

Jame frowned. "I can't see that going down well."

"It was stupid," said Gorbel bluntly. "For once, his usual light style of leadership has served him ill. The other lords might expect orders from his father (whether they obeyed is another matter), but Torisen doesn't often show his strength or, in this case, the lack of it. What holds him back, anyway? There's power there, I swear, enough to stand us all on our heads, but he rarely uses it. Maybe he doesn't want to be like his father who, from what I hear, was most effective after he ran mad."

Jame hadn't thought of that. Of course, Tori wouldn't want to be like Ganth. She and her brother both had known what strength born of madness was like.

"Anyway," Gorbel continued, "he amended his order to a demand that no one sign anything until after the High Council meeting on Winter 100, which is still pretty strong for him."

"It's certainly better, but still awkward."

"He's been stumbling more than usual. The word is that he's still suffering from hay-cough, yes, two seasons later. Add to that fatigue, fever, and terrible headaches, or so I hear. Father says it serves him right. Speaking of relatives, I see that Mustard is here."

"D'you know her?" Jame asked, surprised.

"Of course I do. She's my half-sister."

Jame had thought that Must might be part Highborn, but this was more than she had expected. "Can you tell me about her?"

Gorbel blinked slowly, like a lizard. "Well now. A mystery for a mystery? Not that her story is one, really. Just sad. All right. My father is her sire, and he's possessive about all of his offspring. We played together as children.

Even then, Tiggeri had his eye on her. Grown, she served in the Crown. Then word came that I had passed Kothifir to become a third year cadet. There was a party, more drunken than most, which is saying something. This was on Summer's Eve, while I was still with the Southern Host. Tiggeri didn't take kindly to my promotion. As I hear it, he raped Mustard. My father heard about it and expelled her to the common quarters. Then she disappeared."

Poor Must.

"Will you tell Caldane or Tiggeri that she's here?"

Gorbel thought, pouting out his lips and frowning. Jame could almost see him deciding whether or not to bargain on this point since he had let the other slip past.

"No," he said, clapping hands to his knees. "After all, why should I? If she wants to be here of all places, she must have her reasons." A thought struck him. "Could it be . . . no again. Whatever her secret, it belongs to her. Let her go. Now about my father . . ."

His turn to change the subject. Jame waited with a catch in her throat.

"He's left you alone so far and may for some time to come. My guess is that he's plotting something that he doesn't want disrupted, perhaps in regard to the High Council meeting. But he hasn't forgotten your little establishment or that you may have had something to do with Lyra's disappearance—she is all right, isn't she? I thought so. Walk wary, though. He may not be very bright, but he never forgets a grudge and he's got one against you, Ancestors know why."

Jame remembered the tent near the Cataracts, the Builders' crystals tipped into Caldane's cup.

"This is a rather potent vintage," he had said, sipping. "Luckily, I have a very strong head for wine . . . hic!"

And with each hiccup he had risen another inch into the air.

Caldane was afraid of heights. Truly, that day she had given him something to fear.

"I'll be careful," she now said, wondering if care was protection enough. "It will be dinnertime soon. You and your servant will join us, of course, and we have guest quarters if you would like to spend the night."

"I wouldn't say no to a real bed," he said, rising. "Hard hunting is all very well, but there are certain luxuries . . . speaking of which, is there somewhere I can bathe? I must stink to the skies."

He did.

"We have a room level with the river at the forward end of the island," said Jame with a grin. "Open the ducts and you get sprayed, hard, with ice water. Will that suit you?"

"Ha. A likely drowning chamber. And I thought that Restormir's dungeon was wet."

With that, he scooped up Twizzle, who had been warily regarding Jorin (assuming one knew which end of the pook was which) and clumped down the stair shouting for Bark.

V

DINNER WAS A SUBDUED AFFAIR, the mess hall rather like a pond into which a large predator has been dropped. Gorbel, surprisingly, wore an elaborate, much wrinkled court coat that he had stuffed into his hunting pack. He didn't comment on the lack of exotic fruits at the table. Although he irritably pressed it down, his scanty hair still stood up at the back in a wet cowlick. His bath, he said, had been "stimulating."

After the meal, they retreated to Jame's quarters and talked there awhile longer about inconsequential matters. Jorin sniffed cautiously at Twizzle and jumped back when the wrong end of the pook barked in his face. Eventually Gorbel gathered up his pet and descended to the guest room that had once been Lyra's.

Jame slept poorly that night.

Again in her dreams mortar trickled—*tick, tick, tick,* a sound to drive one mad—and then, suddenly, stones fell.

The way is open, said a bell-like voice in her mind, somehow bearing the impression of golden eyes. *He is coming.*

Jame found herself on a blasted hilltop under a scuttling night sky. The air stank like a thing long dead. Rank grass whined about her knees as if seeking to cling.

Go. Don't go. Go. Don't go . . .

Distant lighting forked the sky, limning the keep in the hollow below. How well she remembered that shape, half-sunken as if the land itself gnawed at its foundations. On its steps, before a closed door, sat a huddled form.

Don't go. Go . . .

Where? Away, or down? That figure drew her with both compassion and exasperation. How lonely and miserable it looked but, if so, why didn't it leave?

More lightning. Above the keep loomed the facade of the Master's House, every line of it a melting abomination down which fetid water poured. A light shone in a high window, and a figure stood against it, gazing down. From the whole massive pile came a grinding, creaking noise as it edged forward out of Perimal Darkling into the Haunted Lands like some monstrous blind worm.

Darkness rushed in again with a clap of thunder.

Another flash.

Over the swelling hills, what were those strange shapes crawling, shambling, running? Down they went into weed choked hollows and up again toward the shattered sky, down and up . . .

Here they came over the crest of the hill on which she stood. All of those faces sloughing off the bone, all of those dead eyes, staring, those reaching hands . . .

It was Winter's Eve. The dead had come out.

Jame woke with a gasp, in sweat-soaked sheets. *I've forgotten something*, she thought. *Somehow, this is all my fault . . . but how?*

It was dark. Sleet tapped on the slate roof overhead. Prowling thunder growled outside.

Something was growling inside too: Jorin, crouched at the foot of her bed, all of his fur on end.

Another flare of lightning.

The Kendar Winter stood over her, dripping. Big hands sought to hold shut the wound from Ganth's sword Kin-Slayer that had nearly cut her in two. Swollen, rotting intestines oozed over her fingers. Her short hair was burned away on one side as was much of her skin, and her teeth showed through a flayed cheek. Oh, the stench . . .

"Child," she said in that rasping, beloved voice. "Beware."

Someone surged up behind her and swung an axe. It cut deep into her shoulder. She turned, clutching a wound with each hand as if to hold herself together.

"Cousin," she croaked.

Corvine swung again, and again, and again. *Thunk, thunk, thunk*. It was butcher's work, although the shuddering flesh still moved. *She's dead*, Jame told herself. *She can't feel it* . . . but, oh, how did one know with a haunt?

Her former nurse fell, yet Corvine continued to hack until the haunt's severed head rolled away. Gorbel stopped it in the doorway before it could bounce down the steps.

"What in Perimal's name . . ."

"They're in the keep," Corvine panted, and staggered away down the stair, almost knocking Gorbel over.

"I'll arm," he said to Jame, and disappeared.

Jame fought off her tangled blankets.

"It's all right," she said, somewhat distractedly, to Jorin, as she snatched up clothing at random. "Stay."

Below, the courtyard swarmed with shadows. One lurched toward Jame, reaching with ragged nails. Berry rammed into it, her twin sister Buckle a step behind.

"Lady!" they cried, speaking as one. "Get to safety!"

And where might that be, Jame wondered, looking around, if she should feel so inclined? The garrison had instinctively snatched up swords and axes, the better to hack with. Dismemberment seemed to work best, even if severed limbs continued to twitch. The ground was greasy with blood. Luckily there didn't seem to be many haunts, a dozen at most, most wearing the tattered garments of Skyrr from north of Tai-tastigon. How Winter had fallen in with such a band, one would probably never know.

Sweet Trinity, Winter . . .

The battle was almost over. Dar took a short sword from Mint to halt her hysterical onslaught on a fallen invader.

(" . . . but it won't stop moving!")

All paused to catch their breaths.

"What in Perimal's name just happened?" someone asked plaintively.

Jame stood before the unbarred gate. The stones, indeed, had fallen, pried apart by frantic nails that had left smears of blood and skin behind. If she stepped closer, she would be able to see over the crest of the hill, down to the keep where she and Tori had been born. Would that solitary figure still be huddled on the threshold?

She refused to look.

"That was what I forgot," she muttered to herself. "Lyra left the other two gates ajar. Why not this one too? And I did nothing to secure it."

"Well," said Gorbel, coming up behind her. "This isn't quite the hunt I expected when I came north. What are you doing with a back door into the Haunted Lands?"

"Getting rid of it, I hope. Dar, see that this is walled up again, immediately. No trick stones this time. Gorbel, will you tell your father?"

"Huh. Would he believe me?"

"What do we do with these . . . er . . . remains?" Jerr asked, for once not making a joke.

"You mean, how do we kill what's already dead but won't lie still? They need to be burned. Does anyone here know the pyric rune?"

Heads shook. Such matters were left to the Kencyrath's priests, of which Tagmeth had none.

"Then we'll have to make do. Get dry firewood, also tinder, also oil. A lot of each."

"You're going to need that wood later," said Must at her elbow. Jame hadn't noticed that the Caineron and Randir *yondri* had been heavily engaged in the struggle. "Why not just throw them in the river?"

"Because they would only wash up down-stream, still kicking. Corvine, fetch Winter."

With that, she began to shiver and couldn't stop. Brier dropped a coat over her shoulders in passing, then went off to see to the pyre.

They constructed it in a corner of the lower meadow and, after considerable unpleasant hauling, transported all of the miscellaneous fragments down to it. The sleet had stopped. Now, hesitantly, it began to snow. Someone brought a torch and thrust it into the pile. Flames leaped and spat. Was it the waves of heat or did the bodies still move even as the flames consumed them? Jame didn't want to watch but made herself, for this was Winter's true pyre, after so many years.

"Good-bye, Winnie," she murmured. Good-bye, childhood.

Movement caught the corner of her eye, and she turned just in time to throw her arms around Corvine. The Kendar surged forward toward the flames, dragging Jame with her, but other hands caught them both, pulled them back. When Corvine continued to struggle, Brier hit her on the head with a piece of firewood. She collapsed on top of Jame.

"This place is a madhouse," said Gorbel, extricating her. "You must feel right at home."

VI

KELLS HAD WRAPPED a bandage around Corvine's head and another around her forearm, savaged in the fight. Jame sat by the Kendar's pallet waiting for her to wake, thinking over the night's events.

Most of the latter were fairly straightforward, as such things went.

No one in their right mind would build a gate to the Haunted Lands, but that part of Rathillien hadn't been contaminated in the old days, before the Kencyrath's arrival, even before that of the Builders. Now, a gate ajar would draw haunts as an open door does flies, especially with fresh meat on the other side. And these last hours were the dregs of Winter's Eve. Jame remembered the much more benign dead of the Merikit village emerging from their wicker coffins to join their descendants' feast on such a night as this two years ago. The Merikit revered and preserved their dead, down to trapping their last breaths inside leather suits, then sealed with wax. How different from the Kencyrath's obsession with pyres.

Jame had been present when Winter had received her death blow, but not for her cremation. That, obviously, had been botched. She imagined it now. Would Father have had the nerve to attend? Perhaps. Perhaps not. The Kendar should have stayed to feed the flames all night if necessary, as a ten-command was doing now in the lower meadow, in the falling snow. Maybe it had rained that night on those blighted hills. Winter, crawling out of the smoking embers, half charred, dead but oh, so horribly aware. . . . The average haunt was mindless, except for an all-consuming hunger. (Did hunger imply that they also felt pain? Did she dare ask the haunt singer Ashe?) The average undead would have been drawn back to the keep. She guessed that Winter had resisted. To be alone, cold, and starving, for years and years . . . the thought made her cringe.

But Winter had come back to warn her. *Child, beware.* Of what?

The way is open. He is coming.

"The way," obviously, was the gate, but who was "he"? Please Trinity, not the Master himself. She wasn't ready for that.

Moreover, who had voiced that tocsin in Jame's mind? "Golden eyes" only meant one thing to her: the shadows in the Master's House who had taught her the Great Dance which, if misused, reaped souls.

But there was one of those strange folk whom, perhaps, she could trust. Her name was Beauty. She had first come to Tagmeth as a darkling wyrm but, several metamorphoses later, she had emerged from her chrysalis as a shadowy child with gold-veined wings and a sweet, innocent smile. Thinking of her seemed to summon her back into Jame's mind, still smiling in a wreath of diaphanous hair.

The way is shut, her soft voice said, *yet he will come.*
Corvine groaned.

Jame raised a cup of cool water to the Kendar's chapped lips and she drank before fretfully pushing the vessel away.

"Oh, my head. Why did you stop me?"

"Winter was your cousin? She was my wet nurse and later one of my tutors. That gash across her stomach . . . she got it protecting me from my father. I know that you're upset about what happened to her—Trinity knows, so am I—but to choose self-immolation . . ."

Corvine gave a harsh bark of laugher. "D'you think that's why I tried to walk into the fire?" She tore away the bandage on her arm and brandished the bloody marks of teeth.

"I only wanted a clean death."

"Oh."

"Dammit, are you laughing at me?"

"N-no. Of course not. It's just that . . . here, look."

Jame rolled up her sleeve. Old scars showed white on her arm.

"I was bitten by a haunt too, once, and the wound festered, but good people nursed me through the fever and I recovered. You only become a haunt if you die of the injuries that they inflict, as Ashe did. It also helps to die in the Haunted Lands, where nothing stays dead forever. To walk into the fire would complicate the situation, but probably just make it worse, and a lot more painful."

Corvine looked blank. "Just another wound . . ." she said, fingering it.

"A nasty one, though. Take care of it."

With that, she rose to leave. The Kendar's voice stopped her in the doorway.

"You never thought of letting me go, did you?"

Jame paused. "Frankly, that never occurred to me."

Then she stepped out into the crisp morning, onto a blanket of crackling snow.

CHAPTER XI

In Stranger Fields
Winter 10—35

I

SOON AFTER THAT, the nightmares began.

At first, Jame found herself again standing on the hill in the Haunted Lands. The gate behind her had disappeared. Somehow she knew that, although she was unable to turn her head or even blink. A fold of the land hid the keep that had once been her home. Was that desolate figure still huddled on its doorstep? A step to one side would have shown her, but she couldn't move. Across the rolling, blighted expanse the Master's House loomed. Someone stood in an upper window as before, black against the sickly witch glow within, apparently staring back at her.

The next night it lurked in the House's doorway.

The next, it was on a nearby hilltop.

They are coming.

They?

Jame never saw the figure move nor could she make out its features. The distance between them remained the same even as, between episodes, it advanced. Framed by the window, it had looked painfully thin. In the open, its outline blurred and seemed surreptitiously to seethe. The wind moaned. The grass whined. The House creaked. Sometimes silent lightning flickered around its battlements against the midnight sky and a growl came from its depths.

It is coming.

It?

Jame always woke chilled, hoping that it was only a dream, fearing that it wasn't.

"Child," Winter had said. "Beware."

But of what?

Meanwhile, cautious exploration of the gates continued.

"After all," Jame said to Brier, "we can't just ignore them."

The Kendar snorted. "Oh, can't we?"

It was true, though, that winter had arrived and with it the end of possible supplies from the south, even assuming that the Caineron would let them through. Anyway, the last messenger had reported that most of the Riverland would be on short rations soon. Tagmeth certainly didn't have enough to last the season. Jame also thought wistfully about discovering such bounty that she could share it with her startled brother. Already she was considering a shipment of fruit from the oasis, if she could somehow contrive to sneak it, unfrozen, past the Caineron. That would show Tori that she was neither helpless nor useless, and worth at least a letter.

Then there were grander dreams. In accepting the Riverland keeps, the Kencyrath had trapped itself here for nearly two thousand years, perennially short of provisions, forced to lease its fighters to whatever petty ruler could afford to hire them. That in turn had tied it to the economies first of the Central Lands, then of Kothifir, and now of the Seven Kings again. Much that now distorted the Three People stemmed from these evils. Ah, to be free of them . . .

But the gates had also shown themselves to be potentially deadly. Brier argued against further exploration, but finally gave in. However, she didn't want Jame to go with her and insisted on choosing the next gate—on the southeastern side of the courtyard, for some reason—and took a heavily armed ten-command with her. Jame and Jorin sidled through on their heels.

On the other side was a rolling plain clad with scattered trees and thick, lush grass. Here it appeared to be spring or summer, the weather deliciously warm after Tagmeth's chill. A pack of animals, perhaps big cats, regarded them from a distance, making Jorin chirp with excitement when Jame saw them. Closer at hand, a buck antelope regarded them warily as his herd grazed. Stark mountains reared to the west. To the south, the land rose into tangled, misty green.

"Any idea where we are?" Brier asked without looking at Jame, whom she had been studiously ignoring.

"Somewhere south of the Riverland, at least. It doesn't look like the Central Lands, though."

"Huh. Are you even sure that it's Rathillien?"

That was a disturbing thought. Jame remembered the room in the Builders' city with its view through bars of their lost, doomed home world far down the Chain of

Creation. However, she was fairly sure that these step-forward stones had been set by natives of Rathillien, if only because they were so efficient. The Builders, sometimes, had been too clever for their own good.

"Reasonably sure," she said. "This would be a wonderful place to graze our herds."

"Assuming the local wildlife doesn't eat them. Assuming there aren't any predatory neighbors. Assuming we can get them through the gate to begin with."

"Usually, those cows can defend themselves, but Char's ten-command can stay with them. First, though, we should scout for natives. As for the gate . . ."

They all turned to regard it. There it stood incongruously all by itself on the plain without the usual surrounding wall. In case anything should rush them on the far side, they had left the barrier up but ajar and had edged past it. Whether they could get cattle to do the same seemed unlikely unless, perhaps, they were blindfolded.

Jame had wondered what role the barriers played besides being not-very-efficient obstacles. After all, the haunts had torn one apart with their bare fingernails. True, however, before Lyra's discovery everyone had assumed that the gates were simply walled-up, blind arches, a ruse that had worked for centuries. Perhaps that subterfuge was more than enough.

Brier was regarding her askance.

"You really want to make use of these gates, don't you, despite what happened."

"If you mean the invasion of haunts, yes, despite that."

She paused, thinking this over. "We've been on Rathillien longer than anywhere else since the long retreat began. Even now, Perimal Darkling is just across the Barrier, on all sides of us. Much of Rathillien has been swallowed, but we're still here. Something about this world has resisted for over three thousand years. It's unique in the Chain of Creation, and none of us understands it properly. Most Kencyr don't even want to try, why, I don't know, unless we're afraid to admit that we've utterly lost control."

Brier snorted. "When, since the beginning, have we controlled anything?"

"That's just it. We haven't. Maybe, though, just maybe, we can start here, now."

"With the gates?"

"With something. I'd like to talk to the Earth Wife about this development, but perhaps only after we make it work. If we can."

"Dreamer."

"Well, yes. I would so like to create something before it all gets smashed to pieces. When we get back, let's see about replacing the stone barrier to this place with a wooden cattle door."

"After our scouts report back," said Brier stubbornly, and turned to give the ten-command their orders.

II

THE NEXT TIME Jame wanted to explore a gate, Brier was even pricklier.

"It isn't your job to go blithely jumping off into nowhere," she said, with a glower into the fireplace in Jame's room.

It was a bright, cold day and the fire was welcome, but not all that fascinating. Jame stood at the other end of the mantelpiece, trying to catch the Kendar's eye. They were apparently going to have another of their rare fights, and she didn't want to conduct it with the malachite stud in Brier's left ear. The way that dark red hair swung forward in a curtain, she couldn't see the other's face at all.

"It's my job to lead," she said, trying to sound reasonable. "If there's unknown danger, I should face it first."

"You should not. Tagmeth can't spare you."

"And it can you?"

"More easily, yes."

"What, I should replace you with Killy? Oh, he would love that."

"Who . . . oh. Him." The corner of her mouth twitched. Jame had almost made her smile. "Then pick someone else," she said. "Dammit, why do you insist on throwing yourself into harm's way?"

"The savannah was a good find, wasn't it? Char says the herd is settling in nicely."

"I could have found it without you. So we now have pasturage, fruit, and grain. Isn't that enough? What else are you looking for, a nice vegetable garden?"

"I wouldn't say no to one, although it does occur to me that the oasis has enough water and the orchards enough adjacent land to plant our own."

Brier made an exasperated sound. "Always, always, you push, and things keep getting stranger. What happens when your luck runs out? Are you a gambler who can't leave the table?"

"With so many cards left to play? Seriously, practical

considerations aside, aren't you at all curious about this mystery, this opportunity, that we've been handed?"

Brier's fist hit the mantelpiece with a crash, for a wonder not cracking it.

"D'you take me for a coward? Of course I'm curious, and I do see the possibilities. But I'm also responsible for our people, for this keep. So are you."

Jame fought down a surge of anger. She should have seen this coming. Tori also complained about his people obsessively trying to keep him safe—"swaddled in cotton," as he put it. After all, without him their whole world would collapse. Though only Brier was bound to her, the other Kendar at Tagmeth were concerned too, as she had seen during and after the yackcarn stampede. That was nice, in a way. It made her feel as if they were really creating a mutual home here. But her habit of risk-taking was obviously tying Brier into knots. That wouldn't stop her, though.

"There are some things I have to do," she said. "You forget: I'm commander of this keep, a third-year randon cadet, and my brother's heir." Also a potential nemesis of the Tyr-ridan, she could have added, but didn't. "In fact, there are some things that only I can do."

"Fine," Brier snarled and turned to storm out of the room, nearly braining herself on the low lintel.

III

THEY AVOIDED EACH OTHER for a time after that—without difficulty given that each had more than enough to keep her occupied.

The cold was only just settling in, no doubt with the savage storms of the north to come, especially with the Tishooo still absent to blow moderating breezes from the south. The horses, it was decided, would winter in the island's lower meadow except in the worst weather. Before that, the subterranean stable had to be prepared while hay, grain, and apples were brought in through the gate from below the peach orchard.

Meanwhile, exotic fruit arrived steadily from the oasis. Gatherers reported a sense of being watched, but saw nothing, reminding Jame of her own first experience in that fertile land. Perhaps, the Kendar said, the place was haunted. Those who tried to explore the hut on the shore found themselves yards back from it every time they attempted to step over the threshold.

Every day Cheva and Tiens led out the hunt in search of fresh meat to supplement the smoked yackcarn of which they expected soon to be heartily sick.

Sometimes they found unexpected tracks, for one the huge pug-marks of the blind Arrin-ken known as the Dark Judge, melted through the snow crust. The giant cat seemed to be restlessly circling the keep. Sometimes far-flung patrols heard his desolate howl in the night:

Come to judgment. Come!

More than one Kendar had had to be forcibly stopped from responding.

There were also blurred footprints near unfrozen ponds and sometimes beside fresh kills. A wandering hill-man, some thought. A solitary hunter, or a lunatic. From the reports, these prey had been torn apart by tooth and claw.

And there were other human tracks in the snow,

within sight of the keep but still at a wary distance. These, some guessed, might belong to Caineron spies. It made sense, after all, that Caldane would want to keep track of his unwelcome neighbors. Jame counted Tagmeth lucky to have gone as long as this without interference.

Meanwhile, the Caineron and Randir refugees continued to gather firewood as well as gorse and bracken and to shelter underground as the nights grew colder. True, it was warmer there and would be all winter, like the cave that it was, but oh, it was so damp. Jame worried about Must. What could she do, though, without slighting her own people? Dammit, she would not be blackmailed.

In the end, though, the lure of the gates brought commander and marshal back together, to the latter's disgust.

"You shouldn't go," said Brier stubbornly, still not meeting Jame's eyes. "Dangerous work like this ought to be delegated."

They were standing in a courtyard swept clean of the morning's snow, Jerr's ten-command of second-year cadets ready behind them, pretending not to listen. Everyone knew that they had quarreled; gossip was every keep's staple, and the spice of Jerr's life.

"Nonetheless," said Jame, ignoring his avid interest, "I mean to go. Your choice. Again."

It was a challenge.

With a grunt of disgust, Brier waved at the gate next to the one that led to the savannah. Perhaps she assumed that if one were safe, the other would be too.

Fine.

This was another with cracked mortar. More dust fell

as Brier pried it open, and dank air breathed out of the darkness beyond. Jame called for torches.

Brier glowered at her. "You know where we're going, don't you?"

"I could be wrong. Watch your step inside."

They edged past the barrier. Instead of the other gates' short tunnels, this one seemed to go on forever. The cadets entered it cautiously, gaping at the expanse before them of dripping walls revealed by their flaring torches. Soggy lichen squished under foot. Luminous albino crickets swarmed over stone, shrilling an alarm, reminding Jame of the verminous cave behind Mount Alban where Bane's dark soul sat guard over the Ivory Knife and the Book Bound in Pale Leather. The cadets murmured, unsettled.

"How far?" Brier demanded.

"D'you want to turn back?"

"Huh."

They kept going. A chasm opened on one side of the path and dark things whirred out of it.

"*Quipp? Quipp?*"

One of the cadets flailed with her torch at the darting shapes until Jame stopped her.

"They're only foxkin. Friendly, if inquisitive."

"Y-yes," said the cadet, steeling herself as a bat-winged creature clambered over her shoulder and stuck a sharp, curious nose into her ear.

"See?" said Jerr. "Nothing to worry about."

Nonetheless, he held his own torch close enough to his head to singe hair.

More troubling, however, were the beady eyes

catching the torchlight in the abyss that now yawned beside them.

"What's down there?" another cadet asked nervously.

"Trocks, I think. The Builders' pets, gone feral, and they can eat through anything. Watch your feet."

"Why is this tunnel different than the others?" Brier asked, in a voice that grated against the nearest wall and plunged eerily down the opposite chasm.

Could she be afraid?

"It's not so bad," Jame said. "Trocks only move in shadows. We have torches."

One guttered out. The cadets huddled closer together.

"As for the tunnel," she continued, as much to fill the shuddering silence as to answer her marshal, "if the Builders adapted the work of native Rathillienites in order to reach their gardens, it stands to reason that they would also need a link back to their own city in the Anarchies. Ancestors know where this originally led. The Builders obviously made it their own like the ones to the temple sites."

"And do we want to go to the Anarchies?"

"Not really. Not now. I said I wasn't sure where we were going."

One of the cadets yelped with pain. "My foot!"

"I said, watch your shadows!"

It immediately became clear that however one stood, one cast an eclipse. Claws chittered on stone. Pinpoint eyes advanced in waves, before and behind them, although a frantic sweep of torchlight revealed only furrowed, fist-sized rocks. Someone else swore.

"Bugger this," said Brier.

Jame found herself swept up and slung over the Kendar's shoulder.

"Back," Brier said, driving the cadets before her.

Every stride she took punched Jame in the gut.

"Brier—*huh*—slow down! You're pan—*huh*—icking again!"

Dammit, Jame thought, her nose bouncing off the other's back, trying to catch her breath, *this is ridiculous.*

Her first impulse was to punch Brier in the kidneys. At best, though, that would make the Kendar stumble and they both might fall into the abyss, toward those swarming, waiting eyes.

Never say things can't get worse . . .

Reflected light glinted behind her, close to the ground, filling Brier's shadow. Ahead, there was a wild scrabble as trocks gave way before the oncoming torches.

Here was the gate, the barrier, the stones scraping against her buttocks.

Brier dropped her in the courtyard.

"Enough," said the Kendar. "Never again." And she stomped off, the chewed tatters of her boots flapping at her heels.

"Well," said Jame to Jerr, sitting up, gingerly rubbing her bruised stomach. "That was pretty definitive."

IV

ANOTHER PERIOD of strained silence followed between Tagmeth's two leaders.

"This is no way to run a keep," Marc commented,

stirring a bowl of batter. "I don't have any candied ginger for this. Would it upset you if I added a handful of fermented dates?"

"Will they explode?"

"Maybe, but I doubt it. For someone in other respects quite ruthless, you do have a soft spot for fruit."

"Also for cats." She rubbed Jorin's furry tummy with her foot as he stretched out on his back before the kitchen fire, his toenails extended through their enclosing tufts of fur. "Also for cooks. What am I going to do, Marc . . . and am I really that cruel?"

"Not cruel, exactly, but on occasion, yes. When you have to be. That's how leaders are."

Jame felt her face flush, not from the fire's heat.

"You're thinking about my berserker flares."

"Then, truly, you are terrifying, and I say that as a friend. After all, it's bred into you."

"What a terrible thing to say."

"Is it?" He fixed her with a mild eye. "We all have our roles to play. You happen to have been born both Highborn and Shanir. Yes, I know that you don't like either. Neither does your brother. I've wondered about that. You and Torisen are both very private people. Does responsibility frighten you or are you just afraid of letting folk down?"

"Are the two mutually exclusive? Neither of us was raised to rule. I think we were both meant to be puppets, Torisen of our father, I of the Master. I did tell you about that, didn't I? It makes one very aware of what misused power can do, a lesson that our father, not to mention Gerridon, never seems to have learned."

The big Kendar added milk.

"You should also remember Lord Caineron," he said, breaking eggs and beating them into froth. "Brier grew up under his rule, and there I lived for many years. He wants control, at whatever cost to others."

Jame snorted. "Orders given, but his hands clean of their results. The end justifies the means. In turn, 'I was only doing as I was told, sir.' Honor's Paradox again."

"Yes, at its most brutal. But don't underestimate the cost, day by day. One maintains one's integrity in part by distancing oneself from corrupt influences, and by extension from anything outside one's control. Brier must fear that. Her self-respect and her honor are at stake. On top of that, here not only was she responsible for a command of scared cadets but also for her liege lady, upon whom she has staked her very identity."

Jame wriggled. "You make me feel ashamed."

"I didn't mean to." He tipped the eggs into the batter, coated the bottom of a heavy skillet with oil, and poured in a small amount of the mixture. "Everything is a compromise, one way or another. One problem with our people is that we make precious few allowances for that. Now, how about a nice stack of spiced pancakes?"

V

SEVERAL DAYS LATER Jame rode out on Bel to investigate another mysterious kill site. Something a scout had said about the hunter's footprints there had sparked her curiosity and, when she saw them, they were indeed curious. That gave her much to think about on the way back, until she began to feel increasingly uneasy without quite knowing why. Bel's walk lengthened to a trot, from that to a canter, from that again to a gallop.

Rue grabbed the Whinno-hir's hackamore and stopped her with a jerk as they plunged, sweat-soaked, into the courtyard. Jame slid down and gently detached the cadet's anxious grip.

"What's the matter? Where's Brier?"

"That's just it. Soon after you left, she took Corvine and her ten-command and opened a new gate. That one there. They haven't come back yet, and it's been hours."

That was it, of course, only she so seldom touched her bond to the Southron that she hadn't been sure what she was feeling. Jame swallowed her anxiety as best she could and regarded the arch in question.

"It would have to be westerly."

Marc came up, frowning, in time to hear. "That makes a difference?"

"If I'm right about gates facing the directions toward which they lead. Dammit, she deliberately waited until I was gone."

As usual, the stones looked solid, but gusts of wind edged around them, alternately hot and cold, stinking of brimstone. White flakes swirled out, mixed snow, sleet, and ash.

"It wasn't like that when they went in," said Marc.

Rue grabbed Jame's arm. "You aren't going after them, are you?"

Other anxious faces stared at her in a growing ring. They would stop her if they could. They must not. She gave Rue a hard look. The cadet gulped, let go, and backed off. So did the others. Her eyes met Marc's worried gaze as he loomed over the loosening circle.

I'll give you "ruthless." Let's see how you like it now.

"I will do what I must," she said, turning to sweep them all with a challenging glare. "Never forget that." Was this the precursor of a berserker fit? Feeling as if sparks were snapping from her fingertips, she curled them inward until extended claws bit into her palms. Control, control. . . "Someone, get me a long, strong rope. Did Brier take one? I thought not. Listen: I'm guessing that the visibility on the other side isn't good, and we don't want whatever's out there sweeping in on us."

"But how will you find them?" someone protested.

"Brier Iron-thorn is bound to me, isn't she? I can follow that link, or try to. If I tug on the line, haul me back. Fast."

Someone had fetched a thick coil of cord such as the engineers had used in rebuilding the outer wall. Jame started to knot one end around her waist, but let Marc finish the job when she found that her hands were shaking. The Kendar slung the remaining loops over her shoulder, retaining their nether end.

"I'll bring her back," she said, and gave him a fierce hug. "My word on it."

"Just remember to return safely yourself," he said, returning her embrace, then snubbing a length of rope across his own broad shoulders.

Jame edged past the barrier. Beyond was a short, dark tunnel, then a wall of white blowing savagely this way and that. Jame took a deep breath and plunged out into it.

Within a stride, she was soaked to the skin with sleet and sinking into mud. The ground shuddered continuously beneath her feet. For the most part, she couldn't see a thing. As the wind changed, however, amorphous caverns opened within the maelstrom and just as suddenly closed. Inside them, the very air seemed to die. Without, oh, the bitter taste of ash and gas. . . . The gate had disappeared behind her. As the wind tried to pluck her off the ground, she was very glad for the weight of rope pinning her down even as she paid out its loops behind her.

What drove her forward, she realized, was not just anger as she had at first thought, but an equal portion of guilt. It was her fault that Brier had come to this terrible place, bringing others with her, because she, Jame, had failed to give the Southron the leadership that she needed. Brier had been flailing around in a vacuum perhaps no less terrifying to her than this howling wilderness. One way or another, Jame must make that right.

For a moment an expanse of air cleared. Far off to the left there was a burning, spitting mountain—the source, no doubt, of the ash seeking to clog her lungs. Ahead loomed a tall, white tower. Beyond that, a black hill seemed to be rolling toward her. The next instant she recognized it as a wave and the sudden land's end beyond the tower as a clifftop. The wave smashed into the cliff. The ground shook. A wall of water exploded upward to shatter against the tower.

Then the driven ash closed in again.

Jame threw herself down flat. The next few seconds of waiting seemed to last forever. When the rest of the wave crashed down on top of her, it was like being caught between an earthen anvil and a coldly molten hammer. She clung by her claws to the sodden ground as bitter salt water rushed over her, taking her breath with it. Just when she thought she would have to inhale brine, the flow reversed. Now it was the rope's tension that held her in place.

It seemed to her, as her ears cleared, that she heard a fell cry somewhere overhead: "Aaaieee . . . yike!"

With her other senses confounded, the sixth drew her staggering sideways, into the tower's lee. There she paused for a moment on one knee, coughing, until her eyes cleared enough to see ash-caked figures huddled against the structure's flanks. Two rose—tall Brier and burly Corvine. The former seized Jame by the collar, jerked her off her feet, and shook her until her teeth rattled.

"You little fool," she shouted into Jame's face. "Why did you follow us?"

Corvine intervened, breaking Brier's hold. "You two. Stop it."

Jame had tumbled backward, landing with a muddy squelch on her rear. She scrambled up, every bit as angry as the Southron.

"Someone had to, you damn idiot!"

Another wave smashed into the tower. Fanged sheets of spray slashed around it, then the water was sucked back into the abyss as everyone braced against its pull.

"Now," said Corvine, ever practical, "how do we get out of here?"

"Get them up," said Jame, fumbling with the rope.

Corvine roused her command and pushed them one

by one to stumble toward Jame. Peering into their red-rimmed, dazed eyes, she reminded herself that they had been breathing this poisonous air much longer than she had, and already her own head felt light.

"Hang onto the rope," she told the first groggy face, and wrapped a loop around his wrist when he seemed not to understand.

Then she gave the line a sharp tug.

A hard jerk on the other end tightened the coil and yanked the Kendar out of sight, into the howling storm. Quickly she secured the next in line, and the next, and the next, until only Corvine and Brier were left.

"Now you, lady," said Corvine.

"No. Me last. I insist."

"Huh," Corvine said, accepting the judgment of her superior, and with that departed.

Only Brier remained.

The Southron stood glaring as her, big fists opening and closing.

"No," she said thickly.

"Yes."

The Kendar lurched forward and enveloped Jame's gloved hand in a crushing grip. What she would have done next would never be known for she had also stepped into a fallen coil of rope just as it snapped taut around her ankle. The next moment she was face down in the mud, the one after, dragged backward. Jame tried to hang on to her, but her glove came off in the other's grip. Then she was gone.

Her abrupt departure jerked the remaining loops off Jame's shoulder and with them their anchoring weight.

The next gust of wind knocked her off her feet and into the air, where the storm engulfed her.

It was a whirling maelstrom. Up, down, sideways all disappeared except for the frequent, violent checks of the rope's end still secured around her waist.

Like a damned kite, thought Jame with a gasp, wondering if she was about to break in two, hoping that at least she was still being reeled in.

Ash stung her eyes and coated her throat. Her cap had come off, her Merikit braids uncombed by the wind so that long black hair whipped in her face. The uproar was a vast abomination that shook her as a Molocar might a rat, as if bent on unknotting every bone from bone.

Where was the tower? If she should smash into that. . . . Instead beneath rolled black water. She was out over the cliff's edge.

". . . aaaiieeee!"

That cry again, closer.

Something, someone, tumbled toward her from above, shrieking. She had barely seen it before it crashed into her. Bony hands scrabbled at her clothes. A stringy beard whipped her face.

"Let me go, let me go!" wailed a voice in her ear.

Abruptly the air cleared and the wind died. Jame stared up into a familiar, bewhiskered face.

"Oops," it said.

Then they were falling, clinging terrified to each other, back into the storm. As chaos clapped down on them again, the rope tightened with a bone-jarring jerk.

The other's weight bore her down, although not as much as she would have expected. By now they were both tangled in the cord. A dark arch appeared in the confusion. They were dragged through it, abruptly, into clear air. Instead of falling, Jame was dragged upward by her companion until the rope suddenly unrolled, releasing him, and he tumbled up into the sky in a swirl of blue robes, with a trailing shriek. Bemused, Jame hadn't time to realize that she was plummeting to earth until waiting arms caught her. They set her down on trembling legs. She plucked futilely at the length around her waist, now pulled so tight that she felt cinched to a wasp's span. Someone had the wits to cut it with a knife.

"Ah . . ."

And here came Brier, looking half-demented with her usually neat helm of red hair ash-clotted and her glaring eyes bloodshot.

"You . . . you . . ." she sputtered, and threw down Jame's glove. "How could you be so childish, so . . . so selfish, as to play a trick like that? Not only are you too fragile for such games but, in case you haven't noticed, the people here depend on you. You can't risk yourself just for the fun of it anymore. Dammit, grow up!"

Jame, listening, felt her temper give way.

"Quiet," she said to Brier.

The Kendar stopped short although she continued to shake like an overwrought horse.

Jame began to circle her. *Tick, tick, tick*, went her flexing, unsheathed claw tips against the outer seams of her pants as if implacably counting stitches. *Tick, tick . . . tick. Tick . . . tick, tick*. The rest of the garrison drew back a step, then another, then another, until they pressed against the court's inner walls.

"Fragile." She heard the velvet purr creep into her voice as if the word were a mouse with which she played. "Shall I tell you what horrors I have survived? Would it please you to learn? Oh, I think not, unless you wish to revisit the worst nightmares of your childhood. Remember the old songs. Think of yourself living them. Certain people stand between you and that fate. *I* am one of them. Be glad of us. And beware: Such times may come again, sooner than you think."

The wind drove wisps of snow about the courtyard. More crunched under her pacing feet, the only sound in that breathless expanse until Brier's teeth began to chatter. Jame flicked a particle of ash out of the other's hair with her nails.

"Shall we talk?" she asked softly. "I think we must. Later."

Then she withdrew. Winter played around her, cutting into her wet clothing. One cold replaced another. She began to shiver.

Rue tossed a blanket around her shoulders.

"Get warm cider," she snapped at the nearest kitchen worker. "Don't you know shock when you see it?"

VI

THIS TIME, people left Jame alone, for which she was glad, at least at first. The kitchen provided honeyed cider and hot buttered bread. A new-laid fire leaped and crackled on the hearth, its light playing across Jorin's white stomach as he cuddled up beside her, paws in the air. Sounds rose from below as workers bricked up the newest gate. There was no need to revisit the Western Lands anytime soon, Jame thought, or perhaps ever. The very thought of them still chilled her. Lost, lost, like so much else of this world, and all because of her own people.

A tentative knock on the door roused her. At her bidding, Marc ducked under the lintel, the balding crown of his head entering first.

"Well?" she asked him as he stiffly lowered himself onto the hearth beside her. "Is everyone still in shock?"

"You gave them something to think about, and that's no lie. About time, too."

"Truly?"

"Truly. You've heard this before, lass, and it's no less a fact now as then. Looking as you do, so slight that a strong wind can literally bear you away, people are bound to underestimate you. I've told them before that that's a mistake. Maybe now they will listen."

"I didn't mean to scare them."

He chuckled. "Sometimes that's unavoidable. It occurs to me that it would be no bad thing if your brother occasionally threw a tantrum of his own, just to wake people up."

Jame laughed, a bit unsteadily. "You have an odd view of us."

"That doesn't make it any less valid."

Soon after, he left to help with the preparations for dinner. Jame waited awhile longer, then dressed and slipped out of the tower. Sure enough, noise clattered out of the mess hall. If her garrison had been shocked by her behavior, it seemed to have recovered itself. She did wonder about Brier, though, and pictured her sitting mute amidst the uproar. Well, there would be time to deal with that later.

Caineron and Randir refugees moved out of her way in the inner ward, some sketching salutes as she passed.

Horses stirred in the island's lower pasture, aware of her presence. It had begun softly to snow again. Bel emerged from the flakes to nuzzle her hand, others following her. Their breaths were plumes of smoke, their muzzles velvet dabbed with melting white.

One looked up, then another, then all including Bel scattered, snorting in alarm.

Jame gazed upward, seeing at first only the swirling onset of night.

"... *aaaiiiee* ..."

The Falling Man plummeted down toward her out of the muffled sky, stopping some ten feet short of the ground but seeming, in his way, hardly to slow his descent. As always, one cringed in expectation of a bloody smash that never came. Jame carefully stepped back, swallowing her heart.

"Tishooo. Old Man," she said. "Or should I call you Your Majesty, the Witch King of Nekrien?"

"Oh, please. Aren't we friends?"

"I'm the one, back at Urakarn, who suggested that you investigate the Western Lands. Have you been stuck there all of this time?"

Rathillien's air elemental tried to shake some order into his tumbling clothes and hooked his long, scraggly beard over one ear to get it out of the way. His blue robe,

Jame noted, was frayed at the edges and trailing loose silver threads. He achieved some poise at last by seeming to recline in midair, his chin propped on his fist.

"Oh, I was there awhile," he said, with a nonchalant wave of his free hand. "It isn't all quite as bad as the bit where we met. Mercy! The elements seemed to go mad there, didn't they?"

"That may be because we were up against a Kencyr temple."

The Tishooo's start set him gently spinning. "That white tower? I should have guessed that you Kennies were involved somehow."

"Up to our eyebrows, I should think," said Jame ruefully. With the Four, it was best to be honest and besides, not much good to lie even if the Kencyrath's god had allowed it. "As I figure it, the original architects of the gates linked one to the western coast. Long afterward, our Builders used Tagmeth's ring to place at least one of our temples there, only one more easy step for them from the Anarchies. I don't know if our own priests are active there now, but it was starting to hum."

That might have been a grin, but by now the Old Man was hovering upside down so it was probably a scowl.

"What are the rest of the Western Lands like?" Jame asked quickly to forestall an outburst.

"Hurrumph. A mess. Every part of them is prey to one disturbance or another, mostly perversions or exaggerations of Rathillien norms. If any people still live there, I didn't see them. And you tell me that this is all due to that Perimal what's-its-name?"

"As far as I can make out. It's already swallowed whole

chunks of this world, and before now you really didn't notice?"

The Tishooo had come upright again, which meant that he had to hold his robe down over spindly shanks to keep it from flying up over his head, a pose not much in accord with dignity.

"I was busy," he said huffily. "Besides, everything changed when you people arrived. How was I to know what it was like before that? Whatever's gone wrong now, it's all your fault."

And that, apparently, was his last word for now on the subject. Besides, his clothes were getting badly out of hand. With a thin shriek, in a bundle of flapping fabric, he tumbled back up into the sky and was gone.

Jame sighed. Somehow, she still had to convince the Four that while the Kencyrath might be to blame, the problem was theirs too.

When she turned, it was to find herself in a circle of curious horses, staring *yondri* and a handful of bemused guards.

"It's been a strange day," she said to all of them, and went off to bed.

☙ CHAPTER XII ❧
Tracks in the Snow
Winter 36—63

I

WINTER DEEPENED.

Day after day, the sun hung lower in the sky, sometimes haloed with a double rainbow of ice crystals. The shadows it cast were black fingers that ran up to the indomitable shade of evergreens at dawn, groped across snowy fields at noon, and crawled back into the valley at dusk. The cold sent birds shivering to the heart of trees. The wind boomed down the throat of the ravine above Tagmeth.

Wooden shutters had long since been crafted for most of the keep's windows to exclude the wintry blast. Jame's apartment also had screens fashioned of worn-out underclothes stitched together, then scraped with bear grease to render them translucent and nearly impervious to the north wind. Their muted colors reminded her of Marc's unfinished stained-glass map at Gothregor. Scouts had collected many samples beyond the gates from lands that the Kencyrath had never before visited, enough to keep him well occupied if—when—he eventually returned to make new glass.

Two more gates had been explored. One led to a turbulent seacoast somewhere in the south. Once, there might have been a harbor at the foot of the cliffs there, suggesting trade with other ports, or perhaps fishing. Kencyr were not, as a rule, seafarers, but the hope of a piscine harvest had spurred enthusiastic if somewhat peculiar experiments in shipbuilding.

The other gate opened into a tangle of giant, vine-draped trees. Scouts were still exploring the wilderness there to see what it might hold besides strange plants and stranger creatures. As for where it was located on Rathillien, no one knew.

As growing cold gnawed at Tagmeth, ten-commands took turns beyond the milder gates to thaw out. Oddly, most didn't want to stay away long, seeming edgy about leaving the keep shorthanded. Jame wondered if this was another sign of their growing attachment to their new home. Perhaps places, as well as Highborn, inspired loyalty. Interesting, if true. Certainly, her Kendar had put enough work into Tagmeth by now to consider it home.

Early on a sharp morning, she emerged from her tower to find the courtyard already a bustle with the ten-command currently assigned to Cook Rackny in the kitchen.

"Yes, we're always up first," said Marc, greeting her on the threshold. "I'll tell you a strange thing, though: Sometimes we arrive to find the yard already brushed clear of snow."

"By whom?"

"We don't know. Maybe someone can't sleep, or lie abed idle, like you. It's a change from our joker, anyway. Here. Have some fresh shortbread."

Jame accepted a finger of the treat.

"Ginger, allspice, and cinnamon," she said, tasting it.

"Also cardamom. If we're careful with our supplies, we may have enough to last until the midwinter feast."

"Very good. Now, where is Brier?"

He regarded her askance. "So the time has come, has it?"

"She and I need to talk. Maybe no more than that. Certainly no less."

"She's in the subterranean stable, helping Farrier Swar. Lass . . ."

Jame touched his arm. "I know. I'll try."

Most of the horses were still in the lower meadow, but a few had been brought below for shoeing or other maintenance. Unobserved, Jame settled on a bale of hay to watch Swar float the teeth of Brier's chestnut gelding. Brier herself held her mount's thick tongue sideways out of his mouth to quiet him as the farrier applied a file to the overgrown hooks on the outsides of his back teeth that prevented hay from falling out of his mouth but which, if overgrown, could also rasp raw the insides of his cheeks. The busy file scraped, accompanied by the stench of friction-scorched bone. The horse rolled his eyes and quivered as he stood. Otherwise, Brier's powerful grip held him still.

The fire in the forge struck a red glow in the Southron's short-cropped auburn hair and green in her malachite ear-stud. Her skin had the permanent bronze glow of one born to the Southern Host, her frame the lithe muscles of one accustomed to adversity, her face the strong bones of character. Jame admired that strength, that presence. How sure she must be of herself, of so many things. But here, now, she was wrong.

"Hold hard," said Swar. "Just a few more strokes. There. Done to a turn."

Brier released the chestnut's tongue. He shook his head, that organ flapping ludicrously, then withdrew it and composed himself with a snort as if nothing had happened. Brier clapped him on the neck.

"Good boy."

Jame cleared her throat.

"Are you done?" she asked Brier. "Then walk with me."

They climbed the steps to the inner ward and crossed it to the middle gate. Neither spoke, not until they came into the lower meadow. There, horses had trampled flat the snow and then pawed it up in search of grass despite hay being brought in from beyond the gates. Some days previously an impromptu snowball fight had broken out here, staining the ground red in patches: Someone had thrown barely covered rocks. Jame wondered if the keep joker was responsible. Nothing had been heard of him since the autumn. No doubt he was still in their midst but not, Jame supposed, occasionally sweeping clean that inner courtyard like some helpful sprite. That phenomenon had a completely different feel.

"D'you want me to release you?" she asked her companion.

Although her gaze was fixed forward, out of the corner of her eye she saw Brier glance sharply at her, then away.

"No," said the Southron, stony-voiced.

"Then we need to understand each other better. I gather that you see kind leaders as weak and cruel ones as strong. From the beginning, you've underestimated me and, I think, my brother too. Yes?"

Brier grunted. That might have been assent.

"If so, you wrong Tori. He has had more than his share of problems, especially at present, but they haven't broken him. We grew up under hard discipline, he and I. Both of us were bred to be the tools of other people. One either submits to that or rebels. Have you any doubt what we did?"

"No," said Brier, sounding reluctant. "After all, here you are."

"And so are you. Caldane would also have made you his puppet. Isn't that the purpose of his little tests? Honor is obedience. Obedience is everything, according to him. Remember?"

Brier shuddered.

"Pretending to be a Knorth now, aren't you?" Lord Caineron had said to her on the balcony in Restormir's Crown. *"Not easy, is it, with Caineron blood in your veins? Not possible, I should think. We both know where the real power lies. Let's see your obedience, girl. ON YOUR KNEES."*

His hands had dropped to loosen his belt.

"Kendar are bound by mind or by blood. Such a handsome woman as you deserves to be bound more . . . pleasurably. By seed. . ."

And Jame had leaped down to shout "Boo!" in his face, at which point he had started to hiccup and float, thanks to the Builders' potion that, much earlier at the Cataracts, she had tricked him into drinking. She remembered Brier's glare.

"You don't know what you've done."

"I seldom do, but I do it anyway. This is what I am, Brier Iron-thorn. Remember that."

"And have you forgotten?" she now asked the stony profile opposite her. "Brier. Think. From the start, I gave you fair warning."

No answer.

Jame sighed. "I don't know which is worse, your stubborn lack of faith or my inability to earn it. All right. Here it is in practical terms: Your current attitude is bad for discipline. However you feel, for whatever reason, you have to back me or everything we're trying to build here will fall apart. Agreed? *Agreed*?"

The Southron made a sound in her throat then gave a brusque, reluctant nod.

"Very well. Do I have your support?"

"I said yes, didn't I?"

"After a fashion. I am honored by your service. Someday, I hope you will be honored by my command."

With that, she turned and walked away.

II

SOON AFTERWARD, the first blizzard descended on Tagmeth. Days of snow, cold, and howling wind followed as everyone stayed indoors as much as possible. The horses sheltered underground. So did the Caineron and Randir refugees. The garrison played endless games of gen, or told stories, or sometimes sang as if to accompany the raging wind outside. Lots were drawn to establish who should bring in the next load of firewood. Trips to the garderobe were accomplished in great haste and, among the men, with anxious inspection afterward in case anything had snapped off. Snow drifts climbed halfway up the northern face of the tower. In the courtyard, mere tracks were kept clear leading to and from the principal doors.

On a particularly stormy night, Jame woke suddenly, her heart pounding. She had pulled her pallet up dangerously close to the hearth for warmth and had snuggled into the bracken under a pile of shaggy blankets. Alternate heat from the fire and cold from the room tweaked her nose. The shutters rattled as if under assault. The seams of the screens piped thinly. It was indeed a noisy night, but what had woken her?

Ah. She had been dreaming. Again.

Whatever approached across the Haunted Lands came on and on, but it was making painfully slow progress. Moreover, tonight, something hunted it, getting closer, closer. . . Iron hooves drummed on the swooping hills. A monstrous gray shape heaved itself up the far side of a rise, snorting. Its eyes rolled as white and mad as the dead moon careening overhead. Spume flowed from jaws pried apart by a cruel bit.

"Ha!" cried its rider, lashing its flank.

Crouch, she told herself. *Hide in the dead grass under the weight of a stolen burden. Shouldn't have taken it. He wants it back, not me. Let us go, let us go . . .*

And then, again, Beauty's voice: "They are coming."

Jame gulped. What did it all mean?

Thump, thump, thump . . .

Had a shutter worked itself loose? Was the wind about to lift off the roof? No. Those were feet, stumping up the stair.

Jorin struggled out from under the blankets, growling. Jame tightened her grip on him, wondering for a moment if he was upset enough to claw his way free.

Thump, scuffle, thump.

Not Winter come back from the pyre. Not that terrified fugitive huddling on a moon-stricken hillside. Through Jorin's senses, under the reek of badly tanned hides, she smelled something else, something familiar that roused the memory of a wooden pit and of a small, sour room, too long a prison.

"Huh," said her visitor, and lowered himself with a weary thud to the floor.

She felt his warmth behind her as he settled against her, back to back, and fumbled for the blankets. After a bit of a tussle, she let him have most of them; after all, the fire was on her side and so was Jorin. The ounce stopped snarling, gave her chin an apologetic nuzzle, and snuggled back into the dried ferns, into her arms.

The shutters rattled. The fire popped.

Two of the room's three occupants began to snore.

III

THE NEXT MORNING, Rue woke Jame with a jolt by shouting in her ear:

"Quick, come down to the mess-hall!"

By the time Jame had fought her way out of a cocoon of bedding, the cadet had clattered back down the stair. Jame hastily dressed and followed her.

Overnight, the storm had blown itself out, leaving a vault of celestial blue down from which drifted a few orphan flakes. Those on the ground rose in drifts waist high, crisscrossed by shoveled paths leading to a cleared rim. Half of the garrison crowded the maze, all craning to peer in through the mess-hall door. Jame edged through their ranks.

Inside at a table sat an enormous man clad in ragged clothes and ill-tanned leather. His full, unkempt beard seemed to merge his head into his broad shoulders and barrel chest. The crown of his skull was split nearly to his eyebrows in a crevasse full of tumbled, gray-streaked hair. Someone had placed a bowl of porridge in front of him. With great concentration, he was trying to wield a spoon against it. Jorin sat on the bench next to him, occasionally tapping his wrist as if to say, "Leave it to me."

Jame slipped into the hall, drew up a bench opposite, and sat.

"Like this," she said, and curled his fingers around the spoon's handle. Her own hand nearly disappeared into his huge paw. Compared to his massive claws, her own were so slight as to appear almost dainty.

Marc sat down next to her.

"It's Bear, isn't it?" he said, speaking softly. "The randon who taught you the Arrin-thar?"

"Yes. I suppose, come to think of it, that he must have another name, but no one has used it in years. That cleft in his skull came from a war axe in the White Hills. You could say that my father was to blame: After all, it was his madness that triggered that misbegotten battle. Bear should have died, but didn't."

They had placed him on the pyre where his brother, Sheth Sharp-tongue, had seen him twitch through the flames and had pulled him out. That might not have been a kindness. Lord Caineron had wanted no more to do with his damaged commander, so the randon college at Tentir had taken him in, then confined him after he had been baited into killing a cadet. Jame was the first Arrin-thar pupil he had taught in years, given that she was also one of those rare Shanir with retractile claws. Then too, factions at the college had tested them against each other for battle-madness. That had nearly gotten Jame killed even though, of the two, she was the only true berserker.

Bear made a tentative stab at the bowl with his spoon and grimaced as porridge splashed across the table. Jorin leaned forward to lap it up. Jame corrected his grip again. At least he recognized the spoon as a tool.

"Has he been in the wilderness all of this time?" asked Marc.

Jame did some figures in her head. The brain-damaged randon had escaped from Tentir the spring before she had left for Kothifir. That meant he had already survived one winter on his own and now was well into another one. His clothing might stink, but he had made it himself down to the drawstring bags encasing his feet.

"As bad as it was, his wound didn't kill him," she said. "There's a chance that a Kendar can, eventually, recover from anything."

Marc gave her a sidelong glance. "So you hope, anyway, and perhaps you're right. It doesn't altogether surprise you to see him here, though, does it? Why?"

"Those odd kills, as if done with tooth and claw—as, of course, they were. Then, too, I visited the last site and saw his prints in the snow. Even with those bags on his feet, you can see the trace of his toenails, which probably need trimming. He's our honored guest as long as he cares to stay. Can you see to his needs, and maybe find him a new pair of boots?"

Marc smiled. "Of course, lass. Your friends are always welcome here. How not?"

IV

IN THE PAST, Jame had gone on adventures and had met interesting people. Now she sat still (relatively) and strange people came to her, bringing strange adventures, or so it seemed.

Bear proved a most peculiar house-guest.

The garrison came across him everywhere in the keep, exploring, poking, experimenting. Many things puzzled him, but none frightened him. He was, after all, only an old warrior in a strange, presumably friendly land.

The elder randon treated him with respect, remembering the great war-leader that he had been. The regular Kendar were kind, as was their way.

The randon cadets only knew him as the Monster in the Maze that was Old Tentir, once a faceless dread, now a curiosity to be followed and watched.

Jame hoped that none of the latter would tease him, as had proved fatal in the past. Already, someone had started a sly rumor that he shared more than her blankets at night. Rue, outraged, had taken to sleeping on the stair in an attempt to keep him in the guest quarters below where, in truth, he was happy enough as long as there was a fire, and bedding, and food. Jame was almost jealous to find that Jorin occasionally joined him there.

Marc found him better cured leathers and furs to ward against the cold.

Swar filed his overgrown toenails, but only with Jame's help.

Then they tried to give him a bath and he bolted, wearing only his new boots, with his new clothes in a bundle under one arm. No one saw him for three days after that.

So far, he hadn't discovered the gates.

One morning, however, he found something else.

Wakened by dreams, unable to regain sleep, Jame came down before even the bakers to find two sets of strange tracks in the snow.

Drifts from the storm still clogged the courtyard and, overnight, had shifted to half obscure the paths. Jame cut across toward the mess hall. Bear had come this way before her, she saw, not that his nails showed through his new boots but no one else wore such big footgear, swollen at the toes to accommodate his unusual armament.

Where the path joined the rim trail, another pair of footprints passed. Small as a child's but slim and long, with even longer bare toes.

What in Perimal's name?

Bear crouched before the darkened kitchen, cautiously peering in the doorway. Jame stopped beside him. The path before them was swept clean, the broom dropped in apparent haste. Whatever had made those peculiar tracks had bolted back inside. From the interior came that breathless silence only achieved by someone standing very, very still.

Jame touched Bear's shoulder. They retreated to the path that led back to the tower and paused there, waiting.

Something in the kitchen fell over. Then, in a sudden scurry, a small, gray-robed figure darted out, clutching a loaf of yesterday's bread. It ran past them around the edge of the courtyard before disappearing through the new gate to the oasis, which clicked shut after it.

Jame stood outside. Again, that intense silence of listening. She could almost feel the other's bated breath, hear the muffled, pounding heart. Then it went away.

Bear loomed over her, prepared to pursue, but she held him back.

"If that was what I think it was—but oh Trinity, how could it be?—we need time, and a lot of tact."

Sounds from the barracks announced other early risers. A cough. The murmur of voices. Shuffling feet.

Jame went quickly back to the kitchen, seized the broom, and finished obscuring the footprints.

Marc emerged, yawned, and stretched.

"So, are you our good imp after all?" he called to Jame.

She smiled although her breath still felt tight and her own heart twanged in her breast.

"That remains to be seen," she said.

V

OVER THE NEXT FEW DAYS, Jame gave the situation considerable thought.

The first thing she did was to withdraw the ten-command currently serving at the oasis. This caused some surprise, as also did the lack of an explanation. Every day thereafter she went through the gate with fresh loaves of bread that she left before the white hut on the lakeshore. At first these remained untouched except by birds and mice. Then one morning the entire stack was gone.

Jame spent that day at the oasis, walking among the trees, gathering fruit to eat, lying on the sand until it became too hot. Jorin hunted bugs and slept. She had sometimes wished for time simply to relax, but this was boring. Every time this thought occurred, however, she glanced sideways at the hut and shivered.

At length the sun set and night fell. Jame built a small campfire on the beach a careful distance from the hut and sat before it, trying to stay awake. The flames' warmth was welcome as the desert around her cooled. Stars circled overhead. The last quarter of the moon rose, a sickly crescent. The fire snapped.

Jame woke from a doze with a start. Someone sat opposite her. The form was small and hooded, only the lower half of its face touched by light from the dying fire.

Jame cleared her throat. "Er . . ." she said. "Hello."

"Hello."

The other's voice was thin and high, like a child's, but with a hoarse edge.

What to say next? Jame had thought about this moment endlessly; now, however, her mind went blank.

"I . . . we invaded your home. Took it over. We didn't know that you were here. I'm sorry."

"Sorry."

Was that a response, or was he just repeating what she said? Trinity, why had she assumed that he would speak Kens? Had her kind and his ever even met before?

Builder.

Finally, in her mind, she called this strange creature what, against all reason, she believed him to be. According to legend, the creators of the Kencyr temples had always finished their work and moved on to the next threshold world before the arrival of the retreating Kencyrath. On Rathillien, though, the destruction of their temporary home in the Anarchies and their supposed annihilation had left the temples incomplete, the gates to the next world unbuilt.

She tried again.

"My name is Jamethiel Priest's-bane. Jame."

Jorin trotted out of the night, a limp jumper mouse dangling from his jaws.

"Waugh," he said around the furry morsel, and dropped it beside her.

Then, through her eyes, he saw their visitor and circled the fire to investigate. Jame held her breath. Jorin stretched out his neck, sniffed within the shadows of the hood that turned toward him, and sneezed into the other's hidden face. Then he retreated to Jame's side, reclaimed his prize, and began to munch upon it.

The Builder raised a long-fingered hand to push back his hood. It fell away from a face in some respects like a baby's, but with deeply wrinkled skin. Firelight hinted at protuberant veins lacing a domed, hairless skull but not at coloration. Bright eyes undimmed by age watched her warily from pouches of loose flesh.

"My name," he said, in lightly accented Kens, "is Chirpentundrum. Chirp."

Jame still found herself floundering for the right thing to say. She glanced at the little hut. "Is that where you live?"

"It conceals the entrance, behind a defense of step-backward stones across the threshold. We dwell in quarters underground."

"'We'?"

His gaze lifted. Twisting around to look behind her, Jame suppressed a start. A dozen more small, gray-clad figures huddled there together, regarding her with clear apprehension. A soft twitter of words passed among them as if through a flock of sparrows. Then they were silent again, staring.

"How long have you all been here?"

"Since the white city was destroyed. We were tending our gardens when that disaster occurred. To this day, we do not know what happened, except that all of our kin perished, leaving our work on this world uncompleted and us stranded here."

That meant that these weren't descendants but the original Builders themselves, exiled here for over three thousand years. Before that . . .

"Are you immortal?"

The little man smiled sadly. "We can die, but previously few of us did." He leaned forward, clearly coming to what most concerned him. "Who else besides you knows that we are here?"

"So far, one other." She didn't add that Bear probably had no idea what he had seen. It had suddenly occurred to her that if these people wished to stay hidden, only she stood in their way, and a dozen of them, however harmless they appeared, were standing behind her.

Beside her, a tiny skull crunched in Jorin's strong jaws. Between her and these strange castaways, which was the mouse?

"Who else will you tell?"

Jame frowned, considering. "My brother the Highlord, I suppose. To say that the scrollsmen would be overjoyed to hear would be putting it mildly. . ."

The little Builder shuddered. "Please. Not academia."

Who else, Jame wondered. Would the current lords even care? For most of them, not unless they could use the Builders' skill to their advantage—which, of course, was always possible.

The priests? Yes, to rebuild the temples. Would that be a good thing, though? Only the priesthood and, ironically, the native New Pantheon, used the temples' power. It had never been clear to Jame what else it was good for, except breaking through to the next threshold world if the Three People should need another retreat. Now it was her turn to shiver. To start over again somewhere new, even more damaged than they presently were . . . unthinkable. Whatever the end, Rathillien must be the Kencyrath's last stand.

To prevent more unstable temples from imploding, though. . .

She remembered the destruction of Languidine where so many innocents had died, the bodies surging up around the sides of the boat on which she and her command had fled. Terrible. Then too, Kothifir's temple was incomplete, its fluctuations a constant threat to the city. For that matter, in the midst of the storm she had sensed the Western Lands' structure stirring to life, with no priests to control it.

G'ah. Worry about that another day.

"What do you want me to do?" she asked.

"Leave. Forget that you ever saw us. Take your people with you."

"I don't think that I can do that. We've come to depend on the fruits of this oasis, of all your gardens. Indirectly, the defense of Rathillien may depend on them. Perhaps we can trade for other things. Do you need meat? Milk? Eggs?"

"Those we never eat."

"But you wanted bread badly enough to steal it."

"When we lost our other gardens, we also lost access to grain. One craves what one cannot have."

"That at least we can supply. Please. Can't we find a way to coexist?"

The Builder stirred unhappily. "Our kinds were never even intended to meet. Always, we have gone before, building. What was our charter, our . . . compulsion." His long fingers twitched. He stilled them. "The need still gnaws at us, but what can we do? Our time has passed. We only wish to be left in peace."

Jame clapped her hands on her knees, coming to a decision. "We'll do the best we can. Certainly, no one will harass or hunt you. My word on it. If I may, I would like to talk to you again. There are so many questions . . ."

The Builder unfolded his short, hidden legs and rose. So, reluctantly, did Jame. The top of his bald head barely came to her sternum, but dignity gave him stature.

"Until next time, then," she said, and bowed to him, then to the anxious others, some of whom bobbed nervously in return. With Jorin trotting at her heels, without looking back, she left the shore and entered the trees, where false dawn cast a smoldering golden glow devoid of shadows. Above, all of the birds were waking to sing. It had been a long night and before that a longer day. Her people probably wondered where she had gone, since she had told no one. Thinking about breakfast, she opened the wooden door that replaced the previous stone barrier. Beyond lay Tagmeth's snowy courtyard, still blue in shadow. A cheerful clatter rose from the kitchen, accompanied by the scent of fresh bread baking. She would have to arrange for a daily portion of the latter to be delivered to the oasis. For that matter, never mind the lords, priests, and scrollsmen: What should she tell her own people about their newly discovered neighbors?

The ground shivered underfoot and Jame hesitated, frowning. An earthquake? Inside there was also a pause, then voice questioned voice.

Now came a rumble, growing louder, coming from the east.

Kendar emerged from the kitchen, curious. One of them was Mustard, carrying a basket of provisions. While her condition now notably bulked out her clothing, her face was thinner than Jame remembered, a hectic flush on her sunken cheeks. She looked about with apprehension and seemed to draw in on herself.

Louder, closer . . .

The wooden door to the savannah shattered. Through the gate rushed a tidal wave of massive black bodies, some sleek, others grossly swollen. Eyes rolled white. Nostrils flared red. Horns tossed.

Workers dived back into the kitchen, one through a window.

Must froze.

Jame darted out, seized her arm, and bundled her back into the shelter of the tunnel, none too soon: Already the cows were upon them. One hooked the door with a horn and wrenched it open, off its hinges. Jorin bounced away, all of his fur on end. Must dropped her basket and shrank back against the wall. The stampede roared past the opening in a madness of thrashing limbs and passed on, by the sound of it, into the outer ward, across the upper meadow where horses fled it screaming, over the bridge to the River Road.

People emerged to stare after it.

Char appeared at the shattered door, panting, red-faced with agitation.

"I sent you word yesterday!" he raged at Jame across the trampled courtyard. "Why didn't you send help?"

"For what?"

"I damn well told you! It's their time. They calve in the snow, remember?"

Must gave a faint cry and slid down the wall, clutching

her belly. Jame held her as she spasmed. "Oh no. Not you, too. Help!"

Voices exclaimed. Feet came running.

"It's all right," Jame said, cradling the girl. Never in her life had she felt so helpless. Oh, please, let it be all right.

CHAPTER XIII
Death and Life
Winter 63—66

I

MUST WAS MOVED into the tower's second-story guest quarters, despite her protests that she wanted to rejoin her people in the undercroft.

"I don't intend . . . to impose on you, lady," she told Jame, an edge of sarcasm sliding between bouts of coughing. "So far . . . I've done well enough . . . on my own."

"Ha," said Jame.

Bear took one look at the newcomer and fled.

Rue rushed off to start boiling water.

Kells arrived with his sack of herbs. When he emerged from the room sometime later, having previously driven everyone else out, he looked grim.

"It's true labor all right," he reported, "although she's nowhere near ready to give birth. Then, too, the child is large and she's just a slip of a girl, going through this for the first time. I don't like that cough either. It weakens her."

Jame thought guiltily about that damp, chilly cave under the outer ward. Why had she let Must stay there in her condition? To herself, she acknowledged that she simply hadn't wanted to think about the problem that the Caineron presented, to which she still had no solution.

The morning dragged on, bright, almost warm. Snow banks began to shrink in the sun. Water trickled.

Across the Silver, agonized bellows rose from the wood where some ten cows were also in labor. Things were not going well, Char reported through Killy. Well, how could they? The poor cows were carrying half-yackcarn calves, big enough to rupture them. Damn Bully anyway, yet what he had done was only in accordance with his nature.

Afternoon.

Kells ordered tea made from blue cohosh, dark and bitter.

"She should have had this regularly for the past week," he told Jame. "Even now, though, maybe it will help with the contractions and the pain."

The other Caineron *yondri* and some of the Randir gathered in the courtyard to wait. One, a gruff woman named Girt, insisted on attending Must throughout her ordeal. Kells would have forbidden her, but refrained when he saw the girl's thin, strained face lighten at the sight of the Kendar.

In general, the Knorth garrison kept their distance. They had never favored Must's ambition, which they saw as presumptuous, yet here she was about to produce Tagmeth's first child. Jame supposed that those who had begun to think of the keep as home would see this as a hopeful sign. She was certainly aware that many watched her askance to see what she would make of the situation.

"Maybe it would be best if both mother and child died," remarked Killy, munching on an apple.

Glares met him on all sides.

Jame had noticed that the five-commander was lingering, clearly in no hurry to return to the birthing field.

"Why are you still here?" she demanded of him, more sharply than was her wont. "Go help Char." Killy, grudgingly, went.

Evening.

"She wants to talk to you," said Kells.

Jame nearly demanded, "About what?" but choked back the words. Being defensive didn't help.

"How is she?" she asked instead.

Rue had kindled a fire in the lower guest room and set a kettle to steam over it. Kells poured more cohosh tea.

"This does some good," he said, sniffing the bitter brew, making a face. "However, I'm worried. True, labor can go on for a full day or more and it's barely been fifteen hours. But nothing is moving except the baby. The way has to open. So far, it isn't."

"And that's bad," said Jame. She had never felt more stupid in her life. "Isn't there any other herb you can give her?"

"Lavender, sage, ginger, nutmeg, raspberry leaves . . . I've tried them all, without results. There is one other." He paused, frowning, clearly loth to speak. "Black tansy, sometimes used to end a pregnancy."

"An abortifacient."

"Yes, although only in the early stages. A strong dose now could deliver the baby, but would be very hard on the mother, probably fatal. The alternative, though, could be that both die."

And then, thought Jame, Killy would have his wish. Also, her dilemma would disappear.

"Have you told her?"

Kells didn't answer.

"I see," said Jame, giving him a sour look. She entered the room and shut the door behind her, leaving him outside.

Inside it was fiercely hot, with a raging fire on the hearth. The Kendar Girt looked up. Then, stony-faced, she withdrew to the nearest wall. Mustard lay on the bed, looking ghastly. The flesh on her face had sunken even more than before, in grotesque contrast to the swollen mound of her stomach under the blanket. Her face shone with sweat. The room stank of it and of vomit.

"I'm sorry," said Jame.

Must glared at her. "For what?"

"That things have come to this. A long time ago, Gorbel told me what happened with Tiggeri, but you still decided to keep the child. Why?"

A mixture of embarrassment, anger, and defiance mottled the girl's face.

"If I had gone to an herbalist at Restormir, my lord father would have heard. He's possessive even of his base-born offspring."

"Ah. Then you came north to Tagmeth because you didn't want him to have your child."

"Neither he nor Tiggeri." She spat out the latter name.

"Even when we were little, he tried to play his games with me. Gorbel protected me, but then he went away, first to Tentir, then to Kothifir."

"I'm sorry," said Jame again. "I haven't done very well by you either, but you shouldn't have tried to force my hand."

"Should I have thrown myself at your feet instead?"

"That might have worked better, but you're very proud, aren't you? Pride is all that the Caineron have left you."

"That, and my baby. At least it will be Gorbel's nephew—yes, I believe that it's a boy—if he chooses to acknowledge it."

"Knowing him, he probably will, unless it endangers the child. Gorbel may be the Caineron lordan, but my impression is that his father dislikes him."

"There is that. But . . . but there may not be a child. I've seen the herbalist's expression. Grim." For the first time, she looked scared. "I should have told you sooner. I should have asked for help. For my son's sake."

"And I should have given it without being asked, however my people and brother react."

A spasm distorted the girl's thin face. Girt stepped forward with a cloth steeped in lavender water to wipe her brow. Kells looked in, but Must gestured him away.

"I only want Girt," she said, sounding both petulant and very young. "She has been my nurse all of my life, and my mother's before me."

Another contraction made her writhe under the blanket. Her hand, when Jame took it, was slick with sweat but oh, so cold.

"I see now," she panted. "I have no future, here or anywhere. I'm dying."

Jame wanted to contradict her, but couldn't. Something in her knew the truth when she heard it, smelled it. There was a throat-catching stench on the other's breath, as if of internal gangrene. Trinity, how long had she been this ill? It was a miracle that the baby was still alive, but not much longer at this rate. She swallowed.

"Kells hasn't told you, has he? There's a final potion he can try that might save your child, but probably not you."

Must gripped her hand. "What? There is?" Jame could almost see her collect herself to think, to calculate. Her grip tightened.

"If I don't survive, what future has my child without a protector? If I take this draught, do you swear to accept him?"

"Blackmail again?"

Must gulped. "A . . . a request. Please."

Jame struggled with herself. How could she give such a promise without any idea how to carry it out? On the other hand, how could she refuse?

Honor's Paradox. Should one follow orders, or do what was right? The answer lay in the question.

The girl gasped, going gray. The blanket tangled around her legs began to turn red. Blood's copper tang permeated the room.

"Yes," said Jame, clutching her hand. "I will provide for the child. Kells!"

The herbalist reappeared in the doorway.

"She has decided to take the herb."

"You warned her of the possible consequences?"

"Yes. As you meant me to."

He returned her glare steadily. She was lord, the responsibility hers. Then again, it must be hard for a healer to deliver death. Here too, however, there might also be life.

"All right," she said. "Do it."

In his hand, she saw that he already carried a cup of black, steaming brew. For a moment, she thought that she would vomit. Must still clung to her hand.

"Thank you," the girl whispered, took a deep breath, and let go.

Jame turned blindly toward the door. Enough, enough . . .

Girt stood in her way. "God bless you or curse you, lady. I don't know which."

"Neither do I. See to her."

Outside, Jame leaned against the closed door.

She heard Kells' murmur, Must's tremulous voice:

"Do you promise . . . do you swear . . ."

Still trying to strike a deal, this time with death.

"Drink," said Kells, clearly.

A pause.

"It's so bitter," said Must. "It's . . . oh. Oh!"

Gasps. Thrashing. A muffled cry.

"Hold her," Kells said to Girt. "It's coming. Steady, steady . . ."

A deep groan. A long, desperate pause. A baby's wail.

"He has come," said Kells, "and she has gone."

Jame stumbled down the stairs. Must's people had been sitting around the courtyard's well but rose at her precipitous appearance.

"Your lady is dead," she told them. "You have a new lord."

Trinity, Jame thought as she left the courtyard, the ward, the lower pasture. Why had she said that? True, the child was three-quarters Highborn, but the quarter Kendar blood defined him. If he should prove to be Shanir, though, able to bind other Kendar. . .

G'ah. Too many "ifs."

She found herself on the hillside opposite Tagmeth, without clearly remembering having gotten there or why she had come. Then the latter came to her:

To escape the stench of death.

Because someone needed her.

Night had fallen. The last thin rind of the moon had long since set and clouds obscured the stars, throwing the slope into deep shadow. It was very quiet. A thin wind skittered frozen crystals over the ice crust formed when the sun had set.

"*. . . blaaa . . .*"

What in Perimal's name was that? It sounded young, weak, and desperate. Jame climbed toward the sound, into the deeper shadow of the skeletal trees. Here, she could barely see at all. Roots and rocks protruding from the snow tripped her. Thorns clutched at her sleeves. Through the sharp, clean scent of snow came something else, throat-catching . . . the reek of fresh blood. She was drawn to it, however much it curdled her stomach, as if to death itself. Perhaps that was what it meant to be a

potential nemesis, and in part why Kells had left her to
deliver the dire news to Must. Jame hoped not, but feared
that it was so.

Then she stumbled over something that once, not long
ago, had been alive.

"Don't tread on her," said a voice. Char.

Jame blinked. Night and death must have clouded her
vision. Bene lay at her feet, the snow around her blacker
than the blackest shadow.

"She came to me in agony," said Char, still shrouded
in darkness, sounding dull and numb. "I was supposed to
make it all better. Instead, I cut her throat. Even then,
her belly moved. The calf. . . I cut again."

Jame could see him now, sitting in a nest of roots.
Something lolled in his arms, twitching. It made an effort
and rose on straddle legs. He steadied it. Long legs, short
neck, a head already bowed under the knobs that would
become horns . . .

"*Blaah,*" it said again through as yet toothless jaws.

It looked more like a moose calf than either a domestic
cow or a yackcarn, and more ugly than either. Clearly, it
was a heifer; undoubtedly, it . . . no, she—was going to be
huge.

"The others . . ."

"Dead, I assume," said Char. "If Killy had brought
back the rest of my ten-command in time, we might have
saved more of the babies, if not more of the mothers.
Huh. Perhaps he did right. What future do yackcows have
in our herd? This one is named Malign."

Jame scrambled for the connection. "Short for
'malignant'?"

"*Blaah!*" said the calf again and tottered toward her dead mother.

Char lurched to his feet. "She needs to nurse. I have to find one of Bene's sisters in milk."

"Wait," said Jame as he started to walk off, one arm around the calf's shoulders. "Tomorrow is Must's pyre and, I suppose, the dressing of whatever cows have died tonight. The day after is the winter solstice. Chingetai owes us some cattle, not to mention a proper bull. D'you want to go up to the Merikit village with me to select the new herd?"

Char hesitated, gathering himself. Jame could almost see him turning from death toward life.

"Yes," he said unsteadily. "I would like that."

II

THE NEXT DAY DAWNED overcast and subdued, with a few hesitant snowflakes drifting down. Everything seemed muted. The Caineron *yondri* prepared Must's pyre on the west side of the lower meadow opposite from the site used earlier to burn the incursion of haunts, using finer wood than they had supplied for Tagmeth's various hearths as if this need had been foreseen. The kitchen provided spices; Marc, a flask of precious oil from the storeroom. All day the garrison left tokens among the growing structure in a show of respect that they had not granted the Caineron girl during her lifetime. Jame wondered what exactly they were honoring. As before, she felt eyes on her askance, waiting to see how she would react. The passing Caineron watched her too, with an air of suppressed challenge.

At dusk everyone gathered. Girt emerged from the undercroft with an escort of torchbearers, holding the baby whose name, Jame had learned, was Benj, in honor of the Caineron whom Fash had killed. He was an unusually taciturn infant, with a red, pouting, frog-like face that seemed to hold in some inexpressible grievance. Jame noted how the *yondri* huddled around him and wondered again what his arrival might portend.

More torches. Must's bier approached, carried by her fellow Cainerons. How small and pale she appeared under a rich coverlet. Had Marc provided that, too from some stash of which Jame was unaware? Never mind. She didn't begrudge it.

The garrison stood back. Whatever their feelings, this ritual belonged to others. It was the first time that they had allowed their unwelcome visitors to come to the fore.

Torches were thrust into the matrix of wood. Flames licked up. A Caineron stepped forward and dropped a white cloth into the growing inferno. The fabric folds fluttered open in the updraft, revealing dark spots soon consumed. So. They were indeed treating Must as their lady, each drop of blood representing the life that a bound Kendar would once have given up on the death of his liege-lord.

Jame felt a stir of irritation. The Caineron were making great claims here for Must and by extension for her baby. Whatever, it wasn't her business, she told herself, but doubts lingered.

The pyre burned well into the moonless night. In the end nothing remained but ash, and a child.

III

COLD, HARD DAWN.

Jorin had chosen not to leave their warm bed.

Death's-head, on the other hand, pawed at the ground. Whatever was going on, he wanted to get on with it. Jame tweaked the reins, and was pulled nearly out of the saddle when he ducked his head.

"Bastard," she muttered.

The rathorn snorted plumes of smoke.

In a scrabble of hooves, Char rode up, a limp Malign slung over his roan's withers, snoring gently. The calf was so big that her hooves dangled nearly at the horse's knees. Judging by the latter's pinned ears, he was not pleased at his burden.

"What, you couldn't find a milch cow?"

"Oh, I found one, but she wouldn't cooperate, so I had to milk her myself."

He slapped a bulging leather sack lashed to his saddle. It sloshed. "We'll have to stop fairly often for her to nurse."

Death's-head warily sniffed the calf's rump.

"*Blaa . . .*" said the baby, still half-asleep, and farted.

The rathorn retreated, shaking his head.

They had a good day for their journey, bright and sunny, unseasonably warm. Jame had chosen to ride Death's-head because his legs were stronger than Bel's, but the Whinno-hir mare would have served just as well, except in the shadows where the drifts were still deep. It seemed to Jame that every time she traveled by the folds in the land, her mount chose a different path. This time, once they had left the River Road, the way north led mostly beside streams under whose icy surfaces water still ran fast. It was a slower trip than usual, given how often they had to stop for the calf's sake. By dusk, they caught sight of Kithorn's ragged walls.

Torches bobbed in the keep's courtyard. Drums muttered and chimes tinkled: *Boom–wah-wah-wah . . . ching-ring-a-ching-ching . . .*

"What are they doing?" asked Char. He had the sense to speak softly.

"The Merikit shamans are mumming for the Four, specifically for the Burnt Man. He's the major player at the winter solstice, until it's the Earth Wife's turn at dawn."

"That creature."

Jame had forgotten that Char had seen Mother Ragga at the summer solstice in her guise as a massive tree, cradling Lyra. They never had discussed that strange apparition. Quite possibly, he hadn't recognized the Earth Wife again in the village during the women's mysteries there. Sometimes she forgot how peculiar Rathillien must seem to most Kencyr.

Night fell soon after, moonless, but spangled with stars bright enough to cast black shadows on faintly purple snow. The hill upon which the Merikit village perched loomed ahead, a dark presence against darker mountains. Not a light shone there. It was two years since Jame had last attended a Merikit winter solstice. Then, she had arrived very late, to find only darkness and the village women anxiously gathered, waiting for Chingetai to play his long overdue role. As at the summer solstice, it occurred to her that she didn't know what the Gran Cyd's women did while their menfolk mummed for the gods. Perhaps, again, she was about to find out.

The gate stood open.

Tip-tap, tip-tap went Malign's hooves over the boardwalk inside as she tottered at Char's heels. All of the half-sunken lodges were dark, although low voices sounded ahead in the open space before Gran Cyd's lodge. Char slowed.

"Am I going to have to wear a dress again?" he asked.

"Maybe not, given what a good sport you were last time."

"Here she is!" voices murmured in excitement as a dark shape pushed her way through the crowd toward the queen's tall figure.

"Well then, Feran," said the latter's resonant voice. "What is our clue?"

"Oh, it's a good one, it is. Listen: What has one eye but cannot see?"

"All have heard? Then seek and find."

As the women scattered into the dark, chattering, Jame made her way through their departing ranks to Gran Cyd, who greeted her with a smile in her voice, if nearly invisible on her face.

"This year you have made good time, my favorite. Welcome to you also, friend of the tribe. And who is this?"

"*Blaaa?*" said Malign, raising her muzzle.

A snort answered her from atop the queen's lodge. Jame saw what she had missed before—a sturdy fence and, leaning against it from the inside, the diminutive hulk of the yackcarn bull.

"I wish that my dear mate had not gifted me with such a guest," remarked Gran Cyd. "He cries all night long, such a lonesome sound."

As if in response, the bull lowed and butted the fence. His horns, Jame saw, had been sawn short and bound with iron bands. Around his neck hung a bell that tolled mournfully. A questioning bugle from Death's-head answered him from outside the walls.

"Housebond!" A slight figure rushed forward and threw herself into Jame's arms, nearly knocking her over.

"Lodge-wyf." Jame returned Prid's hug. "Lyra."

The Highborn girl hung back a moment, then walked into Jame's embrace. Such familiarity was not common among their class, although Lyra had previously been more spontaneous. Jame noted that she only sported the smudged charcoal sketch of a mask, although she and the Merikit again wore similar clothes—the traditional loose, belted tunic and trousers of the tribe. What else might Lyra have learned in all of this time from her hosts, and they from her?

"Prid," said Cyd gently. "Go seek."

Lyra grabbed Prid's arm and the two girls rushed off, giggling. Lyra had already been out of breath. Jame wondered what she had been up to.

"What are they looking for?" she asked.

"Ah, yes. You came too late for this the year before last. All of the fires are out and, by lot, Feran was chosen to hide my tinderbox. We must find it before the men return."

"Oh," said Jame, and turned to explain to Char, the previous conversation having been conducted in Merikit.

"Oh," said Char, looking dubious. No doubt, after the summer solstice, this sounded rather tame.

Women's voices echoed through the dark, calling back and forth. At first they sounded happy, even excited, but then a note of anxiety crept in.

"It should not be this hard," said Gran Cyd, listening. "The riddle was a feeble one."

"Why does it matter so much?" asked Jame.

"You do not understand. The tinderbox is a present from the Earth Wife, back from her days as a mortal. Since then it has passed down from Merikit queen to queen. We were never to forget, she said, that our fire kindles that of our mates. They must not come to us until we are ready. Chingetai, though, only sees the significance of fire. He thinks that the power of the box should be his."

"Huh."

"As you say."

Merikit women drifted back to the lodge, speaking to each other in low, worried voices.

"But it was in my sewing chest," Feran could be heard to protest. "One eye that cannot see. A needle. Who could miss that?"

"Now what?" asked Jame.

"This has never happened before. It would not matter so much if Chingetai had not made such an issue of it. Now, will he come to court or to force?"

Jame took her meaning and shivered. "Can such a

thing really create such a change? Surely, that can't be true for all of the Merikit men."

"Not for most, but some listen to him. Hatch is one."

Someone laughed nervously in the darkness.

"Lady, you needn't fret," Lyra said. "I saw where Feran hid the box, and took it. It was only a joke."

A few women sighed with relief. Others grumbled. Jame had the impression of a dark mass gathering opposite Lyra, eyes hidden but still accusatory.

"Give it to me," said Gran Cyd, holding out her hand.

Lyra fumbled in her pocket and flinched. "It—it isn't there. I must have dropped it."

Prid burst into tears.

"It's only a silly toy," Lyra protested, trying to embrace her.

Prid thrust her away. "Oh, how could you? We women took you in. We gave you shelter. Is this how you repay us?"

"I don't understand," cried Lyra and, clearly, she didn't.

Gran Cyd took her by the shoulders. "Think, child," she said, giving the girl a little shake. "Where did you last see it?"

"In—in Feran's lodge."

"Where have you been since then?"

"Oh, all over the village. We followed the hunters, you see. It was so funny."

"Look!" cried several voices.

A light had appeared at the top of the slope to the north. The men were waiting.

"We have to signal them," said Prid, looking frantic, "but how? All of our fires are out."

Upslope, torches descended in an inverted V as the Merikit hauled their log over the crest of the hill. It appeared to be much smaller than the fifty-foot monster that had nearly rammed in the village gates two years ago. Also, only some of its branches had been lopped off, leaving the rest in a hedgehog's ragged spine.

Perhaps it was an accident, or perhaps Chingetai lost patience, but the tree tipped and began to descend, bouncing on the stubs of its limbs. Lights fell as the Merikit men threw their torches aside and scrambled to straddle the moving spire. Despite its lurching descent, it was coming fast. Had Chingetai fitted it again with the metal skid that had nearly caused disaster once before?

"I quarreled with him about that," said Gran Cyd, as if reading Jame's thoughts. "This is something new. We still need to set it ablaze when it arrives. The Burnt Man, winter, must be burned and buried, otherwise spring will never come."

"Does Chingetai understand that?"

"What my mate does or does not comprehend is sometimes beyond me."

As the women huddled together, watching and murmuring nervously among themselves, Jame looked around. With clouds momentarily obscuring the sky, it was truly the dark of the moon, so black that the earth seemed like a reproach to all life, but she had a Kencyr's keen nocturnal vision and so saw what the others had missed: a faint light that rimmed Gran Cyd's door. Leaving the women, Jame crossed to the stair and descended the steps. A push opened the door. The royal lodge appeared to be empty, but more light seeped around the hanging behind the queen's judgment chair. Behind that was a second door, ajar. Jame slipped through it into the Earth Wife's lodge.

She suspected that normally it wasn't there. Mother Ragga, the Earth Wife, turned up in the most unlikely places whenever she was needed, and that would certainly be on the winter solstice when light and dark, life and death, hung in the balance.

Tonight her lodge was as Jame remembered it from two years ago, full of hibernating beasts, the Earth Wife herself asleep, snoring, on the hearth.

The main difference was the circle of little girls sitting crossed-legged on the floor around a small, silver box, feeding its tiny flame with wisps of kindling. Around them, glowing, bleary eyes blinked in the gloom, and a towering cave bear yawned with fanged jaws fit to snap up any one of them.

Jame carefully shut the tinderbox.

"But it needs to eat," Tirresian protested in the sudden darkness.

"And they need to sleep. Hush."

She herded her seven daughters out, among unseen, grumbling forms, and carefully shut the door behind them on renewed snores.

Outside, Cyd confronted Chingetai beside the log, which had finished its descent and come to rest near the village gates.

"What, my lodge-wyf," he was saying with mock reproof, "have you no fire with which to light my hearth? What, then, shall we say of my passion? Clearly, you have tended neither properly. Is that my fault?"

"Housebond, you do not understand. If we do not kindle this log, winter will never end."

He laughed. "Do you truly believe such old wives' tales?"

"The Earth Wife's tales, yes."

Jame approached with Tirresian clinging to her hand and Malign trailing after them. She proffered the box. "Here. We found it in Mother Ragga's lodge."

Lyra's voice sounded in the background: "But I never went there!"

Cyd accepted it with a sigh of relief and drew a small key out of her bodice. This she fit into hole in the box's side and turned so that within steel struck flint to produce a spark. Jame wondered how Tirresian had started her own fire. Moreover, where had she found the priceless artifact and how had she drawn her half-sisters to her in that secret place? As her mother had said, though, this child was special.

And my daughter, she thought with pride, squeezing small fingers, if a bit alarming.

Gran Cyd applied the spark to a branch. Dried needles kindled, but only at the tip where they burned like a candle's fitful flame.

Jame looked more closely at the tree trunk. "This is ironwood," she said. "It seems to be dead, but just the same it's going to take a long, long time to burn."

"Ah!" said the women, glaring.

"Oh," said the men, with a glance at Chingetai who stood by with a self-conscious smirk.

Cyd drew Jame aside. "This is serious," she said, under cover of the abuse now flying back and forth. "My dear housebond has presented us with a problem, but we will solve it. The Four be praised that it is only a sapling and, as you say, dead wood, but still expect no early spring nor soon thaw of the Silver. In regard to that, you must take your young friend away. I might blink at her theft from a host, but come the vernal equinox, who will be chosen to be the Ice Maiden, bride to the Eaten One?"

Jame remembered Prid's terrified face when she had found the small, crystal totem in her bowl of stew at the spring festival and the awed, fearful murmurs around her:

"The fish is caught, the fish is caught . . ."

And then, oh, the water's icy grip, the surging scales and glassy eyes . . .

"I thought that was a matter of chance," she said.

"So we tell ourselves, but I have observed the ritual for many years, back to when Chingetai's little sister was chosen. Whatever our shamans say, however they manage it, the sacrifice is not only always a maid but even then not random. If she is still here, it will be Lyra's turn next."

To one side, Prid raged at Lyra.

"All of our hopes and dreams, hospitality, friendship, sisterhood—thrown aside for a stupid joke!"

Lyra burst into tears. "I didn't mean . . . I didn't think . . ."

"You never do!"

Lyra threw herself into Jame's arms. "Oh, let me stay! I don't want to go back to Restormir!"

Jame detached her gently but firmly. "The lodge belongs to Prid. I am only her housebond. Think: Do you want to stay where you are no longer welcome?"

Lyra drew a sleeve across her streaming eyes and nose. "When am I ever welcome, anywhere?"

"Come back to Tagmeth with me and we will see."

Grunts came from the still-darkened village behind them: "*Huh. Huh? Huh!*"

There was a thud,.then a drumming of hooves on the wooden walk.

"*Squeee!*"

Merikit scattered as the yackcarn bull burst through the gates. Jame stepped in front of Malign.

"Don't you dare. She's only a baby."

The bull veered off, saw Chingetai, and charged. The Merikit chief looked as if he meant to tackle that hurtling black form. However those menacing horns, even cut short, instead made him dive sideways at the last moment in among the bristling stakes of the ironwood log. The yackcarn paused, pissed on the ground, and rushed off into the night, which immediately hid him, except for the clang of the bell around his neck. Starlight glimmered on white hide as, with the taunting flick of a tail and a flourish of heels, the rathorn galloped after him.

Chingetai struggled out of the branches, shouting for ponies and dogs. A hastily assembled hunting party scrambled after him into the dark, pursued by the women's hoots:

"Lost your manhood, have you, little boys? Then go and seek it!"

Jame found Char standing beside her.

"You let him out, didn't you?" she asked quietly, under the general uproar.

"I may hate the ugly brute, but he didn't belong in a pen."

From out in the night, under the shadow of the mountains, came the receding triumphant cry:

"*Squeee . . . huh, huh, HUH!*"

IV

JAME AND CHAR spent the rest of the night in Prid's lodge, Lyra in Gran Cyd's.

Jame emerged near dawn, her breath a plume on the crisp air, her gloved hands shoved into her armpits for warmth. The women had dragged the ironwood log into the village and placed it in front of the royal lodge. The tips of all its branches were crowned with tiny flames and a pit had been dug under it to bed a fire now burned down to embers but continually fed. So far, the log's bark had barely been scorched. It would be a very long winter.

Tired dogs streamed back into the village and went whining for food to their respective lodges. Perhaps, like the dwellings themselves, like most Merikit possessions, they belonged to the women rather than to the men. The men followed them, also looking tired and dejected except for Chingetai, who looked furious. No need to ask how the hunt had gone.

"You owe us ten cows and a bull," said Char, coming up to the fire, not to be swayed from essentials by tact or timing.

Chingetai drew himself up. "P'ah. Our bull is gone due to that wretched rathorn of yours. Our ponies could have overtaken him and our dogs pulled him down if that white monster had not crossed our path again and again. He even found some way to free the yackcarn of his bell, no doubt by hooking it off. We owe you nothing."

Cyd emerged from her lodge in time to hear this, a fine red shawl threaded with gold wrapped around her white shoulders. Lyra trailed after her. From the girl's puffy eyes, it appeared that she had not slept well.

"Come, housebond. Did you not tell me that you sealed your bargain with spit, water and earth as your witnesses?"

Chingetai snarled at her. She handed him a mug of steaming beer and patted his arm, then stroked it, tracing his tattoos with a fingertip.

"Come now," she said again with a smile. "Is the yackcarn bull really such a loss? What did he have that you do not?"

The corner of Chingetai's lip twitched. "Quantity, perhaps, rather than quality?"

"There speaks my man."

With that she stood on tiptoe to whisper in his ear, and he laughed outright.

"Well then, come along, boy, and we will find you some cows. The bull I leave to your choice, if you have the eye to choose."

Malign trotted after them, trying to convince Char that he hadn't already fed her.

"Find me a willing milch cow," he said, as they passed out of sight, "and I might blink."

An hour later, after the others had had a breakfast of bread and fresh goat milk curds, they were back, apparently still in good humor with each other. Char had picked out his new herd and announced with pleasure that one of the cows had let Malign nurse.

"She's uncommonly large for the valley breed," he reported. "There may well be some yackcarn blood in her."

"What about the new bull?" Jame asked.

"Oh, he's all right—bigger in some respects, smaller in others."

Gran Cyd presented Lyra with the dapple gray pony she had been riding during her stay—Dewdrop, she called it.

Lyra had been unusually subdued, but cheered up some when Prid rushed up at the last minute to embrace her.

"Maybe we can be sisters again someday," the Merikit girl said tearfully. Then, to Jame, "Good-bye, dear housebond, good-bye, good-bye!"

The ride back to Tagmeth was uneventful. The new cows seemed better behaved than their sisters farther south and their presence put the bull on his best behavior, as did Death's-head. Malign trotted most of the way at her new foster-mother's side, only to be carried across Char's saddle bow when she tried to steal naps.

Lyra mostly remained quiet. This was so unusual that Jame didn't press her to talk. Better that the girl should think about what had happened than be lectured about it, which in the past had done little good.

In the late afternoon they rejoined the River Road and at dusk they reached the gorge above Tagmeth. The sound of rushing water and mist covered their descent.

Likewise, the latter prevented them from seeing the fortress until they emerged at the rapid's foot. Then they stopped short, staring.

The field opposite the keep was full of tents and campfires. Armed Kendar—a good three hundred of them—passed back and forth between them while a legion of horses fretted on a picket line, no doubt annoyed to find the grass snow-covered and already close-cropped. Flags hung around one tent of lordly proportions and a fire leaped before its door. A large carcass turned over the fire, its grease feeding the flames beneath. The succulent aroma of roast beef drifted up.

"That's one of my cows," said Char, indignant, and would have started forward if Jame hadn't stopped him.

A flag stirred in an errant breeze. Fading light barely picked out its emblem, a golden serpent feasting on its young.

The Caineron had come to Tagmeth.

◄━ CHAPTER XIV ━►
An Enemy at the Gates
Winter 66—74

I

"THE GOOD NEWS," said Brier, as Rue handed Jame a mug of warm cider, "is that it's only Tiggeri, not his lord father Caldane. You were barely out of sight when he turned up on our doorstep. The bad news is that he wants Mustard."

"Well, that's a problem, isn't it? How did he know that she was here?"

"We've guessed, remember, that Caldane's scouts have been spying on us. More likely, though, your friend Gorbel told him. If so, neither brother would know about her death."

Jame sipped the amber brew, frowning. "Gorbel as much as promised me he wouldn't tell, and I believe him. Yet," she waved a hand, "as you see."

Her gesture took in the busy Caineron camp on the other side of the Silver, spread out beneath the parapet on which she, Brier, and Rue stood. It was the morning after her return to Tagmeth. As on the previous night, Knorth Kendar guarded the bridge and, downstream, the River Road. To the best of Jame's knowledge, there was no closer ford to the south than Restormir. For once, she was glad of the keep's unusual setting.

A figure dressed in hunting leathers emerged from the grand tent and paused for a moment on its threshold to don his gloves. Then he stumped down to the New Road.

"Hello!" he shouted, waving to them. "Good morning! Permission to approach?"

"We may as well talk to the fellow," said Jame, and gestured broadly toward the bridge.

Brier put a hand on her arm. Jame looked down at it, then up into her marshal's eyes. They hadn't clashed over her risk-taking since Jame's sortie into the Western Lands. This was no time to resume that conflict. Brier let go.

Meanwhile, Tiggeri—for surely it was he—had waved acknowledgement and set off northward up the road.

Corvine's command held the bridge span while Damson's ten stood nearby in reserve. All were fully armed and armored, and very much on the alert. Glittering spear points came down on either side of Jame as she stepped forward.

She watched Tiggeri approach. They had never met before, although, thanks to Brier, she knew his reputation.

"Smarter than the average Caineron," the Southron cadet had said, "but not as funny as he thinks he is."

He had the stocky build of his family and, like them,

was no doubt inclined to put on fat, but his face was surprisingly comely, or would have been if not for the wide grin that split it.

"Hello, hello!" he said again, rubbing his hands together as if in anticipation of a particularly sumptuous feast. "How is it that we have never met before? I see that I have denied myself a treat."

Jame blinked. What big, white teeth. What cold eyes.

"I won't say 'welcome,'" she said, "since you've already made yourself at home. To what do we owe the pleasure of this unexpected visit?"

"Oh, I was hunting in the area and thought I would drop in. You have some of our runaway *yondri* whom I would like to reclaim. Also, I understand that my sister Mustard is here. After we finish our business, I will be happy to escort her home."

"And what exactly is our business?"

"Surely you've guessed that, a clever girl like you. I'm here to reclaim this keep for the Caineron, of course. It is ours, after all. Who else's, given the work my great-grand-uncle put into it and its proximity to Restormir? Oh, no doubt you've had fun here, but the time for summer forts and playing randon is over. These two"—he indicated Brier and Corvine—"have probably egged you on. They made a poor deal when they left our house for yours so, of course, they would like to give us a black eye. It's high time, though, that you outgrew their petty games and returned to your true role."

"Which is?"

His grin widened. "It needn't be unpleasant, being a woman."

"Shall I ask Mustard about that?"

His grin remained but it showed, if anything, more teeth, bared in a sudden, ferocious rictus.

"My sister is mine. She always has been. She always will be. She knows that."

Jame nearly went back a step.

"Even when we were little," Must had said, "he tried to play his games with me."

"You will understand," she said carefully, "why I don't invite you in."

"What, not even for breakfast?"

"You ate one of our cows last night. Are you hungry again so soon?"

Tiggeri made a face. "We expected the game to be more plentiful, this far north. You must be short on rations too, with no one in a position to resupply you and so much of the winter left to go. Wouldn't your people be more comfortable back at Gothregor?"

"No," said Jame, and left.

"Now what?" Brier asked as they walked back to the keep.

"He doesn't know that, thanks to the gates, we're well supplied. A siege isn't going to work. And, even at three to one, Tagmeth isn't readily open to assault. I wonder if he came on his own, as he seemed to suggest, or if his father sent him."

"Huh. A bit of both, perhaps. My sense is that Lord Caineron isn't ready to move against us himself, openly. On the other hand, Tiggeri couldn't take so large a force, surely every Kendar sworn to him personally, out of Restormir without being noticed."

"Not a hunt, then?"

"It's possible, but unlikely. From the sound of it, Tiggeri—somehow—got word that Mustard was here and came on an excuse. At the least, his father didn't stop him. Trying to seize Tagmeth could be both revenge and a sop to daddy."

"Which suggests that Caldane won't back him up if he fails. That's something. Are the rest of the cattle safely back inside?"

"Yes. He found one of the cows that we missed, perhaps already dead. There wasn't time to send the dogs out to search for more. So, we wait him out?"

"No one has to leave Tagmeth at all except, eventually, me, and that won't be until the High Council meeting toward the end of winter."

Brier frowned. "You mean to attend?"

"I'm my brother's lordan, aren't I? Besides, I want to see what Tori has been up to all of this time."

II

THE NEXT several days passed quietly enough.

Every morning Tiggeri cheerfully hailed the keep.

Every afternoon his randon officers conducted maneuvers outside the camp while he and his young kinsmen went hunting. His idea seemed to be that the Tagmeth garrison would take the hint from these martial exercises, come to their senses, and give up. Or perhaps he was only putting on a show as a joke. With Tiggeri, it was hard to tell.

Meanwhile, the keep continued to guard the bridge and road, but otherwise went on about its business, if with many a wary glance across the river.

For herself, Jame tried to ignore her unwelcome neighbor. That was hard, however, with so insouciant a foe camped on her doorstep, making so much noise. Although she told herself that this was a waiting game, daily she fought the urge to bring it to an end. But how?

In the evenings, Lyra haunted her quarters.

When they had returned to the keep so precipitously, in such a confusion of agitated cattle, the Caineron girl had jumped off her pony and scuttled through the open gate into the oasis. Jame didn't think that anyone had noticed her arrival or abrupt departure. Since then she had stayed out of sight, but crept back into the keep at night for food and company.

On the sixth evening, Jame watched as the girl wolfed down a cold dinner of chicken and pea-pasty. With no one to help her dress, she had become quite disheveled, her hair a tangled mess and the charcoal mask sketched on her unwashed face nearly smudged away. She was also still unusually quiet.

"I used to admire brother Tiggeri," she said suddenly. "He's always so funny."

"Is that admirable?"

"I thought so. You see, he never lets anything hurt him."

"Is that what you fear, being hurt?"

Lyra regarded her half-eaten pasty, not meeting Jame's eyes. "Of course. Doesn't everyone? Well, maybe not you. You don't seem to care."

"I care. I just don't let it stop me."

"But you're strong. I'm not. All of my life, I've been at other people's mercy, or lack of it. It's helped that they don't take me seriously. 'Lyra Lack-wit.' Even you call me that. And it's true—isn't it?"

Jame considered. "I don't think that you're stupid, just immature."

Lyra flushed. "I'm only a child. No one seems to remember that."

It said something about Lyra's state of mind that she would make such an admission, but it was true. Jame didn't know exactly how old Lyra was. Among the long-lived Highborn, however, she wouldn't come of age until she turned twenty-seven, many years from now.

"Sorry," she said. "Technically, I'm still a child too, but I've had a lot more experience than you. Then, too, I keep running into you in difficult situations."—Which Lyra usually mishandled. Small surprise there, considering. "But you've started asking yourself questions. You want to understand."

"Do I? What's so wonderful about growing up? Grown-ups get hurt all of the time."

"True. Even Tiggeri."

Lyra shot her a sidelong look. "D'you think so?"

"I think that right now Tiggeri is in considerable pain, for all of his jaunty air. He's lost perhaps the only person he's ever loved, and he doesn't even know yet that that loss is forever. When he finds out . . . well, let's just hope that he doesn't. But you said that you used to admire him. Don't you anymore?"

"I—I don't think so. He's caused a lot of trouble,

hasn't he? I was beginning to think, even before this, that people around him suffered more than they should, for all that he made his friends laugh. Then I—I played that joke in the Merikit village. It wasn't supposed to hurt anyone, but Prid was so angry and Gran Cyd made me feel so—so small. I still don't entirely understand why everyone was so upset, but they were. Being funny isn't enough, is it?"

"No. You have to consider the effect on others. Not that humor is always bad, or the only way to cause pain. Trinity knows, I'm not very funny myself, more like absurd, and I've hurt a lot of people. Well, yes, sometimes on purpose, but not always. It just happens. The best I can do is to try to be responsible."

Soon after, looking thoughtful, Lyra slipped away again to take shelter in the oasis. Jame wondered if she had encountered her Builder neighbors yet, and guessed that she hadn't. Talk about doing harm. How were the little people managing with this continuing invasion of their refuge? Surely, one way or another, they had suffered enough already. However, the keep needed the fruits of their labors, especially now with the enemy at its gates. She should talk to them again, soon, if they would grant her that privilege.

Sleep that night brought troubled dreams.

Tai-tastigon shook to its foundations with the untempling of the gods. Whose fault was that? There was Bane on the Mercy Seat, flayed alive, and Bane again, presumably dead, in the pesthole behind Mount Alban, guarding the Book Bound in Pale Leather and the Ivory Knife.

"That knife may have been given to me to use," she had said to the haunt singer Ashe. "What if I need it someday?"

"Then call. I think that he will bring it to you . . . with help."

Jame shuddered. Into her mind came the image of that "help": a trail of disintegrating victims ridden and discarded as Bane ate the soul out of each in turn.

"Sweet Trinity. Whose responsibility will that be?"

"His, who feeds. And hers, who calls."

The Book and the Knife. Only two of us, Kindrie and I, have begun to face the possibility that we are part of the Tyr-ridan. Mine is the Knife. The Book—Kindrie's or Tori's, when neither knows how to read the master runes?

Oh, Tori. Something had haunted him. Again she saw that pitiful figure huddled outside the Haunted Lands keep, unable to face what lurked within. Ganth was bad enough. What could be worse?

The Book and the Knife, yes, but what of the Serpent Skin Cloak?

Golden eyes, a voice softer than the shadows that enfolded it: "He . . . it . . . they are still coming, but slowly. Wait."

For what? For how long?

Dammit, no one told her anything, and she was supposed to save the world—or was that to destroy it?

I don't want to hurt anyone, so why do I keep doing it?

She had forgotten something. What?

Jame woke with a start, to the muted light of early

morning snow and Jorin's grumble of complaint from under the blankets.

It was seven days since she had last seen Bear. Where was he?

III

IT HAD SNOWED HARD over night, leaving a foot-deep blanket, heavy and white. Those Kendar out first into the island's lower meadow quickly discovered that this bounty was perfect for another snowball fight. Projectiles were flying when Jame arrived to see what the shouting was all about.

A snowball sailed over the river and hit a cadet with a wet smack on the shoulder. Tiggeri's guards had joined the fray. In a moment, the air over the Silver was full of taunts and hurtling balls, more and more as Kendar joined the battle on either side.

This was as it should be, thought Jame, watching their joyful play. Kendar should only fight Kendar in jest. Anything else was . . . obscene.

Brier, beside her, caught a snowball before it could hit her in the face.

"Huh," said the Southron, brushing away the icy crust to reveal an embedded rock.

The trickster was back.

Jame regarded the laughing ten-commands— Damson's, Berry's, and Char's. No one looked back at her, too intent on their fun, no doubt needing it after the past week's tension.

Someone on the far bank yelped in pain. From the blood trickling down his face, he also had been stuck by a rock.

Soon after, randon arrived to break up the game. Jame recognized one of them from the randon college at Tentir, an instructor named Acon who, while hard, had always played fair despite house politics. As annoyed as she was by Tiggeri, as upset by the thought of a traitor on her own side, it cheered Jame to recall the good Caineron she had known, including the Commandant and Gorbel, assuming the latter hadn't betrayed Must's presence here to his brother as Brier supposed.

Soon afterward, the opposite camp began to stir uneasily. Passing Kendar glanced at the grand tent, from which Tiggeri had yet to emerge. Others huddled together, murmuring. His young kinsmen arrived in a rush, pushing aside the guards. Someone in the tent cried out—oh, such a sound of pain, and grief, and rage. Then all was ominously still again. Jame found herself on the parapet watching the scene across the river.

"What is it?" asked Rue, trying to hand her a bowl of porridge that she ignored.

"I don't know. Something bad."

Tiggeri appeared in the tent's door and stood there for a moment, breathing hard. He saw Jame, but didn't salute her. Even from this distance, she felt the heat of his eyes. Then he headed for the bridge.

Jame went to meet him.

"Oh, you diddled me prettily," he said when they were face to face.

Behind him, his kinsmen glared at her with even less

control than he had so far managed. Jame wondered if they were bound to him and feeding off the core of his rage. Her own guards as one lowered their spear points to cover her. Brier and Corvine slipped through them to tower at her back.

Tiggeri didn't seem to notice them. "When were you going to tell me that Mustard was dead?"

"How did you know that she was here?"

He sneered, too angry to dissemble. "Even your own people know what an unnatural thing you are. One of them told one of my scouts. Then, this morning, I received this." He brandished a wrinkled, bloody paper in a shaking hand.

Jame felt her heart sink. "It was wrapped around a stone, wasn't it?"

"See? You can be truthful when you try."

Brier surged forward a step, but Jame held her back.

"Think," she said evenly. "I am a Highborn, a lordan, and a randon cadet. I always tell the truth. To do otherwise would be the death of honor."

Tiggeri smiled, showing all of his teeth.

"You randon," said one of his followers, also grinning.

"Always so honorable," said a second.

"Always so superior." A third.

Yes, they were mirroring their liege lord, and some of the Kendar as well, who shuffled forward half a step wearing ugly expressions.

"I want my son," said Tiggeri.

"The child is under my protection. That was his mother's dying wish."

"What does that matter? I want him."

Jame didn't answer.

Tiggeri's teeth audibly ground. Abruptly, he turned on his heel and stalked off, his people withdrawing with him.

Jame wondered, was that it? She was also about to retreat when someone shouted, "Shields up!"

All around her, shields were unslung and raised overhead, barely in time. A flight of arrows plucked at their hardened leather covers, one finding a gap and plunging through to pin a Kendar's foot to the ground.

Caineron yelled their battle cry.

The reserve Knorth ten-command surged up.

Caught in the midst of Kendar half again her size, Jame was lifted off her feet and shoved backward out of the crush.

"Tagmeth to the rear!"

Brier picked her up. "After all," she said, "you are unarmed."

IV

THE BATTLE on the bridge raged, intermittently, for the rest of the day. Because the way was too narrow to carry by force, wave after wave broke against the defenders, both sides fighting in relays of fresh troops. More flights of arrows stitched the sky, some aimed into the keep itself, until, it seemed, the attackers ran out. Casualties remained light, but they did occur, especially among the Caineron.

"Hard slogging," Marc commented as he and Jame

watched from the battlements. "Can't they see that this isn't going to work?"

"I think Tiggeri is past reason and so, therefore, are many of his troops. Watch. Some throw themselves into it; others are just trading blows with us, and we're only trying to hold them back. At this rate, though, even with replacements, both sides are going to fight themselves to exhaustion."

"Then what?"

"Trinity only knows."

Marc again presented her with the bowl of soup that he had brought up with him from the kitchen, and again she waved it away.

"No breakfast and now no lunch?"

"This takes away my appetite." Below, a space had cleared between the combatants as it did periodically to allow for the removal of the wounded. "Kencyr shouldn't fight Kencyr. Even the ones that want to kill us—that's only because they're bound to a Highborn madman."

"You really do idolize the Kendar, don't you?"

"D'you think so? What about any of this conflict is natural?"

"That depends on how you define 'nature.' It has happened before. It will happen again. That's just the way things are."

"Then 'the way things are' stinks."

Marc smiled at her, a bit sadly. "I hope that we never give cause to disappoint you, for our sake more than for yours."

Marc had a way of making her feel very young and very naïve. Just the same:

Some things need to be broken, she thought, scowling. *Surely this is one of them.*

Dusk brought the reluctant withdrawal of the attackers. The garrison continued to man the bridge under flaring torches and the faint light of a crescent moon. By turns, ten-commands went in for a hardy supper of yackcarn roast and baked apples. Jame, again, had no taste for either.

She was at the parapet, half dozing where she stood, when Brier touched her shoulder.

"Look."

Figures had gathered on the opposite shore. Dark shapes edged out into the current.

"God's claws," said Jame, staring. "They're trying to ford the river."

Their rafts were logs bound loosely together, ridden with their legs in the water. Jame wondered why they weren't swept away. Then she saw that ropes connected the two shores, anchored on the island's side by the wall around the lower pasture. Had they shot them across attached to arrows, or had the trickster been busy again? Whichever, they now edged out into the current, hauling themselves hand over hand.

They came in silence, but even so their approach was noted. The Caineron *yondri* lined the wall, waiting.

Jame experienced a moment of doubt. Perhaps they meant to help their former colleagues. Perhaps, in fact, the trickster wasn't Knorth after all.

Downstream, water swirled. A whirlpool was forming, thin moonlight glinting on the ribbed spiral of its deepening throat.

The rafts were drawn toward it.

The ropes attached to the far shore gave way. *Yondri* grabbed the other ends and tried desperately to reel in the would-be invaders.

"Pull, pull," Jame heard herself urge as she beat the parapet with her fist.

The logs upended, spilling their riders into the watery maw. It closed over them. Timber shot back to the surface, but no bodies.

Slurp, said the River Snake.

Tiggeri stood on far shore, watching, his followers behind him. He turned and walked back to his tent through their silent ranks, which closed behind him.

Jame descended from the battlements to the courtyard. The gate to the oasis stood open. She entered.

Night lay soft on the garden within. Night birds called sleepily to each other from rustling trees. Bats flitted from palm to palm. The moon had set and the eastern sky held the least hint of dawn. By the lakeshore, Jame started a campfire and settled down beside it, facing the water.

"Hello!" said Lyra behind her. "What are you doing here?"

"Thinking."

"Couldn't you do that in bed? It's late."

"Then go back to sleep."

"I'm awake now." She stifled a yawn, sat down, and snuggled up beside Jame, head on her shoulder. "Tell me a story."

Jame opened her mouth, then shut it again, considering. She wasn't much good at storytelling. Just the same. . .

"Once there was a little girl . . ."

"Was it me?"

"No. Be quiet. She lived in a terrible place until one day her father saw her dancing, mistook her for someone else, and threw her out."

"It was a mistake, then?"

"Not really. He meant to do it and never, as far as I know, regretted it. She went to live somewhere else even worse."

Lyra yawned. "That was silly of her."

"She didn't have much choice. Did you, when your father sent you to Karkinaroth?"

"Fathers do things like that. Now he wants to send me to the Ardeth at Omiroth, but I ran away."

"So did she, and ran, and ran, until she came to a great city, but again she was driven out. She did meet many good people, though, including good Kendar like the folk who raised her."

"I like the Kendar. They pay attention, and don't make you feel silly."

"Sometimes they do, when you are, but they care. Mostly. It was a great shock to her when she discovered that some didn't care at all. Rather, they listened to their lords and did whatever they were told. That's called Honor's Paradox. Trust the Highborn to come up with something so vile."

"I don't think I like your story. It doesn't have a plot, and where's the happy ending?"

"Sorry. That's just life, which doesn't have much of a plot either. As for happy endings, well, that remains to be seen."

Behind her, sand crunched, the barest furtive whisper of a sound. Jame pulled herself together.

"The thing is, she . . . I owe the Kendar a debt that I'll never be able to repay. All Highborn do. They are our moral compass, ignored at our peril. Now a group of them has taken refuge with me, but their lord's son is at my gate and I can't guarantee their safety. One of them is just a baby."

"A baby!" said a voice behind her.

Lyra squeaked with surprise, but Jame stopped her from turning around.

"Don't. If he doesn't want to be seen, it would be rude. Hello, Chirp."

"Thank you for the bread," said the Builder, sounding rather breathless.

"You're welcome. Have my people been treating you with respect?"

"Most still do not know that we are here. The rest . . . well, these are Kendar. As you say, they have been discreet and kind."

"With your permission, I would like to settle my refugees with you as a permanent colony."

The tiny Builder circled around the fire, looking disturbed, causing Lyra to exclaim again.

"Oh, he's just like a doll!"

"This is Lyra Lack-wit, who is not discreet. Lyra, this is Chirpentundrum, who is probably older than all of your ancestors combined, and much wiser. Behave."

"A permanent colony. . . Permanence, to us, means more than it does to you. Still, a baby. . ."

"A newborn boy."

"Oh! Our kind reproduces so very rarely. I have not held a baby in a dozen worlds. Would you let us help care for him?"

"You would have to ask his guardian, a Kendar named Girt, but I see no reason why not."

"You didn't say that Girt would agree," Lyra pointed out as the Builder wandered off in a daze of delight.

"Sometimes you surprise me. No, I didn't. We'll worry about that later."

Back in Tagmeth's courtyard, in the kindling dawn, Jame summoned the Caineron *yondri* and told her that she and her people were moving into the oasis.

"They say that it's nice there," said Girt wistfully, hitching Benj up on her shoulder and gently burping him. Her fellow *yondri* hadn't been part of the troop rotation in and out of the garden. "It's really too damp underground for a newborn."

"You'll . . . er . . . have some neighbors there—small, gentle folk. Treat them respectfully and, please, listen to any requests they may make."

"Such as, lady?"

"I'll let them speak for themselves, if they aren't too shy. You need to move quickly, though. This morning."

Brier approached. "There you are," she said. "Acon is at the bridge, alone. He wants to talk to you."

Now what, Jame wondered. After the long night she was both tired and very hungry, but she went to see.

Acon waited for her, standing stiff and straight. His was a hard face, not given to expression, certainly not betraying his errand, whatever it was. They traded wary salutes.

"Hard fighting," said Jame, both as a comment and a compliment. She didn't add how wasteful she had found it.

"You've given my lord a proper bloody nose. He doesn't take well to such things."

"What's to be done, then?"

"Will you give up the child?"

"No."

"I didn't think so."

He glanced off toward the keep, not meeting her eyes. Jame's eyebrows rose. Whatever he had to say, he didn't want to say it.

"We . . . er . . . understand that you have also given your protection to a randon known as Bear."

"He lives here, if that's what you mean, and I am honored to give him shelter. He has never needed my protection."

"Well. Scouts have seen his tracks. This morning, Tiggeri set out to hunt him."

Oh, schist. Jame had learned that Bear had left the keep when Must had been brought to child-bed in his quarters, but she had hoped that he would at least keep a safe distance. Not far enough, it seemed.

"What are you doing to do?" she asked Acon.

"That depends on you."

"Then we have to catch up with Tiggeri."

Brier's hand closed on her shoulder. *Beware*, she might as well have said. *While true, this could be a trap to draw you out.*

"That can't be helped," she told her marshal, giving the Southron's fingertips a reassuring touch.

"Then the rest of your randon will go with you. This is our business too."

They passed through the Caineron camp, watched warily by Tiggeri's Kendar. What did they think? It was all well and good to consider the Kendar in aggregate as noble, but they had to live where they found themselves. Not many, like Corvine, were able to escape a bad situation, or a bad lord.

Corvine herself came up behind Jame as she entered the forest above the meadow and overtook her. Acon was already pulling ahead on his long legs through the deeper snow under the trees. Jame floundered in their wake, stumbling over concealed, fallen branches and into hollows. Others passed her—randon officers, sergeants, and cadets, Knorth and Caineron, all intent on what lay ahead. Hounds and horns sounded. Could Bear really have stayed so close to the camp? So it seemed.

Panting, a stitch tearing at her side, Jame emerged into a clearing. Randon lined its edge with dogs straining at their leashes. Bear stood at bay against a rock face. His massive claws were out, unsheathed.

"Huh," he said, and swung them idly as if weighing possibilities.

Tiggeri stood out before his hunters, a boar spear in his hand.

"Well?" he said, impatiently, over his shoulder. "What are you waiting for? Take him!"

No one moved.

Tiggeri swung around to face them. His eyes were hot, his face blotched with red.

"You dare?" he snarled. "This is more of Sheth Sharp-tongue's insolence, isn't it? Don't think that he won't pay. So will his misbegotten brother. So will all of you."

He turned, leveled his spear, and charged at Bear. Bear batted the spearhead aside and grabbed the shaft. Tiggeri refused to let go. They wrestled for a moment, scuffing up snow, then Bear gave a mighty shove and Tiggeri went down on his back. With a grunt, Bear sat on him. The shaft was between them, gripped by both. Slowly, implacably, Bear bore down on it until it pressed across the Caineron's throat. Tiggeri began to gag.

Jame left the margin and went to Bear's side.

"Enough," she said, touching his shoulder.

Bear glanced up at her, grunted again, and rose. After a moment, so did Tiggeri, one hand on his bruised throat. He looked enraged enough to gibber, but with a great effort controlled himself.

Jame stood between the two.

"Enough?" she said again, this time making it a question.

"I didn't know that he was your pet," said Tiggeri hoarsely, with a lopsided smile that was half a baring of teeth.

"And I didn't think you had the courage to tackle him alone. That was impressive."

"Well. Now what?"

"I invite you and your randon to join me for breakfast, provided you take my word for it that the boy is no longer at Tagmeth."

"Oh? Just like that?"

"He was in danger, so I sent him away; and no, I won't tell you where. Have you any other good reason to attack us?"

"We Caineron still claim the keep."

"I said, a *good* reason. Be sensible. You've seen that we can't easily be taken by assault."

His chin jutted. "I can still starve you out."

"Come judge that by the table we set."

He eyed her. "You're a strange girl, quite possibly mad. All right. I'll come. We all will."

V

IT WAS A PECULIAR PROCESSION that returned to Tagmeth, wondered at both by the camp and the garrison, although Jame had sent word ahead to the latter what to expect and how to prepare for it.

In the island's meadow, she pointed out the site of Must's pyre. Tiggeri looked stricken.

"How many days ago?"

"Eight."

"So recently. And I missed her by only that much."

Then he saw the larger bare patch caused by the haunts' pyre and cheered up.

"I see that you have had other deaths. Many of them. Not easy, is it, to establish a keep in such a wilderness?"

Jame didn't correct him.

They found the courtyard swept clear of snow with tables and benches set out surrounding the well. A purposeful clatter arose from the kitchen. Helpers ran in and out. Breakfast was usually a casual meal, but Marc and Master Rackny were preparing for a feast, a week's cookery gone in one burst from whatever could be prepared quickly or had been started the night before.

Jame saw Tiggeri glance around. The gates were there, of course, closed and looking innocent—unless one asked where they led. Otherwise the courtyard appeared neat and well maintained, also its people, who arrived looking trim and fit, but understandably wary.

While most of the regular garrison would eat outside, tables had been prepared in the mess hall for Tagmeth's guests and its randon. The doors stood open, billowing fragrant steam into the chill outer air. The fireplaces at either end of the hall roared. Jame showed Tiggeri to a seat at the high table and gestured for wine, a precious bottle of which had been broken out of storage. Master Rackny's current assistants ran out of the kitchen bearing platters of spiced toast with almond sauce and luce wafers.

Tiggeri drank without pausing to savor the vintage which, Jame supposed, was just as well. At least the stuff was strong.

"You're up to something," he said. "I know it."

"What, if not to heal the breach between our houses?"

"That you will never do. Our enmity goes back too far and runs too deep. My son . . ."

"Is gone." Trinity, she hoped that that was true. Girt and the Caineron *yondri* at least were nowhere in sight, and she had told them to hurry.

"Do you doubt her word?" asked Acon, from her other side.

"Oh, to call a randon a liar—you would love that, wouldn't you?"

"No, my lord. Lies befit no Kencyr."

Platters of smoked pike salad in pastry, baked lamprey, and brie tarts were set down before them. Tiggeri glowered at the bounty, ashes to his mouth, no doubt. If nothing else, this repast should convince him that Tagmeth was not readily to be starved out. Still, he couldn't resist. As he truculently tucked in to the feast, Jame bent toward Acon.

"What did he mean," she asked under the mess room's growing clamor, "about the Commandant's insolence? That doesn't sound like Sheth Sharp-tongue at all."

"Nor is it." Acon also spoke quietly, almost as if not addressing her at all. "Sheth is still at Restormir, largely because Lord Caineron can't decide what to do with him. He doesn't say much, but his very presence, I fear, is a reproach."

"Are things so bad there?"

Acon applied himself to a fig stuffed with cinnamon eggs. Jame suppressed a grimace. She had told the kitchen not to serve anything exotic, such as fresh figs, for fear that Tiggeri would ask where they had come from. However, he didn't seem to have noticed the lapse.

"Restormir is . . . on edge. The Caineron Matriarch is dying, and Lady Kallystine seeks to take her place. I confess, we did not realize what a check on our lord his great-grandmother was. Is. I mean, who credits Highborn women with such power?"

Only fools, thought Jame, but that was hardly fair. The Randon weren't aware of the interplay between Highborn men and women. For that matter, she was the first Highborn female in at least a millennium to undergo randon training. Curious how, despite her connection to That-Which-Destroys, the links she made between people, ideas, and powers kept ringing true. Who was it who had said that a potential Tyr-ridan would be close to all three faces of their god until he or she came to maturity? In that case, so far so good. Ancestors help her, though, with whatever came next.

God-born. God-cursed. Was there a difference?

She became aware that at a neighboring table Killy was speaking rather loudly.

"You wouldn't credit it," he was saying, "that doors could lead out of this world, or maybe into it. Rathillien is amazing. Think about it—people moving from here to the other side of the world just by walking across a threshold!"

Jame stiffened. Tiggeri wasn't paying attention yet, but Damson was. She shot the cadet a look. Damson wrinkled her forehead and Killy began to choke. Char hit him on the back, without result. Then he followed Damson's gaze, raised an eyebrow at Jame, and put a hand under Killy's elbow to raise him.

"Excuse us," he said.

That caught Tiggeri's notice.

"Early in the day for a drunken garrison, isn't it?" he asked as Killy stumbled toward the door between his two escorts. In the doorway stood Lyra. She recoiled as Killy was led past, then raised her eyes to meet those of her half-brother.

Trust the girl to nose out a feast, Jame thought

despairingly, and then not have the sense to use the back door.

"Well," said Tiggeri, putting down his cup. "That's one mystery solved. We wondered where you had gone. Greetings, little sister."

Lyra looked ready to bolt, as well she might, but where? Any serious search of the keep would no doubt betray the gates. Would Lyra think of that? Would she care?

"Your great-grandmother needs you," said Tiggeri. "Darling Kallystine has scared off most of her attendants, even if she can't entirely strip Cattila of power. She's dying, you know, although she is fighting it every inch of the way. How not? A tough old bird, our Gran. Also, our father has had a falling out with Dari of the Ardeth, so you needn't fear being made his consort. Will you come back?"

It was a surprisingly tactful plea. Jame wondered if he actually cared about Cattila and Lyra, or just the credit he would gain by returning his runagate sister, especially after failing so abysmally to reclaim either Tagmeth or his own son.

Lyra wavered, a fawn about to bolt. She gulped and looked at Jame as if for guidance, but this must be her own choice.

I can't help you, Jame wanted to tell her, *but, oh, think of the damage you might do!*

"All right," said Lyra. "I'll go back with you. Maybe I'm not very clever, but I can try to be responsible."

For her, that was a surprising concession.

Soon afterward Tiggeri and his randon left, with Lyra at his side trying to assume a dignified pose. Jame wondered what her position would be when Cattila was gone, also if Lyra had thought about that. But it was no answer for her to hide anymore. One eventually had to face one's life.

At the bridge, Tiggeri suddenly turned and enveloped Jame in a bear hug that was virtually an assault.

"Don't think you've won," he hissed, hot breath in her ear as spear points clashed down around them on both sides. "I will have my son, and I will have Tagmeth. Just wait."

Then he thrust her away, or maybe she did him, and he stalked off. There went a bad enemy.

Then, when Tiggeri had at last broken camp and gone, she turned, reluctantly, to deal with Killy.

VI

DAMSON AND CHAR had taken him to her quarters and there he waited under their watchful eyes.

"I made a mistake," he burst out, as soon as Jame entered the room. "Anyone can do that."

Jame sat on the edge of the table, folded her arms, and considered him. "Oh, it was a mistake all right, blurting out Tagmeth's greatest secret. So loudly, too, in such company. Did you mean for Tiggeri to hear you?"

Killy laughed. "Am I that big a fool?"

"It seems to me that you must be, one way or another."

Now he was growing angry. While generally a handsome boy, a pout made him look both sulky and weak. "You don't give me enough credit. You never have.

Trinity, half of the time you can't even remember my name! I should have been promoted to ten-commander. Like that show-off Dar. Like silly Mint. Like you." And here he sneered at Damson. "But we all know that you favor your freaks."

"The word," said Jame, "is Shanir."

She was watching Killy closely now, prey to a sudden suspicion. "You don't think much of anyone, do you?"

"I think as I find. Even of you, lady. Why does everyone believe that you're so special? Your lord brother doesn't. He only sent you here to get you out of the way."

Char stirred, but Jame quieted him with a glance.

"Do you think that he wants me to fail?"

"Of course! What else? This place is a farce. It always has been."

"You would like very much to prove that, wouldn't you?"

"Yes. No. After all, how could I?"

"Oh, a trick here, a prank there . . . Some of them were almost funny, not that I enjoyed falling off a roof, or almost getting hit in the head by a rock, or nearly drowning in Gothregor's water meadow—although, come to think of it, that last was before Tagmeth. Then someone told a Caineron scout first that Must was here, and then that she was dead, leaving a child. We've had a dozen or more injuries over that, some serious. But Tiggeri didn't know you were the spy, did he? Otherwise, he would have listened."

"No one remembers me!" Killy burst out, and it was clear that this was resentment, not denial. "It wasn't like that. You don't understand. When the Highlord hears how you've mismanaged this keep, he will thank me."

Jame wondered if Killy's thinking was always this muddled or if Damson was playing games with his mind. The former, probably.

"Then you had better go and tell him," she said.

The boy looked startled. "You're throwing me out?"

"That does seem best, all around, doesn't it? Take the gray gelding, the cranky one, and leave. Now. When you get to Gothregor, tell my brother what you like, but only him."

Killy left, trying to swagger, but none too steady on his feet. Char went with him to be sure that he took the right horse, one that most people would be glad to see go. The same could be said for its rider.

"I always thought that he was a fool," said Damson. "The question is: Can he still do us harm?"

"'Us.' I like that." Jame sighed. "He can't say anything that I haven't already reported—assuming that Tori has kept up on his correspondence—but there are different ways to tell any story."

Damson shrugged. "It will be as it may, then. How long until you attend the High Council meeting at Gothregor?"

"God's claws. Twenty-six days."

CHAPTER XV

Meanwhile
Winter 90

I

STEWARD ROWAN dawdled over her bowl of porridge, reluctant to start the morning.

Bake-master Nutley entered Gothregor's mess hall bearing a loaf of new bread. This he placed on the table and then sat down opposite her presenting, as it were, his bosom as he did so. He had taken to wearing a bodice to show off his new cleavage and was growing a fine, black beard. The contrast was . . . interesting.

"You look glum," he said, offering her a slice.

She took it wondering, as usual, how he could tell. Thanks to her branded forehead, her expression seldom changed. It even hurt to smile, not that she felt much like it at the moment.

"I have a hard day ahead."

"How so? The ovens are drawing well and we have enough to eat, if barely and nothing fancy. If it weren't for having to plan a feast for the High Council, I would be happy."

"We can't feed them?"

He made a face. "There's enough for our simple tastes, but they should sup on gruel garnished with mast? If this isn't an elaborate meal, word will spread that we're at famine's door. That won't be good for our prestige."

He didn't need to stress the importance of putting on a show.

Throughout the Riverland it had been an edgy, discontented winter with short rations due to a poor harvest and the Central Lands raising prices to ruinous heights. There were rumors that agents of the Seven Kings had haunted the Riverland since autumn, trying to bargain with the other lords for troops. Wisely, none had come near Gothregor since their expulsion the previous spring. If Torisen hadn't decreed that no one strike any deals until after the High Council meeting, the more self-indulgent lords might already have signed away their Kendar for a handful of luxuries. Lord Caineron in particular must be lusting for his usual treats, although he was one of the few rich enough to buy what he wanted, if he could bring himself to pay the price. The poorer houses had no such choice. That the Kencyrath should have come so nearly to this. . . Rowan felt her world shiver around her, and trembled with it. So much depended on Torisen.

"You're frowning," said Nutley.

"How can you tell?" Rowan bit into her bread. "This is crunchy. Mast?"

"Only for the swine, dear lady. For you, hazelnuts."

The bake-master would tease her all morning if she let him. It was a game that they played, all the more piquant because he knew that she would never betray her

lord's secrets, nor would he want her to. Still, he was also
bound to Torisen and could sense that all was not well.

"You're going to see him now, aren't you?"

Rowan reminded herself that Nut was prescient that
way and, despite herself, she sighed.

"Then go," he said, suddenly serious. "All of our souls
go with you."

He fluttered his beard at her and departed, bosom
bouncing.

Rowan left the mess hall into a crisp, white morning.
Usually the snow had gone by now except for sporadic
bursts. This year it continued to clog the inner ward and
to drift down, lazily, from a milky sky. It would be a late
spring, the older Kendar said. A few of the eldest hinted
that somehow the Merikit were to blame, but no one took
them seriously.

Here was the old Knorth keep, its flanks long since
repaired after the freak storm the previous spring. Here
was the first-story death-banner hall. Perhaps the tapestries
there spoke to Torisen. They only glowered at Rowan as if
to demand, "Have you done your duty?" The second dark
floor was still set up with glass kilns in the eastern corner
towers. The great hall above blazed with jeweled light
through the stained glass window that, although
incomplete, was already Marc's masterpiece. The fused
work stood like translucent iron, while sections of the
transitional cullet had fallen to the winter blasts, admitting
blades of cold air. Rowan wondered if Marc would ever
finish or if the Knorth Lordan was his work now.

Voices sounded down from the northwest tower,
where Torisen kept his meager quarters.

"Where is my other boot?"

"On your foot."

"Oh."

It was going to be one of those mornings.

Rowan climbed and knocked. Burr opened the door, his bulk filling it from post to post like a wall. Then he saw who the visitor was and stood aside.

"Did he get any sleep last night?" Rowan murmured to him as she passed.

"No. He pretended, but I wasn't fooled, not with all of that coughing."

"If you're discussing me," said Torisen in the room beyond, "talk louder."

Rowan stepped into the disordered study. It had always been a mess, despite Burr's best efforts, but these days it also stank of mold and rot and sickness. Parchment crumpled in heaps on the table. Scattered clothes turned green at the seams. The boot in Torisen's hand looked about to fall apart.

So did the Highlord himself. He was more haggard than Rowan had ever seen him, his face gaunt with dark shadows under his eyes. His untidy hair, streaked with white, needed trimming almost every day now, as did his nails. Surely that wasn't natural, thought Rowan, but neither was Blackie. He hadn't been, in more subtle ways, ever since she had first met him as a boy, some twenty years before. He was normally so quiet that one forgot how ancient and strange the blood was that ran in his veins, how devious its course had been over the past millennia.

"I can't find anything," he now said, plaintively. "Where is . . . oh."

He began to cough again, a wet, tearing sound. For nearly three seasons now since the tainted harvest the illness had come and gone—impossible, it seemed, to shake off. Was hay-cough finally developing into lung-rot? Others at Gothregor had died of that, but only in early days. Just the same. . .

"You should send for Kindrie," said Rowan, not for the first time.

"He told me to stay away from my people. And I have. And he was right. Bo recovered. No one else is sick anymore, are they? Not seriously, anyway. Just me. Maybe I should call him back."

Rowan deliberately didn't look at Burr. This capitulation was sudden and unexpected.

"I'll write a note for you, then, shall I?" she said, glad to hear that her voice was as flat as her expression.

"Do that. Do that." His eyes glazed and his head tilted as if he were listening to someone or something else, far away. "Don't tell her that," he murmured. "I didn't run away. I escaped, with the permission of all our Kendar. They knew you would kill me, sooner or later. Anar said . . . Anar said he would take the blame, if there was any. But then . . . then he said, 'I was wrong. Nothing outweighs a lord's authority. Take back the responsibility, child. It burns me. It burns. Set me free. Free us all.' We tried. Kindrie tried. With the pyric rune. But what shame to have bought my freedom with their suffering. My fault. My fault."

Rowan felt creeping horror. Almost, she could also hear a distant, mocking hiss:

"*Yessss. Your fault. And he didn't give you leave to go,*

did he, whatever your precious Kendar said. Coward. Disowned. You, who have the nerve to call yourself Highlord."

Laughter disintegrated into a wail, to the thud of fists against wood.

"*Oh, let me out, you misbegotten bastard, let me out!*"

The madness of Ganth Gray-Lord had been contagious, but Torisen wasn't mad, just . . . preoccupied, or so Rowan told herself over and over again. When he fixed his mind to something he could keep focus. Usually.

Even so, why should he feel such guilt?

Rapid footsteps sounded on the stair. Rowan had barely turned when a young man burst into the study.

"Let me go!" he cried as she and Burr seized him by the arms. "I have to talk to him! You can't stop me!"

"We have so far," said Rowan. "Be off with you."

But Torisen had heard, and his wandering attention sharpened. "You're . . . er . . . Killy, aren't you? One of my sister's folk."

"Never hers. Only yours."

"You were assigned to Tagmeth. What are you doing here?"

"Hinting that he knows great secrets," said Rowan, disgust in her voice, "to whoever will listen, which is few. I won't say that this boy lies, only that he is either deluded or has misunderstood."

Killy sputtered in protest. Torisen raised a hand—the one not holding a boot—and the Kendar stopped, goggling, as if he had run head-first into a stone wall. There was that too: a new sharpness that sometimes emerged like a lightning strike from Torisen's general distraction.

"Tell me."

"Your sister has betrayed you."

"How so?"

This cool reception to so dramatic a charge seemed to flummox the young Kendar.

"S-she hasn't told you all that's gone on at Tagmeth. Those gates to other lands—she hasn't mentioned them, has she?"

Torisen frowned. "I believe that she has, not that I entirely understood. I . . . don't seem to be thinking clearly these days. Then, too, wherever Jame goes, improbable things happen. It's hard to keep up. I expect that, when she arrives for the Council meeting, she will explain."

"She's taken in Caineron and Randir *yondri*. They expect her to bind them. She hasn't yet, but she will, at the expense of loyal Knorth."

"That would be more serious, if she should do anything so improper. Still, fugitives . . ."

Killy began to wax desperate. "One of them was Lord Caineron's half-breed daughter. She died—good riddance—but her brother Tiggeri came looking for her and attacked us. There were casualties on both sides, and now there's that bastard baby . . ."

Torisen gestured vaguely toward the table piled high with parchments. "There's a message here somewhere. I keep meaning to read it."

Killy looked as if he wanted to shake him, but didn't dare approach. "What will Lord Caineron say when he hears that we are sheltering his runaways, even his half-breed grandson? I tried to tell Tiggeri but somehow the words stuck in my throat. That freak Damson was responsible, I'll swear it!"

"If you were about to say something that Jame didn't want Tiggeri to hear, can you wonder? You were assigned to my sister. It doesn't sound as if you've been particularly loyal."

"You can't want her to succeed! It-it's preposterous, obscene. What would your ancestors say? Your father . . ."

Torisen's eyes flashed silver, and everything around him jolted back an inch. "Leave Ganth out of this. I am Highlord now, not he, whatever he thinks to the contrary. Go away."

"But, but, but . . ."

"Oh, be quiet."

Killy seemed to gag on his own tongue.

"You heard him," said Rowan, taking the boy by the shoulders and thrusting him out the door so that he nearly fell headfirst down the steps. "Go."

"Best to keep a watch on that one," Burr muttered to Rowan. "He sounds unhinged."

Meanwhile, Torisen had slumped back into the chair, his eyes clouding. He ran the long fingers of one hand through his disheveled hair and, distractedly, tugged at it.

"Now, where is my other. . ." He looked down at his foot. "Oh."

And another fit of coughing seized him.

It was hopeless, Rowan thought with despair. If he didn't sort himself out before the High Council meeting, the other lords were going to eat him alive.

CHAPTER XVI

The High Council
Winter 95—100

I

"I SHOULD GO WITH YOU."

"No. You're needed here. In case Tiggeri comes back."

Jame tightened Bel's girth, adjusted the stirrup, and swung into the saddle with a creaking of leather. Brier glowered up at her. Clearly, it still came hard to see her lady ride off into potential danger without her, but, since their misadventures in the Western Lands, she had at least learned how to control herself. Mostly.

Jame grinned down at her. "If it helps, think of me as strong and cruel. Keep an eye on Jorin, please, and be sure to check on Girt's people at the oasis."

"Huh. Are you at least going to travel by the folds in the land?"

"I've already told you. That route nearly always happens by accident, and it's never the same twice. There are no maps."

Besides, in her pocket was Sheth Sharp-tongue's laconic message, received the previous day by post rider:

Join me at Restormir. As odd as it seemed, who was she to refuse the Commandant?

With Rue at her side, she rode out to the lower meadow where Damson's ten-command waited for her, along with seven heavily laden packhorses.

They traveled all that day on the River Road, with Bel showing no inclination to veer. That both reassured and worried Jame. She trusted the Commandant, of course, but by this route they would pass both the Caineron stronghold and Wilden, neither well inclined toward her. For that matter, had it been wise to take a ten-command of second-year cadets led, no less, by the problematic Damson? What, had she hoped that other randon would go easy on children? Where did the randon stand now anyway?

Tack jingled. Hooves rang on stone.

Snow still lay under bare boughs, but the sloping, rocky fields were naked except for tangles of dead grass. A few fat white flakes drifted down from a clear sky. Spring, indeed, was late this year. Nonetheless, eagles and black swans soared overhead, northward bound, shrieking or whistling, as was their wont. They, at least, trusted that the year would eventually turn. Jame devoutly hoped that it would. She was tired of being cold.

At midafternoon they came over a rise, and there lay Restormir, more or less at their feet. It was a huge fortress, made up of a compound for each of Caldane's seven established sons and an eighth, the largest, for Caldane himself. Overshadowing all of these was the island tower keep known as the Crown, where Caldane's family lived. On top of the Crown was a garden and set in it, a white dot at this distance, was Cattila's stone cottage.

Even as Jame's gaze fell on it, the earth shivered. Horses threw up their heads and tried to bolt, but Bel spoke to them and they quieted, if with nervous, rolling eyes.

"What d'you make of that?" asked Damson.

"The Caineron Matriarch has been ill most of this year, and she's an old friend of the Earth Wife. Perhaps she's taken a turn for the worse."

Was Lyra up there with her, Jame wondered, and, if so, how was the girl coping? Tiggeri had said that the old woman had virtually been stripped of attendants. Nursing the dying was no easy chore, especially for one as young and inexperienced as Lyra.

"Look," said Rue.

A company of Caineron randon was trotting across the bridge from the keep to the River Road. Jame recognized Cloud's steel-gray coat and the tall figure on his back. She descended to greet Caldane's war-leader, as she supposed Sheth Sharp-tongue still was.

"Commandant."

"Cadet."

The earth shuddered again. Snow and debris cascaded down the sides of the tower from the Crown, where chunks of masonry had already been dislodged.

"This has been going on for a fortnight," remarked Sheth. "Eventually it got on m'lord's nerves. He left four days ago, no doubt to travel slowly and in comfort. With luck, we won't catch up with him until Gothregor."

Jame looked at him askance. "Was that why you asked me to meet you here and why you waited behind—to provide a shield?"

"Do you need one?" he asked lightly. "More often, it seems, m'lord Caineron has required protection from you than the reverse. Say, rather, that we randon should ride together."

If so, it was nice to be included in the ranks. Jame wondered what he and the other randon officers had heard about Tagmeth. Not much, probably. It said a lot, though, that she and her Kendar had lasted the winter there without crying for help.

"Commandant, what's going on?"

"It would spoil the surprise if I told you. Then, too, perhaps things won't turn out as I fear they may."

With that she had to be content.

She did learn, however, that Cattila was still alive, but failing. When Caldane had grown tired of waiting for her to die, and of having his home crumble over his head, he had departed early, taking Lyra and Kallystine with him, the former against her will. Hopefully someone had stayed behind: A sad thought that that indomitable old lady might have been left to die without kith or kin.

The rest of the day passed agreeably enough. To her surprise, the Commandant proved an entertaining conversationalist who made her laugh more than she would have believed possible. In turn, it was tempting to tell him more than she should. At least she was able to set his mind at ease about his older brother Bear and to praise the Caineron randons' respect for him. She said nothing about Tiggeri's abortive hunt. No doubt he had already heard about that from other sources.

"I thought you might be good for each other," he said with a faint smile when he had heard her out, "assuming you didn't kill each other. As for Bear's possible, eventual recovery, well, it's a pleasant thought."

"But not one that you believe in."

"Hope only goes so far."

Some time later they stopped briefly to let the horses rest.

Jame wandered away. As amiable as the Commandant had been, talking to him at length was a bit of strain, like discoursing with a legend. Of course, she supposed that by those standards she was a legend, too, but only one in the making. He, on the other hand, was the Commandant and would never be anything less, whatever his fool of a lord decided.

The fading day glimmered, white snow under dark boughs, limned with blue shadows, and here was a slope of boulders recently shaken down from the heights. Some of them still seemed to be in motion. One reshaped itself as she approached, its blocky lines arranging themselves into the curve of a hunched back, of drawn up knees, of tightly folded arms, of a rough head that slowly lifted at the crunch of her footsteps.

"Mother Ragga."

"Oh," the Earth Wife groaned, and the ground shifted. "Why do people have to die? I escaped death, didn't I? Why can't she?"

"Is Cattila in much pain?"

"It comes and goes. I transfer what I can to the earth."

"Are you with her now?"

"Of course. She is my old gossip. Who else can I talk to when she is gone? Even Gran Cyd wouldn't understand. You?" She made a grating sound and spat out pebbles. "Don't make me laugh. We old women have a language all our own. Such days we have seen. And it's been fun, listening to all of your problems."

"Mine?"

"Yours, true, but also those of your people. Oh, you are a strange race, or collection of them. Who else would worship such a god, not that you really do, or take on such a world-spanning task, not that most of you seem to believe in it anymore. You, though, child; you believe."

"My experience gives me little choice."

"Ha. There it is, that wry acceptance. Should I believe you, though?"

"I know what I know. Rathillien is my home too. I love it. I want to defend it. What can the Three do, though, without the Four?"

The Earth Wife irritably gummed more rock and dribbled gravel. "I dunno. I'm thinking. Why do we have to have this conversation over and over? Try turning the world sideways on its axis, that's me. Oh!"

Another shudder of the earth, another displaced mortal tremor. Boulders tilted and rolled, including the one that had been the Earth Wife. Jame scuttled backward. It ground to a halt face down, nearly on her toes. Then all was still again until voices below called anxiously to her.

She went back to join the others.

II

NOT LONG AFTERWARD, at twilight, they came to

Mount Alban. Kedan, who was both Lord Jedrak and Lord Jaran by that house's eccentric reckoning, meet them at the gate of the Scrollsmen's College. With him were the college's Director Taur, its lordan Kirien, and Kindrie.

Jame could tell at a glance that something had changed between the latter two. What, she didn't guess until at dinner she saw them with their heads together, sharing a private joke.

"All right," she told them later. "I'm stupid. Congratulations."

"Were we that obvious?" asked Kindrie, blushing furiously.

"I don't really have the experience to answer that, but I think so. Never mind. No one will mind as long as you don't plan on having children anytime soon."

Kirien regarded her, head atilt. "I know what I'm doing. Do you?"

"Point taken. I think so, but I'm not ready yet to put it to the test. Besides, with whom?"

"What?" said Kindrie in confusion, looking from one to the other.

Both burst out laughing.

"Never mind," said Kirien, patting his arm. "If you need to be concerned, I will tell you."

The next day, augmented by the Mount Alban contingent, the party reached Tentir around midafternoon. There, more randon rode out to join them, including the current Coman commandant. With a sour look at Jame, the latter pushed her back in line and took her place beside his fellow war-leader. He talked a lot to

Sheth, but got little response. Jame couldn't hear most of it. However, she got the impression that the Coman wanted to know why he and his fellows had been called out. The High Council was the lords' business, after all. The randon would have their say on the First of Summer. That last came through clearly, as did the glare that he shot back over his shoulder at her.

"You have no friend there," murmured Kirien, who had also been listening.

"Then we have to hope that actions speak louder than prejudices."

"How often does that happen?"

"Cynic."

Shadow Rock was reached late in the day.

Holly, Lord Danior, had already set off for Gothregor, but had left orders that his cousin be received in his absence. Thus Jame found herself again situated opposite Wilden, and very uncomfortable at the prospect.

"Lord Caineron was there for three nights," Holly's steward told them. "Trinity knows what devilry they were concocting."

He would say that, thought Jame, given the animosity between the two keeps, but still . . .

"Anyway," the Kendar continued, "Lord Randir left for Gothregor yesterday, his lady mother traveling with him."

That last was a surprise. Rawneth hadn't been at the Knorth keep since Kinzi had ordered her out of it many years ago, before the massacre. That she should return now stuck Jame as both odd and ominous.

"I had a strange experience travelling nearby, last

summer," said Kindrie, standing that evening on the ramparts with Jame and Kirien, all three of them staring across the valley at the dark mass that was the Randir fortress. "Someone was wandering the streets, knocking on doors."

"'Let me in, let me out,'" murmured Jame.

Kindrie looked at her in surprise. "Yes. How did you know?"

"She came to a gate that opened, and her guards rushed inside. They killed whomever answered her summons. The next day they accused that entire household of treason, apparently for seeing what they shouldn't have. The family chose the White Knife. Some Kendar escaped, though, and took refuge with me at Tagmeth. That's how I heard the story."

"Was it Rawneth?" asked Kirien.

"So the Kendar said. So I believe. Apparently she doesn't sleep well these days. Cousin Holly thought he saw something strange the night that Tori slept here on the way back from Mount Alban, but he didn't say what. At the time, I was trying to remember a dream of my own. Now I wish that I had pressed for details."

She was beginning to get an idea, though.

III

THE NEXT MORNING they set off again, intending to reach Gothregor that night. However, at Falkirr they caught up with Lord Caineron. It was only midafternoon, but Caldane had already stopped to enjoy Brandan hospitality and, Jame suspected, to cajole Brant, Lord Brandan. Politics already curdled the air.

"I have to stop here," Sheth told her. "You can ride on, though."

Jame wished that she could, but the valley was clogged with camping Caineron, too many having arrived to be housed in the fortress. As for striking east into the hills, Bel hadn't yet shown any desire to leave the road. Would she if Jame turned her head that way? Would they be followed if she did?

As Jame was pondering this, a message arrived from the keep. Lord Brandan and Lady Brenwyr requested her presence at dinner.

Her contingent and that of Mount Alban camped outside the walls, glad enough not to share a roof with the Caineron before they must.

The meal that night was finer than Jame's last at Falkirr, but only in terms of its participants being better dressed. Caldane was certainly gorgeous in scarlet damask trimmed with spotted ermine, looking as broad as the setting sun on a cloudless day and as incandescent of face. As Gorbel had hinted, he had spent the winter eating and now required a double bench rather than a chair, even then overflowing it on all sides. Brant and Brenwyr shared the high table with him, the former in a plain coat of good quality, the latter, perhaps defiantly, in the brown jacket that encased Aerulan's death banner.

Jame fingered the collar of her own coat. It had been presented to her on her departure from Tagmeth, a tailored crazy quilt composed of the Kendars' best scraps, many of them heirlooms. It hadn't previously occurred to her that such things were valued relics, carried in one's permanent kit, rarely used except, perhaps, in one's eventual death banner. She had been deeply touched to receive such a gift, and unsure at first if it or another constituted her finest gear. The latter would serve for the Council Meeting itself, for many reasons. In the meantime, she felt quite elegant as she was.

Caldane talked a lot and frequently laughed, all the while leaning toward Brant. On Brant's other side was Kallystine, who gave the impression of having crammed herself into the high table. When she bent toward Lord Brandan, she exposed an expanse of spectacular white cleavage over cream velvet sprinkled with opals. Her face, however, remained veiled and she ate little.

Kirien and Kindrie sat with Jame along a side table.

Opposite them were Gorbel and Lyra, the former glowering, the latter miserable, trying to catch Jame's eye. Trouble there, thought Jame.

Caldane leaned toward Brant, overturning a cup with his trailing sleeve and planting his elbow in the resultant flood. "All of this fuss over procedure! Don't you think we should be looking forward rather than back? What is the past but a pyre of failed hopes, dead promises, and corrupt traditions? It's time for new ideas."

"Ask the Highlord when he thinks of such things," said Brenwyr tartly.

Caldane smiled, as if to say, "Ah, the dear ladies."

"I understand," he said to the matriarch, "that you have also been summoned to Gothregor. What is all of that about, eh?"

Behind her mask, Kallystine appeared to simper.

"No doubt Adiraina will inform me when I arrive," said Brenwyr, and turned away to signify the end of that conversation.

When the meal concluded at last, the Tagmeth and Mount Alban parties returned to their campsite. It was a cool, crisp night under a glorious array of stars. The moon's last thin crescent had long since set. Tomorrow it would fall into the dark, an ominous thought.

Something was ending, thought Jame, poking at the fire to rouse it, too restless herself to sleep. Maybe several things.

They had camped under the spreading boughs of an enormous oak, on ground raised above the general snowmelt by a lacework of roots. Last year's dried leaves rustled overhead and arthritic twigs creaked uneasily, although there was no wind. The night held its breath.

Everything ends, darkness seemed to whisper. *Eventually.*

Voices sounded. A sentry came into the firelight, escorting a slight figure bundled in a cloak. Jame rose in time to receive Lyra's rush of an embrace.

"Oh, take me home, take me home!" the girl sobbed, clutching the plain jacket that Jame had exchanged for her finery. "Gran is so sick and Kallystine made me leave her and oh, I just want to go h-h-home!"

"There you are."

A second muffled figure emerged from the shadows, Caineron guards looming behind her. Knorth and Jaran randon coalesced silently, warily, around them.

"Easy," Jame said. "These are guests. I think."

Kallystine pushed back her hood. Eyes glinted through a slit in her heavy veil.

"Dear little sister. Why did you run off? If you were upset, you should have come to me."

Lyra clung to Jame. "You? Never! You made me leave Gran and-and you said that Father was going to contract me to Lord Randir f-for an heir!"

"If I did, when he does, how will it help to complain? The match has my sanction. His, of course, will follow. As for your precious Gran, she has lived her day—in fact, an age of them. Didn't you hear Father? It's time for new things."

"Would you put Cattila on her pyre before her death?" Jame asked. "Would you turn your back on the past?"

Kallystine laughed. "Gladly! So should you. What has our history offered but pain? Ah, I admit that I don't know much about your previous life. No one does, it seems— not even your brother. But something like you doesn't spring out of nowhere. Could it be our past again to blame? With your ideas, you and dear Torisen are both relics. Archaic. Our people have moved on."

"Yet the past made us all, and marred us. I'm sorry about your face."

Kallystine all but spat at her. "Hypocrite! At least I paid you back. You are also damaged goods."

Jame had to think about that for a moment. "Oh. You mean this." She touched the scar on her cheek. "What of it?"

Kallystine grimaced in frustration. "How can it signify so little to you? I should have guessed it, though, unnatural creature that you are. No wonder the Women's

World threw you out and no man will offer for you except as breeding stock. Not for long, however. Your house is all but spent. Soon, soon, we will wipe your name off every scroll, out of every song. No one will know that you ever existed."

Jame smiled. "Be that as it may, I'm here now and so are you. What next?"

Yet again the earth stirred. Lyra yelped. Jame hustled her off the spread of roots as it began to writhe underfoot. Overhead, boughs as thick as limbs shifted, groaning. Leaves crackled, then ignited as embers from the disturbed fire rose to kindle them. The deep fissures of its trunk gaped and shifted. A seamed face formed. Toothless mouth, hanging jowls, furrowed cheeks, poached eyes . . . it screamed with a mighty rending of wood, then muscles went slack and fissures drooped. The fiery crown burned out. Night returned, to the distant cry of horses and the sense of a diminished world.

Kallystine clapped her hands.

"Don't tell me. The hag is dead. At last! Now I shall be matriarch!"

The oak settled with a groan. A crack ran up its trunk, jagged as a lightning bolt, and half of the tree fell with a hideous shriek. If not for Kallystine's guard sweeping her out of the way, she would have been crushed.

"Just the same," said Jame, in none too steady a voice, "if she had wanted, she could have killed you."

Kallystine made a choking sound and caused her veil to flutter by breathing hard behind it.

"Be that as it may," she croaked. "Lyra. Come with me."

"You have to go," Jame said gently to the stricken girl. "Things will work out."

"Do you promise?"

"How can I? But I'll do what I can."

IV

THEY REACHED GOTHREGOR the next evening after a long, slow ride on the heels of the Caineron contingent. It was the 99th of Winter.

Jame and Damson's ten-command settled into their old quarters in the barracks. Rue grumbled that Jame, here on official business and the Highlord's heir to boot, wasn't given something better. Jame pointed out that they were lucky to have a roof overhead at all. While Gothregor was huge, most of it was either ruins or occupied by the Women's Halls. An extensive tent city had sprung up outside its gates, including one enormous, luxurious structure occupied by Lord Caineron and his retinue. Receptions started there as soon as the canvas was up, promising to continue long into the night. Meanwhile, people walked from tent to tent to visit after the winter's isolation and, no doubt, to discuss the coming meeting. Politics again, thought Jame. Only a few people, she noted, came into the fortress itself, and those left early.

She stepped outside the barracks and looked across the inner ward to the old keep. In the southwestern tower where Torisen kept his sparse bedchamber, a solitary candle flickered like a distant star.

Rowan joined her.

"I won't say that you can't see him tonight, of course, but I would prefer that you didn't. Burr is up there now, trying to get him to sleep."

"How bad is he?"

Rowan shrugged. "I've seen him worse. In some ways, on some topics, he's surprisingly sensible, when he can keep his mind fixed. If he doesn't sleep, though . . ."

"How long has he been awake this time?"

"Ten days. Again, I've known worse, but still. . ."

It was, Jame thought, quite bad enough, even without the morrow to think of.

"I'll leave him in peace, then," she said. "In the meantime, I have something for you, or rather for the kitchen."

She led Rowan back to the barracks and presented her with the packhorses' burden, reduced to enough sacks nearly to fill her small bedroom. Rowan stared at the puckered orange placed in her hand.

"There are lemons, tangerines, and papayas too," said Jame, smiling at her expression, or rather at the lack of it. "Also dried figs. Pears and apples, unfortunately, are out of season, and the strawberries aren't ripe yet. There's also smoked yackcarn."

"Where did you get all of this?"

"Tori knows. It would be better if you didn't, though, and certainly no one else. Will they be useful?"

"Oh," breathed the steward. "We were so worried that we couldn't provide the lords with anything special. It's been a lean winter here. With all of this, though . . . I'm no cook, but I wager our kitchen can turn this bounty into a feast the Council will never forget."

V

THE NEXT DAY dawned clear and bright.

Jame dressed and stood before Rue, who would have to act as her mirror.

"Well?"

The tow-headed cadet regarded her judiciously. "Going to war, are we? Just the same, it's impressive. We'll set them on their heels this time, for sure."

Jame laughed. Two years ago, Rue had been chagrined at her commonplace garments. It was something, at least, to please one's servant.

She found the other lordan gathered in the inner ward, wearing a rainbow of court coats. Timmon approached her, his golden hair shining above a jacket of ochre and bronze embroidery.

"What," he said, "is that?"

Jame turned before him, despising herself for still feeling anxious. "What do you think?"

"Well, the inner coat is the rathorn scale-armor byrnie. I remember it from our stand outside Kothifir against the Karnids. Good luck for you that blood doesn't stain either rathorn ivory or rhi-sar leather. A wealth on your back, my girl, enough to buy a quarter of this keep. The outer coat, though . . ."

"That you might not recognize. Cadets embroidered it at Tentir onto unsanctioned Kothifiran silk, which didn't survive, except where the stitches held it down."

"It looks like words floating on lace," said Timmon,

leaning closer to stare. "'Then the rathorn colt surprised her at the swimming hole.' Oh, I remember that. To get away, you dived under a cloud-of-thorns thicket, naked, and came out the other side looking like a flayed rabbit."

"Kindly stop reading my chest."

Movement at the ward's edge caught the corner of her eye. The randon had gathered there, several hundred of them from up and down the Silver. Whatever the Commandant feared, so did they, hence their presence here, so they mingled regardless of house, quietly talking. What had been that jerk of motion, though, ducking out of sight behind them? Could that scarecrow have been Killy?

Kirien and Kindrie approached, followed by Gorbel. The latter wore a gorgeous, if snug, coat depicting the Snowthorns at sunrise, all smoky blue and gold fretted with the suggestion of autumn leaves. Kirien, as usual, looked trim and neat in dove gray while Kindrie sported a new coat the color of spring grass.

"So, here we are in all of our finery," said the Jaran scrollswoman lightly. "I like yours. It's refreshingly simple in hue but complex in design."

"Now, that makes me blush."

"Really? The truth shouldn't."

Gorbel squinted at her collar, breathing down the back of her neck. "'The Caineron Corrudin asked her to do the unspeakable. She told him to back off and he did, out a window.' He hasn't forgotten that, by the way, nor stopped backing up."

"I'm beginning to regret this."

Boom. Boom. Boom, boom, boom.

Gothregor's main gate swung open. Horns sounded, and the lords entered in a grand procession.

Caldane came first, borne on a litter by six sturdy Kendar, wearing a cloth-of-gold coat the size of a small tent. The sun glittered off it and sent spangles of light to the far corners of the ward. He seemed half of a mind to wave graciously to the assembled randon, half to ignore them.

After him, in plainer array, came the Ardeth.

"That's not Adric," said Jame.

"No. He's ill. Cousin Dari is taking his place."

Jame gave Timmon a sharp look. "Not you, his heir?"

Timmon tried to shrug this off, but looked uneasy. "I wasn't consulted. Mother was . . . well, you can imagine. Then again, what could I have said or done in a full Council meeting, against them?"

"Got to make up your mind and take a stand sometime," Gorbel grunted.

Timmon glared. "Would you know?"

"About some things, yes."

Jame glanced at him. "Gorbel, what is your father up to?"

"If I knew . . . look. There's the Commandant."

Sheth Sharp-tongue had been pacing the procession along the sidelines. Now he joined the end of his lord's segment, calling no attention to himself. Simply by being there, though, he somehow shifted its center of gravity.

Jame's sense of unease grew.

The Randir followed the Ardeth, Kenan riding on a high-spirited stallion whose mouth bled from a cruel bit, likewise his sides from crueler spurs.

The Brandan and Jaran came on together quietly, on foot, surrounded by their Kendar. Kirien twitched. Did she belong with the lordan or among the scrollsmen following her uncle Kedan? Jame touched her sleeve. Here she was, where she must stay by her house's will. Kirien gave her a fleeting, rueful smile.

Tiny Coman, Edirr, and Danior brought up the rear, to no fanfare.

"Caldane arranged this, didn't he?" Jame asked Gorbel.

"Yes."

"I thought so."

Then time passed. Before the lords began to discuss current business, traditionally their lordan were presented to the Highlord, who acknowledged each with some paltry token. Two years ago Jame had gotten a small carving, lost since her childhood, and Timmon a ring, still on his father's finger. Not so paltry, perhaps, after all.

"What's the delay?" Jame asked Rowan, who had drifted close to her as if by accident.

"The Matriarchs have asked for an audience."

"Don't they handle their own affairs?"

"Usually. I hear that this has to do with the contested admission of a new member."

Kallystine, thought Jame. Then, with an unreasoned jolt of fear: *What if Rawneth is there too?*

The Matriarchs, of course, would have entered by the back door abutting the inner courtyard. Jame made for the front door to the old keep. The lords had shed their retinues outside. These looked at her askance as she brushed past. The Knorth guard at the door, however, saluted and stood aside, almost with an air of relief. Kinzi regarded her anxiously from the weave of her death as she crossed the tapestry hung lower hall.

Girl, protect your brother.

Yes, great-grandmother. I hear you.

Jame ran up the northwest spiral stair, past the second floor strewn with artifacts of Marc's artistry, up into the Council Chamber.

There she paused on the threshold, catching her breath. Hoarse panting behind her indicated that, drawn by whatever obscure impulse, Gorbel had followed her.

Burr stood to one side of the door just within the room.

A broad ebony table ran east to west down the hall and at this the lords sat, four on one side, five on the other counting the twin Lords Edirr.

Torisen stood at the far end, under Marc's stained-glass map. Jame had never before seen him so thin nor the shadows under his eyes so dark. He wore black with silver embroidery as before, elegant in its way, but how tightly that belt cinched his slender waist. And his now white-streaked hair was long enough to be caught by a silver clasp at the nape of his neck.

However, he wasn't wearing the Kenthiar. That struck Jame as a mistake, here, where he most needed to stress his status as Highlord.

The Matriarchs were drawn up opposite with Adiraina at their head, looking small, trim, and rigid with indignation.

Kallystine glided back and forth before them in a diaphanous blue gown spangled with sapphires that radiated out from the twin white moons of her breasts.

"I . . . we regret having to bring this matter before you," she was saying, all sweet milk and honey. "Of course, you have more important business to discuss. Still, the Caineron Matriarch is dead. Someone must represent our house's interests within the Women's World. Who better than I?"

The jeweled eyes sewn into Adiraina's mask glittered. "We already told you, lady. A matriarch is expected to have experience, which you do not, except of fruitless contracts."

"Ridiculous!" Karidia could be heard to mutter from farther back in the throng. "When put to the test, has a Caineron lady ever been known to breed false?"

"Well," said Trishien, "there is a song about one soon after the Fall who bore a litter of blind puppies . . ."

"Oh, trifles!" said Kallystine, impatiently brushing these remarks aside. "All of life is politics and power. Those I know. Was I not once consort to the Highlord himself?"

With that she circled Torisen as if coyly to twine the trailing cloud of her skirt around him, but he drew back with a shudder.

He's not going to say anything, thought Jame. *Will anyone?*

Around the table, the lords' expressions ranged from stony to impatient to embarrassed.

Kallystine stomped her foot in exasperation, as best she could while wearing such a tight underskirt.

"Father, see here: There is business pending between the Caineron and the Randir." She slipped among the grove of assembled Matriarchs and, with difficulty, hauled out a shrinking Lyra. "Who if not I will sanction the union between this child and Lord Kenan, whose mother quite rightly wishes him to sire an heir?"

Caldane slapped the table with a beringed hand. Wood rang.

"Wretched child, not even your great-grandmother would be so presumptuous! Your sanction? Yes, I have promised Lord Randir a daughter, but I didn't say which one. Kenan, here are two. Which do you prefer?"

Lord Randir languidly regarded them, one stiff with terror, the other with outrage. "Virgins are such a bore. What say you, lady? Shall we make a match?"

"But . . . but . . . but . . . oh, look, damn you!"

Kallystine ripped off her veil and bared perfect, white teeth at them through a mere hint of lips. Papery skin stretched taut over cheekbones sharp enough to cut. Her lavender eyes were still lovely, but seemed about to pop out of the skull that was her face.

Kenan waved all of this away. "Oh, put that mask back on. Faces are boring too. At least your hips are broad enough for the purpose."

Caldane flipped a pudgy hand. "So be it. Daughter, you are contracted."

"Think of it," said a coolly amused voice from the back on the crowd, "as the gaining of necessary experience."

Kallystine was led away, sputtering with incredulous fury and incoherent threats. Lyra watched her go, her mouth agape, then realized that she was being left behind and bolted after the departing Matriarchs. One only remained.

Rawneth's gown echoed a direhound's coat, the body

pearl white, the sleeves, mask, and hem shading from gray to black. Like Torisen, she looked painfully thin and unwell, but compact in malice. When she turned her chill smile on him under the shadow of a hood, even a tilted glimpse of it made Jame shiver.

"Fetch the Kenthiar," she said to Burr.

The Kendar twitched, suddenly aware of her presence, and turned. The thin silver collar was already in his hands, its sullen gem glowing purple and blue with shifting hints of red. Jame took it, careful not to touch its inner surface, and walked down the hall to stand a pace back from her brother, to one side. She had felt the lords turn to watch her pass, but Torisen's eyes remained locked on the Randir Matriarch.

"Leave," he said. "Now."

Rawneth fell back a step with an adder's hiss.

Kenan half rose. "Now see here. . ."

"Hush, my son. Remember who speaks and judge accordingly."

With this cryptic utterance, she gave the assembled company the ghost of a bow, turned, and departed.

"Now, that's the way to handle women," said Caldane, not looking at either Kenan or Jame. "Who are they to think they have a say in anything?"

With that he was off on a rambling bluster to which his peers listened, bemused. The presentation of the lordan, it seemed, had been forgotten.

The collar was very cold in Jame's hands, numbing her fingertips. Was this another of its defenses against someone who wasn't supposed to handle it? That limited its use to Tori, but then so she had always been given to believe. Why hadn't he donned it when he had risked his neck so often by doing so before?

"'Cursèd be and cast out,'" murmured her brother, as if answering her question, and maybe he was. "'Blood and bone, you are no son of mine.' By what right, therefore, do I claim my father's rights? A voice in my mind whispers that the true Highlord has yet to come, or is it that he has yet to return? I stand in his way. Do my people suffer thereby?"

"Tori." She poked him with an elbow. "Be quiet."

He jerked as if waking. "I refuse to hurt. . . Jame. What are you doing here?"

"You sent for me. Remember?"

"Oh."

". . . and that is why individual houses should have the last word in such matters," Caldane was saying. "Moreover, the strongest house should have the loudest voice. I speak for over twelve thousand Kencyr, the Randir for only some eight thousand."

"Eighty-five hundred," murmured Kenan.

Caldane gave him a gracious nod that made his many chins bunch. "Granted. But Kallystine is also my daughter; therefore, I spoke first in this matter, and the Highlord not at all."

Torisen did in fact have the right to interfere in any contract, although he rarely used it. His continued silence now, though, was allowing the others to ignore him.

"Say something," she hissed, forgetting that she had just told him to shut up.

"What?"

"Anything!"

The flicker of a smile crossed his tired face. "I just did."

Ill or not—and she could see that he was—damn this abstraction of his. She had felt unexpected power stir when he had ordered Rawneth out, but now he was in a fog again, listening to voices she could not hear.

"It would be foolish, would it not," Caldane continued, "to let such lesser houses as the Danior, the Edirr, and the Coman have a say in such matters. Why, even the Knorth number only a paltry two thousand."

The others stirred uneasily.

"One house, one vote," said Holly, planting his elbows on the table and leaning forward.

"Ah, tradition." Caldane sketched a gesture as if to wave this away. "See how well it has served us in the past."

"So, how about one lord, one vote?"

"Hush," said Kedan, touching Holly's sleeve. "We tamper with such arrangements at our peril."

Caldane appeared to be doing sums on his fingers. The Randir and Coman for the Caineron. The Ardeth, Brandan, Jaran, and Danior for the Knorth. The Edirr? Who knew or cared?

"No. It has to be by garrison. Some twenty-four thousand on my side, some fifteen thousand on yours. There. That works."

"Only if we change the rules," said Brant. "I for one vote that we do no such thing."

"And I." "And I." "And I." "And I."

Brant leaned forward. "Torisen? What say you?"

The time had come. Jame stepped forward and raised

the Kenthiar, its hinged jaws open. It snapped shut around Torisen's neck, neatly severing his gathered fall of hair and the clasp that held it.

"Ah," he said, blinking, then giving himself a shake. "Now, what were we discussing? Oh yes. Why would I remove myself from power, especially with four houses behind me?"

"Five," said Essien and Essiar, the twin Lords Edirr.

"There you have it, then."

Caldane glared. "This isn't right. This isn't fair. And it doesn't matter anyway. We are gathered here to establish whose mercenary troops go where to fight in the spring. Well, I already know the destination of mine. I have leased a company to Prince Uthecon of Karkinaroth, another to King Ostrepi, and a third to Duke Pugnanos."

"But," said Brant, clearly distressed, "the first two are fierce rivals, with lands abutting each other, and Pugnanos is across the Silver, a blood-enemy to them both."

"So?"

"Have you at least written the contracts so that Kencyr won't face Kencyr?"

"Trifles, as my dear daughter would say. I leave it up to my war-leader, Sheth Sharp-tongue, to stand between them." Caldane snickered. "Oh, he thinks himself so superior. All randon do. We mere Highborn don't know the meaning of honor as well as they, oh no. We will see. Be it on his head if he fails his precious code."

Jame edged back from Torisen. She could feel his anger growing, and the strength of it astonished her.

"Do I understand," he said, beginning to pace slowly

down the table's length, "that you have put in place no other safeguards? These are your people. Would you have them slaughter each other?"

"As in the White Hills?" Caldane laughed again, but now he looked nervous. "That was the trick your father played."

"No trick. Rather a tragedy. Are you no better than he?"

That seemed to rattle Caldane. He pushed back his chair and struggled to rise. Gorbel, who so far had stood back, moved to assist him to his feet.

"You Knorth. You think you know so much and are worth so much more. Again, all by our accused god's will! My father died in the White Hills. I was left to fight for the survival of my house in the shambles that he left, all because Ganth's madness took him. Well, never again. Your day is done. None of your house is left except for you and this succubus of a sister. Have you slept with her yet? How long until you do? That was the end for Gerridon and the Dream-weaver. Don't say that hunger doesn't live on in your blood."

"I remember now: your son attacked Tagmeth. He should not have done so."

Caldane backed away. The other lords on his side of the table hastily rose to make room for him with a great scraping of chair legs. Wine glasses tipped over one after the other with no hand near them, and a decanter shattered. Jame glanced uneasily up at the window where cullet crumbled and fell.

"Did you sanction that assault?"

"No, no . . . it was Tiggeri's idea. Heh. Boys. And what

of it? Tagmeth by rights belongs to the Caineron, and we will have it yet, when that witch brat of yours leaves."

"Who says that she will? By my reckoning, this past winter makes the keep hers. Perhaps I will give her permission to bind more Kendar to garrison it. Why not? How many of your vaunted numbers are actually bound to your sons?"

"You're insane, just like your father! I knew it . . . we all knew it . . . and madness is contagious. Stay away from me!"

Torisen poked him in the chest with a long forefinger. "Boo."

"Hic!" said Caldane, and looked aghast.

His feet scuffed the floor, desperately seeking traction. "Hic!"

As Caldane floundered, he began to rise, watched with astonishment by the other lords. None seemed to remember that this had almost happened two years ago when Jame had first been presented as Torisen's heir. Then, Gorbel had held his father down until the seizure had passed. Now the Caineron lordan sprawled on the floor, wheezing from a flailing parental elbow to the pit of his stomach.

"HIC!"

The Caineron began to rotate. His cloth-of-gold coat inverted over his downturned head, leaving pudgy, wool-clad legs to thrash in midair. There was a draft in the hall, coming from the stairs, breathing out between the multicolored panes of glass. Caldane bobbed in the latter direction. He bumped up against the window like a gaudy bee in a bottle but couldn't see enough to catch the glass's edge. Here was an opening. He bobbed against it, then through, then away, screaming.

Gorbel scrambled to his feet, clutching his stomach, still short of breath.

"Which way did he go?"

"Up," Jame said. "Don't worry. Eventually even your father has to run out of hot air—or is it gas?"

"Huh."

Gorbel plunged down the stairs. Below, he could be heard shouting for a horse.

"I suggest," said Lord Brandan, "that we call a recess." He was regarding Torisen askance with concern. "Immediately."

ᘒᙎ᙮ CHAPTER XVII ᙭ᙏᘂ
Blood on the Floor
Winter 100

I

AS THE HIGH COUNCIL filed out, some lords hustled, complaining, by others. Torisen leaned against the table.

"My head hurts," he said, and began to cough. Dark blood spattered the ebon surface between his scar-laced fingers.

Jame caught one arm as he sagged, Burr the other. Between them, they helped him up the nearest stair to the study, clumsily, single-file, for the way was narrow. Not good, thought Jame; they should have gone by the southwestern tower to the bedchamber. Burr apparently realized this as well and kicked open the door leading to the catwalk between the two western towers. They lurched out onto the spidery way—no problem normally for those not affected with height-sickness—but with Torisen lurching from side to side between them, even Jame felt dizzy.

The ward below seemed to be full of randon, looking

up—with what hopes, what fears? She caught the Commandant's dark, intent gaze. Had he guessed what a snake pit his lord had designed for him, for them all?

"It would spoil the surprise if I told you. Then, too, perhaps things won't turn out as I fear they may."

But they had. Damn Caldane anyway, that selfish, jealous, stupid man.

"Hold on," she murmured to her brother's bowed head.

The walk jittered to a rapid footstep. Jame let go of Torisen but had only half turned before the other was upon her.

"Apostate, traitor, freak . . ."

Killy slashed at her. The knife ripped her embroidered coat open across the shoulder (oh, so many memories unraveling) and skidded off the ivory beneath.

Killy struck again, wildly askew.

. . . not even competent as an assassin . . .

"Highlord!" he cried past her, through a mask of tears and snot and shattered illusion. "I would have died for you!"

"Killy, stop it. Please."

He gaped at her. Could compassion disarm him?

You shouldn't exist, Char had said.

Her people had been starved of reality for so long, leaving so many desperate for meaning.

With a sob, Killy gathered himself to strike again. The catwalk lurched. Trinity, if he should cut its cords. . .

Panicked disbelief widened his eyes as he stumbled.

"No," he said, and again, louder: "No!"

With a thin shriek he lost his balance and toppled over

the outer guideline. Jame didn't see him hit the ground, but she heard the crunch seventy feet below. Blood and brains spattered the stones in a halo of red and gray. Just outside their range stood Damson, scowling down at his broken body. Then she looked up.

Well?

"Well," breathed Jame, and lunged to catch Torisen's arm.

She and Burr got him into the southwestern tower and into bed, although still fully clothed. He shuddered and curled up on the spare mattress. His skin burned with fever. Another spasm of coughing wracked him.

"Help me," Jame told Burr as she struggled out of her tattered coat, then forced herself to stand still as the Kendar undid the byrnie's laces. Freed, she lay down on the bed and threw her arms around her brother. His hand, groping, caught her braid and clutched it. How many Merikit lives were knotted into it? Enough, surely, to anchor him, and there she was at its root, and he in her arms.

The way to the soulscape led through dreams, and that through sleep.

Trinity, how, frantic with worry as she was? Maybe she should ask Burr to hit her on the head with a brick.

Still, ten days awake . . . not the longest Torisen had gone, but still much too long.

She let his need draw her down, into a ruin of dreams mixed, like broken glass, with memory:

"Blackie hasn't been quite himself since the end of winter."

Tori with his back turned toward her, hands clasped tightly behind him. "So you've come at last."

Oh, I would have come sooner, if only you had asked . . .

"Here, son. Drink to my health."

A drop of blood quivering on a knife's point over a glass of wine.

A plate crawling with maggots.

"Destruction begins with love. The power that seduces, that betrays. . . They are creatures of the shadows, poisoning men's dreams, sucking out their souls . . . Cursèd be the lot of them . . ."

"Who, Tori?"

"Shanir. Women. You."

And he looked at her through Ganth's sick, raging eyes.

No!

Jame blinked hard.

(" . . . but I never cry . . .")

She was sitting at the top of a flight of stairs, a closed door at her back, a circular courtyard at her feet. Beyond the latter's outer gates, gray hills rolled up to a sullen, sunless sky. The wind combed through the coarse grass there as if through the pelt of some long-dead creature, and it stank.

Never, forever, whined the grass. *Forever, never . . .*

"Why didn't you answer my letters?" she asked the boy at her side.

"What letters . . . oh. Those."

"I wrote one every tenthnight, for nearly a year. A lot happened."

"It would."

He sounded exhausted, but also amused, and very

young. However, this was not the helpless, hopeless child whom she had met in this place before, who more recently in a dream she had seen huddling on its doorstep. For the first time in years, they were nearly the same age.

Torisen coughed again. Behind the door at their backs, the hall of the Haunted Lands' keep made a nasty chuffing sound like congested laughter:

Huh, huh, ha. . .

"You seemed to be doing all right," he said when he had caught his breath. "Better than 'all right.' I envied you."

"Oh," said Jame, and felt as if he had knocked the wind out of her. A winter's worth of petty resentment gone, just like that. "Did you mean what you said when you told Caldane that you might let me bind other Kendar to garrison Tagmeth? Can you even do that? I'm not yet of age."

"That hasn't stopped you so far."

"Huh. Brier. And you should know: There was one before her. Caldane's bastard son Graykin—not that that was my idea either. It just happened, as with Brier."

He glanced at her askance. What a nice face he had had as a boy, if thin and anxious. How many years together they had lost. "You are dangerous, aren't you?"

"Sorry."

Voices muttered behind them, the first querulous, the second slyly insinuating.

". . . betrayed, betrayed . . ."

"By your own son, too. By what right does he claim your place, that ingrate, that coward? You made him. You can unmake him. Now, your daughter . . ."

"That filthy little Shanir. Who is she, to look so like her mother? An imposter. A cheat. . ."

"Yes, yes. Even now she sneaks, she spies, she listens. Everyone is against you, and always has been. Poor, poor Grayling."

Torisen shuddered. "I said that I wouldn't listen, but how could I help it? They wanted to drive me mad and almost did; but then I got stubborn and decided not to let them. That meant trying to understand their taunts. I also thought about what you said—did you say it, or did I only dream it?—about the ability to bind Kendar being a Shanir trait."

"Yes."

"Well, logically that makes sense. Not all Highborn can do it, just as not all are Shanir. But those that can, well, those also tend to be the lords. Including me. Including Father. So much self-loathing, for what? It only cripples us. I think that, but then I feel . . . I feel . . . as I was taught to feel. Are some things inherently loathsome? Father says so. But he hates himself. And he's mad. We always knew that, didn't we?"

Jame wasn't sure. He had simply been their father, with only the decency of the Kendar for contrast. Then too, since Tentir, she had seen another side of him as both an abused son and brother. One judged by what one knew—or thought that one knew.

And here was a further doubt:

"Tori, this is a dream. Do you mean what you say, or are you only saying what I want to hear?"

He made as if to pinch her. His fingertips skated on ivory.

"Oh," said Jame, regarding her gauntleted hand. More rathorn scales ran up her arm and down the slight swell of her chest, although, now that she thought about it, she felt a distinct draft up her back, where a young rathorn had no armor. That last convinced her: They had descended into the soulscape.

"I've wanted to say these things to you for a long time," said her brother.

"Why didn't you? Why did you drive me away?"

"Because they wanted me to hurt you, and I was afraid that I would. Things kept happening. Everything around me started to rot. There was that freak storm, then a plague of locusts, then a murrain on the cattle, then the hay-cough. Kindrie says I nearly killed that child Bo. Other Kendar did die. I think . . . I think . . ."

"What?"

"You said, 'There are three of us Knorth now.'" He gave a shaky laugh, coughed again, and wiped a smear of blood off on the back of an unsteady hand. "I can guess what that means although I can hardly believe it. The Tyr-ridan, after all this time. . . . You said we weren't ready. Ancestors know, I'm not. You can only be Destruction."

"That needn't be a bad thing."

"No, depending on what needs to be destroyed. Kindrie is a healer. Preservation. Also with its dubious side."

"If not, why our cherished recourse to the White Knife?"

"Yes. That leaves me. Creation. But to create isn't necessarily good either, is it? Mold, disease, rot . . . Whatever I am, I can't control it, especially in its destructive aspect. Right now, I'm more dangerous than you are."

"We could put that to the test."

"Let's not. I'm glad we finally talked, though, especially now. I think that I may be dying."

He leaned forward, head bowed, and choked as if about to cough out his lungs. Drops of blood spattered the pavement at his feet.

Heh, ha, ho . . . ! chortled the hall.

Jame held him until the paroxysm subsided. "Get Kindrie," she heard herself say to Burr back in the tower. "Quick."

"D'you know who is in your soul-image beside Father?" she asked her brother.

"I didn't . . . until I heard her speak . . . in the Council Chamber." Breath and speech both came hard to him, and he was already exhausted. "Then I ordered her out. Why is she still there? How did she get in . . . in the first place?"

Talk. Keep his attention. Wait.

"When you stormed out and slammed the door behind you, you must have accidentally trapped her inside. That was just after I got to Gothregor, wasn't it? We shared that terrible dream in Lyra's quarters, when you were nearly possessed. 'Foolish, foolish child. As if it were given to you of all people to know the truth.' And you told her that you refused to listen, refused to be driven mad. 'The door is shut,' you said. I thought you meant the inner one, but it must have been the outer. Later that night when we talked, you were much calmer. You even thought it was funny that the Karkinorians had tried to kidnap me which, granted, was amusing. Then you told me to leave Gothregor. I didn't understand at the time."

"Yes. I didn't trust myself. And the randon wanted proof."

"I haven't talked to cousin Holly yet, but he told me that he dreamed he saw someone walk out of the mist from Wilden when you were at Shadow Rock. She's a dream-stalker and a soul-walker, Tori, who apparently needs to be close to her prey. And there you were. You must be stronger than she is, though, or she would have done a lot more harm than she has. Trinity, to have spent such a year and not to have been destroyed by it. . ."

Torisen struggled to his feet. "That's not enough. I want her gone. Now."

He leaned against the door. Obedient to his will, it opened inward a crack with a mighty screech of rusty hinges.

"Rawneth! Bitch of Wilden!" he cried to the seething shadows within. "Come out!"

Darkness rose against the crack, forcing it more open still. A chittering flood of black spiders spilled out, each the size of a child's clenched fist with nine scrambling legs that seemed to shift from body to body. Jame backed up, not sure if she should flee before this obscene tide or stomp it into oblivion. When the edge of it ran over her toes, she stomped. The rest swarmed down the steps into the courtyard. There, arachnid clambered on top of arachnid. A swaying form straightened and rose, swathed in gray spun silk. Atop it, multifaceted eyes leered through a mask of fiddling limbs.

"Sssooo, little lost children." The voice rustled and

crackled, chitinous, dry. "At last I am free. What will you do now?"

"Send you away," said Torisen. "Again. Go."

"Ah, ha, ha, ha. What a bleak soul you possess, little lord, but how much I have learned during my time there."

"Father talked to you, I suppose."

"Oh yes. Poor, lonely Grayling, betrayed by everyone. While he still lives, in whatever form, you are nothing. You never were. And you call yourself Highlord? What will your precious Council say when I tell them how you deserted your liege lord?"

Jame laughed, although she was growing angry, on the edge of a berserker flare. Descending the stairs, she began to circle the nightmare figure. It twisted to face her, but only from the feet up. "What proof will you give them? 'A dead man told me.' And our father is dead, whatever you say, slain by the changer Keral. Only his madness lives on."

"Yessss. Within your brother. Little girl, you would do well to ally yourself with me. Better you than that hag-faced doll, Kallystine, as a consort for my son. Think what a child you might bear."

"I *am* thinking. It turns my stomach. Your son is a changer too, isn't he? Have you ever asked yourself where that blood came from?"

The spider legs that framed Rawneth's mouth writhed into the travesty of a crooked smile. "I know full well. Did I not see my lover's face alter in the Moon Garden, when my dear Kenan was conceived?"

"I believe you that it changed, from the semblance of my foul uncle Greshan to that of the Master,

Gerridon. Consider this, though: What if it changed again, afterward?"

Mandibles clicked in irritation.

"Obscene. Pernicious. As if I could be fooled."

"Couldn't you?"

The silk shroud twisted, winding tighter and tighter around the seething torso. Black, many-jointed legs started to wriggle through it in a grotesque fringe.

"No. You will say anything to support your brother's false claim. I am too clever for you."

"Tell yourself that, and begone. The dead await you in the Graylands. Kinzi, Aerulan, all the other Knorth women slain at your word."

"Ha. And what proof have you of that? We checkmate each other, girl. Secrets are power. Never doubt, though, who will win."

"Oh," said Jame, taking another quarter turn. "I don't."

Silk split. With a thin shriek, Rawneth spilled out onto the ground and fled, a black shadow scrambling across the courtyard, out the gate, across the moaning hills, away.

Jame sighed. The battle wasn't over, for all her brave words, and the adversary far from defeated. Rawneth wasn't her primary foe. The Kencyrath faced layer upon layer of them, back to Perimal Darkling itself. The mind boggled at that. It was the crush of history.

"We aren't ready," Torisen had said, and he was right.

She turned back to the door, but it gaped empty. Her brother had disappeared into the hall.

She entered cautiously, eyes adjusting from dim light to dimmer admitted by two barred windows to the left and right. The smell struck her first, sweet and sickly. Was this the stench of lung-rot, here, in the heart of Tori's soul-image? Then she saw the tables, and the indistinct, hunched figures sitting at them. A breath of air through the outer door caused the latter to stir and sway bonelessly, ghosts spun of spider silk, echoes of a sick past.

A hoarse voice muttered behind the closed inner door and Torisen sagged against its outer surface, listening:

"You have betrayed me, you, and you, and you. You told the boy to go and he went. Traitors, all of you."

Kindrie stumbled into the hall, his white hair in wild disarray, a bruise rising on his chin.

"I was frantic," he panted. "Burr hit me. I think he cracked a tooth. What's going on?"

"Hush."

Jame had recognized the scene before her for what it was: her brother's worst nightmare. Rawneth had assumed that what he most feared was exposure over the rift with his father, but that wasn't it. He didn't regret fleeing Ganth's madness or his dying curse. What ate at his soul was that he had inadvertently left the keep's Kendar to pay for his escape.

"You, and you, and you," said that muffled voice again. "In your hands are knives. Turn them on me, or on yourselves to prove your loyalty."

"No," whispered Torisen. "These men are . . . were . . . my friends. Anar, tell him!"

"Ah-ha-ha. That feeble excuse for a scrollsman is long since gone, whining. Remember? 'I was wrong. Nothing outweighs a lord's authority. Take back the responsibility, child. It burns. Set me free. Free us all.' But you couldn't even do that, could you, because here I still am."

Torisen coughed. "Blood on the floor, on the knife. That's it, isn't it? You didn't just make my friends kill themselves. You tried to blood-bind me as a child. You knew all of this time that you were a binder, a Shanir, and yet you taught me to hate, yes, even my own sister. Damn you, Father, and curse you, always and forever. Leave us alone!"

His hand fumbled on the lock and the door swung open, almost taking him with it. Something black billowed in the narrow way beyond, filling the space from post to lintel to post.

"Oh," it breathed, and condensed.

A figure stood there, thin and anxious, drained at last of rage. "My son, my child, set me free."

Torisen drew deep into his ravaged lungs for that last drop of poisoned blood and spat.

The figure disintegrated into a stifling cloud of ash. The wind behind it from above drove it into the hall where the spun ghosts at the table turned black and brittle at its touch before crumbling into dust.

Ahhhhh . . . said the wind.

Torisen crumpled, gasping, to the floor. Jame went quickly to his side. In and out went the wind. Out and in. The rattle on it had died away. Finally, he could again catch his breath. Jame smoothed the hair off his face.

"That's better," said Kindrie, looking over her shoulder. "Now, all I need is a broom."

"Er . . . what?"

"To sweep out this mess, of course. See, there's one

behind the door. Whenever I need a tool in the soulscape, I can find it."

Torisen's eyelids fluttered open.

"What happened?"

"Your face is less gray and you can breathe again. I think you're going to live."

"Oh. Good."

Jame settled on the floor and took him into her arms.

"I'm confused," he said, sinking into her embrace. "That was Father, wasn't it?"

"I think so. Things in the soulscape don't necessarily align with reality, but he seemed real enough."

"Even at the end, asking for release?"

"Yes. Which you granted him. He was always so unhappy, except with her, and that couldn't last. It's been awhile since I last thought of him as a monster."

"Well, then, let him go. What else haven't you told me?"

"A lot. I'm sorry. You didn't seem ready and then, as Rawneth said, secrets are power."

"You were afraid that I would use them against you."

"Wouldn't you? No. Sorry. It's in part that I guess things that I can't prove. Rawneth had that right. If you knew, too, you might feel compelled to act, and we aren't ready."

"You don't trust me."

"I barely trust myself. Oh, Tori, we come from such a troubled past, and now the future looks pretty murky too. Ancestors know, this move of Caldane's throws everything at hazard, just when other things are starting to come together. How many lords d'you think will follow his lead?"

"The Randir, probably; others as well, if compelled by need. I can't tell them to let their people starve."

"I have some resources now."

"Enough for all nine houses, or only for us and maybe for our allies? That might only make things worse."

"Tori, I'm frightened."

"So am I, and so very, very tired."

"Rest, then," she murmured to him, and kissed the white streak at his temple. "I am here, at last, and so is Kindrie, and so are you. We have come home."

The End

⟨⟨⟨ Lexicon ⟩⟩⟩

Acon	a Caineron randon officer bound to Tiggeri
Adric	Lord Ardeth
Adiraina	the Ardeth Matriarch
Aerulan	Jame's dead cousin; Brenwyr's beloved
Anar	a scrollsman; one of the twins' teachers in the Haunted Lands keep
Arrin-ken	One of the Three People— cat-like immortal judges
Ashe	haunt singer
Bane	Jame and Torisen's half-brother
Bark	Gorbel's servant
Beauty	an unfallen darkling
Bel-tairi ("Bel")	a Whinno-hir

Beneficent ("Bene")	a cow
Benj	Caineron *yondri* speared by Fash, also the name of Must's baby
Berry	a ten-commander at Tagmeth, also Huckle's twin sister; fair
Blackie	Torisen's nickname
Bo	the infant son of Merry and Cron
Brant	Lord Brandon
Brenwyr	Brant's sister, also the Brandan Matriarch
Brier Iron-thorn	Jame's marshal and master-ten
Bully	a stray yackcarn bull
Buckle	A ten-commander at Tagmeth, sister of Berry; dark
Burnt Man	Rathillien elemental for fire
Burr	Torisen's servant
Caldane	Lord Caineron
Cattila	the Caineron Matriarch

Char	a ten-commander at Tagmeth in charge of the herd
Cheva	horse-master at Tagmeth
Chingetai	Merikit chieftain
Chirpentundrum) ("Chirp")	a Builder
Cleppetty	cook at the Res a'Byrr in Tai-tastigon
Commandant, the	Sheth Sharp-tongue
Corvine	a ten-commander at Tagmeth
Cron	a Kendar at Gothregor
Da	a Merikit, mate of Ma
Damson	a ten-commander at Tagmeth
Dar	a ten-commander at Tagmeth
Dari	currently in charge of the Ardeth keep during its lord's indisposition
Dark Judge	a blind Arrin-ken

Death's-head	Jame's rathorn colt
Dens	one of Damson's ten-command, second year male cadet
Dewdrop	Lyra's dappled pony
Dianthe	the Danior Matriarch
Drie	Timmon's Kendar half-brother, swallowed by the Eaten One
Eaten One	Rathillien elemental for water
Erim	a ten-commander at Tagmeth
Falling Man ("the Old Man," "the Tishooo")	Rathillien elemental for air
Fash	a Caineron cadet
Fen	Kendar farmer with the Tagmeth garrison
Four, the	Rathillien's four elementals
Ganth Gray-lord	father of the twins, the former Highlord

Geri	a Danior cadet with a haphazard control over insects
Gerraint	Ganth's father
Gerridon	the Master, renegade Highlord who caused the Fall
Girt	Benj's nurse, formerly Mustard's
Gnasher	the wolver king of the Deep Weald
Gorbel	the Caineron lordan
Gran Cyd	the Merikit queen
Granny Sit-by-the-fire	a primordial story-teller
Gray Lands	where the souls of the stranded dead wander
Greshan	Jame and Tori's uncle
Grimly	a wolver poet
Hatch	a Merikit, in love with Prid
Holly	Hollens, Lord Danior

Immalai	an Arrin-ken
Index	an old scrollsman
Iron-jaw	Ganth's haunt warhorse, then the Master's
Jamethiel Dream-weaver	the twins' mother
Jamethiel Priest's bane	Jame
Jedrak	traditional name for Lord Jaran
Jerr	a ten-commander at Tagmeth
Jorin	Jame's ounce
Kallystine	Caldane's daughter, once Torisen's consort
Karidia	the Coman Matriarch
Kells	a herbalist at Tagmeth
Kenan	Lord Randir
Keral	a darkling changer

Killy	Knorth cadet; five-commander to Char
Kindrie Soul-walker	a healer; Jame and Tori's cousin
Kirien	a scrollswoman, also the Jaran Lordan
Krothen ("Kroaky")	King of Kothifir
Languidine	a lost city in the Southern Wastes
Loof	a complaining acolyte
Lordan	a lord's heir
Lyra Lack-wit	Caldane's young daughter
Ma	a Merikit
Malignant ("Malign")	Bene's calf
Marc, Marcarn, Marcarn Long-shanks	Jame's oldest Kendar friend
Marigold Onyx-eyed	randon in charge of the Knorth barracks at Kothifir
Master, the	Gerridon

Merikit	a hill-tribe community
Merry	one of Torisen's Kendar
Mint	a ten-commander at Tagmeth
Mirah	Randiroc's green-eyed mare
Mother Ragga	the Earth Wife
Mustard ("Must")	an escaped Caineron yondri
New Pantheon	Native gods created in part by the temples' awakening
Niall	a ten-commander at Tagmeth
Nutley	bake-master at Gothregor, Rowan's partner.
Oath-breaker	a Kendar sworn to Ganth who didn't follow him into exile
Odalian	former prince of Karkinaroth
Old Pantheon	The gods before the New Pantheon, risen out of primordial forces
Oreq	an acolyte

Ostrepi	King of a Central Land on the east side of Silver, just above Karkinaroth
Pereden	Timmon's father
Pook	a very furry small dog, used to track game through the folds of the land
Prid	a Merikit girl; Jame's lodge-wyf
Pugnanos	Duke on the west side of Silver, blood enemy of Prince Uthecon and King Ostrepi
Quill	Damson's Five-commander
Quirl	Corvine's dead son
Rackny	the cook at Tagmeth
Randiroc	the Randir Heir
Rathorn	a carnivorous, ivory armored equine
Rowan	Torisen's steward
Rue	Jame's servant
Shade	Lord Randir's half kendar daughter

Sheth Sharp-tongue	Caldane's war-leader, also called the Commandant
Spot	Kindrie's post horse
Swar	Blacksmith at Tagmeth
Talbet	ten commander at Tagmeth
Taur	Director of Mount Alban
Thorns	half horse, half Rathorn, always mares
Tiens	hunt-master at Tagmeth
Tiggeri	one of Caldane's established sons
Timmon	Lord Ardeth's heir
Timtom	A part Knorth novice and Shanir, twin of Tomtim
Tirandys	Jame's uncle and teacher, also a changer
Tirresian	Cyd and Jame's infant "daughter"
Tomtim	Twin of Timtom

Torisen ("Tori")	Highlord of the Kencyrath, Jame's twin brother
Trishien	Jaran Matriarch
Tungit	Merikit shaman
Twizzle	Gorbel's pet pook
Uthecon	Prince of Karkinaroth
Whinno-hir	an intelligent, immortal equine
Winter	the twins' wet-nurse and teacher from the Haunted Lands keep
Wort	one of Damson's ten-command, second-year cadet girl
Yackcarn	a huge, hairy bovine
Yackcow	a cross between a Yackcarn and a cow
Yce	Wolver heir to the Gnasher

IF YOU LIKE...
YOU SHOULD TRY...

DAVID DRAKE
David Weber
Tony Daniel
John Lambshead

DAVID WEBER
John Ringo
Timothy Zahn
Linda Evans
Jane Lindskold
Sarah A. Hoyt

JOHN RINGO
Michael Z. Williamson
Tom Kratman
Larry Correia
Mike Kupari

ANNE MCCAFFREY
Mercedes Lackey
Lois McMaster Bujold
Liaden Universe® by Sharon Lee & Steve Miller
Sarah A. Hoyt
Mike Kupari

MERCEDES LACKEY
Wen Spencer
Andre Norton
James H. Schmitz

LARRY NIVEN
Tony Daniel
James P. Hogan
Travis S. Taylor
Brad Torgersen

ROBERT A. HEINLEIN
Jerry Pournelle
Lois McMaster Bujold
Michael Z. Williamson

HEINLEIN'S "JUVENILES"
Rats, Bats & Vats series by Eric Flint & Dave Freer
Brendan DuBois' *Dark Victory*
David Weber & Jane Lindskold's Star Kingdom
Series
Dean Ing's *It's Up to Charlie Hardin*
David Drake & Jim Kjelgaard's *The Hunter Returns*

**HORATIO HORNBLOWER OR
PATRICK O'BRIAN**
David Weber's Honor Harrington series
David Drake's RCN series
Alex Stewart's *Shooting the Rift*

HARRY POTTER
Mercedes Lackey's Urban Fantasy series

JIM BUTCHER
Larry Correia's The Grimnoir Chronicles
John Lambshead's *Wolf in Shadow*

TECHNOTHRILLERS
Larry Correia & Mike Kupari's Dead Six Series
Robert Conroy's *Stormfront*
Eric Stone's *Unforgettable*
Tom Kratman's Countdown Series

THE LORD OF THE RINGS
Elizabeth Moon's *The Deed of Paksenarrion*
Shattered Shields ed. by Schmidt and Brozek
P.C. Hodgell
Ryk E. Spoor's Phoenix Rising series

A GAME OF THRONES
Larry Correia's *Son of the Black Sword*
David Weber's fantasy novels
Sonia Orin Lyris' *The Seer*

H.P. LOVECRAFT
Larry Correia's Monster Hunter series
P.C. Hodgell's Kencyrath series
John Ringo's Special Circumstances Series

ZOMBIES
John Ringo's Black Tide Rising Series
Wm. Mark Simmons

GEORGETTE HEYER
Lois McMaster Bujold
Catherine Asaro
Liaden Universe® by Sharon Lee & Steve Miller
Dave Freer

DOCTOR WHO
Steve White's TRA Series
Michael Z. Williamson's *A Long Time Until Now*

HARD SCIENCE FICTION
Ben Bova
Les Johnson
Charles E. Gannon
Eric Flint & Ryk E. Spoor's Boundary Series
Mission: Tomorrow ed. by Bryan Thomas Schmidt

GREEK MYTHOLOGY
Pyramid Scheme by Eric Flint & Dave Freer
Forge of the Titans by Steve White
Blood of the Heroes by Steve White

NORSE MYTHOLOGY
Northworld Trilogy by David Drake
Pyramid Power by Eric Flint & Dave Freer

URBAN FANTASY
Mercedes Lackey's SERRAted Edge Series
Larry Correia's Monster Hunter International
Series
Sarah A. Hoyt's Shifter Series
Sharon Lee's Carousel Series
David B. Coe's Case Files of Justis Fearsson
The Wild Side ed. by Mark L. Van Name

DINOSAURS
David Drake's *Dinosaurs & a Dirigible*
David Drake & Tony Daniel's *The Heretic* and *The Savior*

HISTORY AND ALTERNATE HISTORY
Eric Flint's Ring of Fire Series
David Drake & Eric Flint's Belisarius Series
Robert Conroy
Harry Turtledove

HUMOR
Esther Friesner's *Chicks 'n Chainmail*
Rick Cook
Spider Robinson
Wm. Mark Simmons
Jody Lynn Nye

VAMPIRES & WEREWOLVES
Larry Correia
Wm. Mark Simmons
Ryk E. Spoor's *Paradigm's Lost*

WEBCOMICS
Sluggy Freelance... John Ringo's Posleen War Series
Schlock Mercenary... John Ringo's Troy Rising Series

NONFICTION
Hank Reinhardt
The Science Behind The Secret *by Travis Taylor*
Alien Invasion by Travis Taylor & Bob Boan
Going Interstellar ed. By Les Johnson